PRAISE FOR *SUSTAINABILITY TO SOCIAL CHANGE*

T0289617

From Business Leaders

"*Sustainability to Social Change* is a great read. It tells you about our journey (the printable parts), where other forward-looking businesses are headed, and how you can lead your company to a better future—for business and the world. Have yourself a giant scoop."
Ben Cohen and Jerry Greenfield, Cofounders of Ben & Jerry's

"This wonderful book, based on hands-on research, is a practical guide to how companies can help lead social change. I love the examples and user friendly format and will be applying the insights to the corporate boards I am a member of in Asia".
Dato Timothy Ong, Chairman of Asia Inc Forum

"This book is a huge wake-up call for all business leaders. We are either going to live in co-existence with all our neighbors and the planet or there will be no existence. The book clearly demonstrate that hiding behind the current system is no longer an option. The inspiring case studies show that early systems innovators can deliver equitable value to all stakeholders."
Louis "Tex" Gunning, CEO at LeasePlan Corporation N.V.

"A visionary call to action for all entrepreneurs! Instead of trying to sustainably reduce ourselves, Mirvis and Googins challenge us to actively build the future and align a deeper purpose into a long-term vision of what success can look like."
Jason Grenfell-Gardner, Founder of The J. Molner Company

"This book is a comprehensive and focused look at corporate performance at the nexus between business and societal goals. Focusing on the lessons here can help you and your company to 'raise the bar' and uptick performance for all."
Stanley S. Litow, Former IBM Executive, Professor and Innovator in Residence at Duke University, and author of the *Challenge for Business and Society: From Risk to Reward*

"In this insightful book, Phil Mirvis and Brad Googins argue that businesses play a crucial role as a voice for social change. But for that to work, they say business must transform the way it thinks about value. Read their timely account of why so many business leaders are finally embracing the sustainability agenda and how innovators are moving onward to regeneration. They know this is the future of business, markets and, ultimately, capitalism."
John Elkington, Co-founder of Environmental Data Services (ENDS), SustainAbility, and Volans and author of *Green Swans: The Coming Boom in Regenerative Capitalism*

"Phil Mirvis and Brad Googins have long been leaders in the conscious business movement. In this important book, they point out that it is later than we realize; they capture the "fierce urgency of now" and show how businesses can and must take the lead in bringing about social change. This book is an inspiring guide to how to move beyond 'doing less harm' to realizing a holistic vision of flourishing for all stakeholders."
Raj Sisodia, Co-founder and Chairman Emeritus at Conscious Capitalism Inc. and Distinguished University Professor of Conscious Enterprise at Tecnológico de Monterrey

"Phil Mirvis and Brad Googins have written a magnificent book, deeply grounded in the real world, but it's not just for business leaders who want to win the hearts and minds of customers, employees, communities, and partners. It's for everyone who cares about the business of building a better world. This book asks us to look in the mirror. It reminds us that the future is coming at us fast and that history has its eyes on us. But, most importantly, this is a leadership playbook designed to help you to meet the moment and propel your organization forward. It comes alive by showcasing real companies that are successfully transforming whole industries and leading the world's solution revolution to positive prosperity with intergenerational concern and world-changing intention."
David Cooperrider, Char and Chuck Fowler Professor for Business as an Agent of World Benefit at Case Western Reserve University, Honorary Chair of the David L. Cooperrider Center for Appreciative Inquiry at Champlain College, and author of *Appreciative Inquiry: A Positive Revolution in Change*

"In this important book, Phil Mirvis and Brad Googins offer a roadmap for the next stage of business leadership. It takes you *beyond* sustainability to an evolving form of the market, and the role of business and the manager of tomorrow. It offers real examples and tools for developing a new kind of leader, one focused on mastering the domains of commerce while also recognizing that they have an interest and responsibility in maintaining the integrity, stability and equity of the system in which they practice that craft. Rather than exploit a broken market or political system for personal gain, future business leaders must take ownership for stewarding the institutions of the market. This book shows you how."

Andrew J. Hoffman, Holcim (US) Professor of Sustainable Enterprise, University of Michigan and author of *Management as a Calling: Leading Business, Serving Society*

"Mirvis and Googins have produced a tremendously useful book on the role that executives can play in social change. Not only does this book cover the gambit of ideas related to sustainability and social change, it is chocker block full of examples that show how these ideas are put into practice. This book is a must-read for executives taking their company on the journey to social change."

Tima Bansal, Professor of Strategy at the Ivey Business School and Founder of Network for Business Sustainability

"*Sustainability to Social Change* begins with a concise yet comprehensive account of the corporate sustainability movement up to the present. The authors then offer principled, practical guidance on how to focus corporate goals towards social change. A valuable read."

Hannah Payson, Executive Director at the Center for Business, Government and Society in The Tuck School of Business at Dartmouth

From Social Changemakers

"At last, a book that blends the 'why' with the 'how': why it's important to embrace social change in business and how leaders can go about it. Data makes it clear that the public expects much more from the private sector, but business executives—even those who are committed—ask, 'What is it I am supposed to be doing now?' *Sustainability to Social Change* lands at the

right moment; drawing on decades of practical research and observation to show the way forward."
Judy Samuelson, Founder and Executive Director of Aspen Institute Business & Society Program and author *The Six New Rules of Business: Creating Real Value in a Changing World*

"Business leading social change? It's easy enough to dismiss this idea, but *Sustainability to Social Change* shows you that giants like Unilever, Ikea, and Novo Nordisk; smaller companies like Ashley Stewart and Lush and Ben & Jerry's; and B Corps are redefining the role of business in society. Read this thoughtful and timely book to get yourself and your company into the 'next' wave."
Sally Uren, CEO at Forum for the Future

"Corporate social responsibility? Sustainability? All good… but NOT GOOD ENOUGH. So say Phil Mirvis and Brad Googins. They provide business leaders a GPS for the next challenge—to create social innovation and real value for their business *and* the world. The authors use stories, frameworks, reflections and insights from their decades of relentlessly examining and challenging the changing role of business in society to convincingly demonstrate that business leaders today can integrate purpose and profit successfully across the value chain."
Cheryl Kiser, Executive Director of the Lewis Institute for Social Innovation and The Babson Social Innovation Lab, and author of *Creating Social Value: A Guide for Leaders and Changemakers*

"*Sustainability to Social Change* makes a compelling case for businesses large and small to tackle the urgent economic, environmental and social challenges of our time. Mirvis and Googins provide solid evidence and engaging real-world examples of how companies are responding to shifting societal expectations and leading social change. This book shows you why such enlightened leadership is essential and how companies can do it!"
Chris Coulter, CEO at GlobeScan and author of *All In: The Future of Business Leadership*

"*Sustainability to Social Change* will make you stop in your tracks and consider: what is business 'for'? Philip Mirvis and Bradley Googins explain how businesses can creatively address problems of inequality, climate change and much more. This book should inspire everyone in your organization, from new hires to the CEO."
Mark Hurst, Founder of Creative Good

"In one sentence, Mirvis and Googins say it all: 'Learn from the changemakers, and be one yourself.' This book—the result of the authors' unique longitudinal studies of inspiring business practices—is rich in illustrative examples, insightful analysis, memorable tips, and persuasive arguments on *why* business leaders must lead social change and *how* to move social value creation to the heart of your business. So, let's get to work and lead that change!"
Susanne Stormer, PwC Partner and change agent

"The call to action in Mirvis and Googins' new book is important and timely. Business has made real progress over the past decade in addressing societal challenges, but results are 'too little' and 'too slow.' The authors don't stop at calling out the private sector's unhurried pace: they provide practical advice, along with checklists, scorecards, and frameworks for leaders to rapidly evolve their businesses to meet the urgent needs of the world today."
Deirdre White, CEO at PYXERA Global

Sustainability to Social Change

*Lead Your Company from Managing
Risk to Creating Social Value*

Philip H. Mirvis and Bradley K. Googins

KoganPage

First published in Great Britain and the United States in 2022 by Kogan Page Limited

2nd Floor, 45 Gee Street	8 W 38th Street, Suite 902	4737/23 Ansari Road
London	New York, NY 10018	Daryaganj
EC1V 3RS	USA	New Delhi 110002
United Kingdom		India
www.koganpage.com		

Kogan Page books are printed on paper from sustainable forests.

© Philip H. Mirvis and Bradley K. Googins 2022

The right of Philip H. Mirvis and Bradley K. Googins to be identified as the author of this work has been asserted by them in accordance with the Copyright, Designs and Patents Act 1988.

ISBNs

Hardback	978 1 3986 0437 7
Paperback	978 1 3986 0435 3
Ebook	978 1 3986 0436 0

British Library Cataloguing-in-Publication Data

A CIP record for this book is available from the British Library.

Library of Congress Cataloging-in-Publication Data
Names: Mirvis, Philip H., 1951- author. | Googins, Bradley K., author.
Title: Sustainability to social change: lead your company from managing risks to creating social value / Philip H. Mirvis and Bradley K. Googins.
Description: 1 Edition. | New York, NY: Kogan Page, 2022. | Includes bibliographical references and index. | Summary: "Is your company using its talent to create social value? Or is it simply managing risks? To address the problems facing society and business today, sustainability is not good enough. Instead, companies need to do their part to lead social change. In Sustainability to Social Change, leadership and social innovation experts Philip Mirvis and Bradley K. Googins share their hands-on research to reveal how leaders can design and guide their companies to create more inclusive prosperity and become agents of social change. The book reveals the inside story of how socially innovative companies are making the strategic shift from minimizing risk to creating social value. It then outlines the strategies and practices that leaders can use to address the five biggest problems facing companies and society today: Purpose, Prosperity, Products, Planet and People."– Provided by publisher.
Identifiers: LCCN 2021059744 (print) | LCCN 2021059745 (ebook) | ISBN 9781398604353 (paperback) | ISBN 9781398604377 (hardback) | ISBN 9781398604360 (ebook)
Subjects: LCSH: Organizational change. | Risk management. | Social responsibility of business. | Social values. | Social change.
Classification: LCC HD58.8 .M57 2022 (print) | LCC HD58.8 (ebook) | DDC 658.4/06–dc23/eng/20220110
LC record available at https://lccn.loc.gov/2021059744
LC ebook record available at https://lccn.loc.gov/2021059745

Typeset by Integra Software Services, Pondicherry
Print production managed by Jellyfish
Printed and bound by CPI Group (UK) Ltd, Croydon CR0 4YY

To daughters Alexa, Lucy and Suzy, for all you've been and will be
Phil

To sons Nicholas and Benjamin, may your future flourish
Brad

CONTENTS

LIST OF FIGURES

SOURCES

The case material here comes from personal interviews, field observations, our own action studies, and in some instances corporate reports, scholarly papers, journalists' accounts, and blogs. Our ten years of field research involved over 70 companies, select foundations, and think tanks based mostly in the United States, Europe, Africa, and Asia. This is a sample of convenience and not representative of companies worldwide or of any industry. Field research involved face-to-face interviews with executives, CSR and sustainable leaders, and employees at their base sites and at projects in the field. Supplemental information was obtained from fellow scholars and surveys by professional service firms. Our thanks to everyone we met who contributed to this research and informed our thinking.

Select material in this book has been reported in our prior writings, including:

Mirvis, PH (2012) Employee engagement and CSR: Transactional, relational, and developmental approaches, *California Management Review*, 54 (4), pp. 93–117.

Mirvis, PH, Googins, B and Kiser, C (2012) Corporate social innovation, Lewis Institute, Social Innovation Lab, Babson College.

Mirvis, PH (2017) Stewardship and human resource management: From me to we to all of us, in *Corporate Stewardship*, Routledge, pp. 134–55.

Mirvis, PH and Googins, B (2017) The new business of business: Innovating for a better world, Giving Thoughts, Conference Board.

Mirvis, PH and Googins, B (2018) Engaging employees as social innovators, *California Management Review*, 60 (4), pp. 25–50.

Mirvis, PH (2020) From inequity to inclusive prosperity: The corporate role, *Organizational Dynamics*, https://doi.org/10.1016/j.orgdyn.2020.100773

All excerpts and adaptations made by agreement or permission.

Introduction

Business is on the cusp of serious social change. Beyond its tragic toll on human health and wellbeing, the coronavirus stalled economic growth and shuttered over one-third of small businesses during lockdowns (historic numbers permanently). It also accelerated shifts to digital shopping and e-commerce and a hybrid workplace of in-office and remote workers is the new normal. Climate change and extreme weather events—heatwaves, hurricanes, floods, and fires—have a direct impact on 70 percent of the global economy and are already affecting more than one in four organizations worldwide.[1] Social movements concerning racial, ethnic, and gender equity are sweeping into companies and social media has amplified a "cancel culture" where you and/or your company could be publicly shamed and boycotted for transgressions, saying the wrong thing, or failing to take a stand. Add to all of this a global refugee crisis, charged domestic political divisions, plus spikes in disinformation and cyberhacking, and every business, including yours, is facing perils.

Gone are the days when a company could address issues like these with tweaks to work schedules, more spend on digital marketing, better waste and emissions management, a few "diversity" hires, and assorted other risk management measures, all supported by philanthropy and an uplifting PR campaign—and otherwise go about its everyday business. That doesn't cut it anymore. Employees and wired-up consumers see through cosmetic changes and view vacuous virtue signaling with disdain. Instead people want real change; great majorities of the public worldwide are calling on business to step up, speak out, and do more to help solve economic, social, and environmental problems. No more sitting on the sidelines or waiting for gridlocked government to take the lead. As Hamdi Ulukaya, CEO of Greek yogurt maker Chobani, puts it, "In today's world, the private sector is the most effective changemaker."[2] Are you and your company ready to lead social change?

Progress to Date: Good, but Not Good Enough

We have been studying business leadership for decades now. When we got started in the 1970s, most companies had a narrow view of their responsibilities—jobs, profits, and taxes—and were guided by economist Milton Friedman's advice that "the one and only social responsibility of business is to use its resources and engage in activities designed to increase its profits."[3] Today, by comparison, the majority of business leaders say that they are committed to social responsibility and sustainability, and many are changing the way they do business. Why so? Customers, investors, regulators, and the public expect more socially conscious and accountable business behavior. And so do the people in your company.

Over these past decades, progress on this journey has been animated by powerful ideas and calls to action; back in 1987, the United Nation's Brundtland Commission made a plea for sustainable development and in 2015 business joined with the UN to issue global Sustainable Development Goals (SDGs). In the early 2000s, financial institutions began to incorporate ESG (environmental, social, governance) factors into capital markets and public companies could monitor their ESG performance on the Dow Jones Sustainability Index (DJSI) and the London Stock Exchange FTSE4Good Index. Over the next years, thought leaders proposed business models to protect the earth and serve consumers at the economic base of the pyramid (BoP) and outlined how business could profit from creating "shared value" with society—making it a "win–win" proposition.

In 2019, some 180 CEOs of major US companies in the Business Roundtable issued their "Statement of Purpose of a Corporation" which said they would be no longer bound by the single-minded pursuit of profits, but instead lead their companies "for the benefit of all stakeholders—customers, employees, suppliers, communities and shareholders." The World Economic Forum followed this with its *Davos Manifesto 2020*, declaring "stakeholder capitalism" as "the universal purpose of a company."[4]

So why yet another book on this journey? Well, the evidence is in that while the laggards are finally taking their first steps, many of the early movers and heretofore fast followers are slowing down. A 2019 survey of 1,000 big company CEOs found that just one in five (21 percent) are making a meaningful contribution to achieving the SDGs. A 2020 survey of experts reports that the private sector's performance on sustainability has been trending downward. Now, even with a post-pandemic recovery, companies worldwide are "underperforming" in their efforts to reduce inequality and studies find a "huge gap" between what companies say and what they actually do when it comes to meeting their stakeholders' needs.[5]

Some business leaders say that stalled progress is mostly a matter of "implementation"—noting that these things take time, there are pockets of resistance, it is complicated and difficult to put new policies and practices into effect—so just be patient. They remind us too that other priorities, like digitizing the business, responding to cyber threats, and redesigning the workplace post-Covid, compete for a company's attention and resources today. All true, but our concerns are more fundamental and have to do with how business has framed its sustainability agenda (motivation and mindset) and charted its course (route and goals).

Now we don't discount the progress business has made these past decades. We're not advising you to abandon your sustainability programs, nor to stop sharing value with your stakeholders. Each of these movements has yielded strategies and practices that benefited both society and the business bottom line. But, frankly, given the problems we face today, progress to date is good, but... NOT GOOD ENOUGH.

What is needed to get things moving again—faster and toward a better place? Einstein once famously said, "We can't solve our problems by using the same kind of thinking we used when we created them." We believe that it is time to rethink the journey to sustainability and here we make a case for why the time is now. We will show you how some innovative companies are on a new tack—pivoting from managing risks to creating social value—and setting a course to lead social change.

What Needs to Change?

Is business basically greedy, selfish, and evil? You might think so if you read social media maven Arianna Huffington's *Pigs at the Trough* or David Korten's *When Corporations Rule the World* or just about anything by business critic Naomi Klein. Documentaries like *Supersize Me*, *The Corporation*, and *Capitalism: A Love Story* by Michael Moore dramatize the seamy side of big business.

If you find this material too biased or leftish, consider that Edelman's Global Trust Barometer reports that only one in five of the world's public believes "the system is working for me" (2019) and 56 percent agree that "Capitalism as it exists today does more harm than good in the world" (2020).[6] Stated simply, the private sector, historic engine of economic growth, jobs, and trade, source of most goods and services, and driver of progress and the rise of the middle class, is now suspect.

These attitudes are not universal. Trust in business is high in China, where 850 million have risen out of poverty in the past two decades, and in India, whose middle class has increased to over 40 percent of its populace today and is projected to rise to nearly 70 percent by 2030, and also in Singapore, now ranked as the world's most competitive economy. Where is trust in business in the pits? Germany, Japan, the UK, and the US. "We are living in a trust paradox," says Richard Edelman, Edelman CEO:

> Since we began measuring trust 20 years ago, economic growth has fostered rising trust. This continues in Asia and the Middle East but not in developed markets, where national income inequality is now the more important factor. Fears are stifling hope, and long-held assumptions about hard work leading to upward mobility are now invalid.[7]

For 50 years, business models based on maximizing shareholder returns have made the rich richer but created massive income gaps between the well to do (the top 10 percent) and the rest of us (the other 90 percent) in the US, UK, and much of continental Europe, and caused the middle class to shrivel. Globally, 69 of the richest 100 "entities" in the world are corporations, not nations. Young people in particular are turned off by rapacious profit-driven business behavior and growing numbers of people worldwide want to buy from, work for, and invest in companies that do business a better way.

Whether you read *The Economist* or the *Wall Street Journal*, tune into CNBC, Sky News Business Channel, or India's ET Now, or pick up Thomas Piketty's *Capital in the 21st Century*, Paul Collier's *The Future of Capitalism: Facing the new anxieties*, or Rebecca Henderson's *Reimagining Capitalism in a World on Fire*, a consistent theme emerges: capitalism as currently practiced in much of the world isn't working and something must be done to fix it. There is more to this outcry than disillusioned "Maoist Millennials" in the US flirting with socialism or protests by Occupy Wall Street and French yellow vests. And we need something better than the British government ordering schools not to use educational resources from groups seeking an end to capitalism. The "system" *does* need changing. What can you and your business do?

Pledges to promote stakeholder capitalism alongside the shareholder model are a start. Some leading businesses are turning away from quarterly forecasts and short-term profit taking toward longer-term value creation. New ideas and models of a more equitable and inclusive economy are moving from academic circles into business practice. B Corps—now numbering over 4,000 companies—are legally required to produce a "public benefit" for society and/or the environment while earning profits.[8] If not already, these hybrid businesses will soon be your competitors. Companies individually and in partnerships with other businesses, government, and nongovernmental organizations (NGOs) are tackling the world's most pressing problems. To push this forward, the Omidyar Network is supporting the work of hundreds of think tanks, NGOs, and academic associations to "reimagine capitalism" and the US National Civic League has launched a "New Capitalism Project" to bring together the leaders of 90 organizations, across every sector, to share perspectives and align their efforts.

Behind all of this is a new conception of the role of business in society. A report on the *Principles for Purposeful Business* by the British Academy states it in this way: "the purpose of business is to solve the problems of people and planet profitably, and not profit from causing problems."[9] What are the big problems that need solving?

Five Key Problems All Businesses Need to Address

Wherever your company is based around the globe, there are five universal problems that business must address to earn the public's trust and help to build a better future:

1   **Purpose.** The idea that the business of business is to maximize profits and serve only its shareowners is shortsighted, lopsided, and well past its shelf life. CEOs have agreed that employees, customers, suppliers, and communities are stakeholders who should be on the same footing as investors. But, at this pivotal post-pandemic moment, 83 percent of senior executives say that business must take the lead, create solutions, and drive change on today's most pressing issues. Companies driven by such a positive purpose are rated 4.1 times more favorably worldwide than those just doing business as usual.[10]
    Reflect: Apart from its philanthropy, can you explain how your company helps to solve society's problems?

2   **Prosperity.** The top 1 percent of households globally own 43 percent of all personal wealth while the bottom 50 percent have only 1 percent.[11] CEO pay has skyrocketed (to 320 × the average US worker) and pay gaps in companies between men versus women and white majorities versus non-white minorities persist. Business leaders are waking up to fairness: some 88 percent of CEOs believe our global economic systems need to refocus on equitable growth.[12]
    Reflect: What is your company doing to promote equity and inclusive prosperity?

3   **People.** Globally, just 20 percent of the workforce is engaged by their work (34 percent in the US and Canada; 11 percent in Western Europe). The rest just "show up" for their jobs or are totally turned off. Even the comparatively motivated ones want "something more" from their jobs and companies.[13] Research tells us that Millennials (born 1981–1996) and Gen Zers (born 1997–2012) work for purpose more than a paycheck. And some 90 percent want to help solve social and environmental problems on their jobs![14]

   Reflect: Are you engaging your employees as a "whole" person? Are they doing work that is useful for society?

4   **Products.** What we put in our bodies (food) and on our bodies (clothes) is problematic. Chief culprits include processed-food purveyors, fast-food franchises, and fast-fashion brands that exploit labor (overseas and domestic) and produce massive amounts of waste. Consumers worldwide today want brands that both "solve my problems" (85 percent) *and* help to "solve society's problems" (80 percent).[15] Meanwhile, billions worldwide can't get access to banking, technology, or adequate healthcare while overconsumption in wealthy nations threatens our health, shrivels our psyches, and is killing our earth's life support systems.

   Reflect: How do your products or services make the world a better place?

5   **Planet.** The World Economic Forum cites climate change as the #1 threat to business—and humankind.[16] The earth is warming. What's next? Glaciers, snowpack, and polar ice sheets melt and sea levels rise, threatening coastal cities and islands with flooding. Oceans heat up and become more acidic, bleaching coral and dissolving the shells of marine life. Heatwaves increase, wildfires, hurricanes, and storms intensify, and we get extreme weather events. Is sustainability the answer? As Bill McDonough likes to say: "sustainable means 100 percent less bad," which means not adding any more damage. A more ambitious agenda is to help restore our earth that has been ravaged by centuries of industrialization and deforestation.

   Reflect: Can your business help the planet to flourish?

You are surely aware of these five problems, having seen them mount over the past several decades. Each of these is relevant to the success of your business to varying degrees. They impinge on your company's strategy, marketing, operations, supply chains, investment decisions, HR practices, measurements, and reporting systems. You are likely taking steps to address one or more of them—maybe just "baby steps" or perhaps big strides.

This is a book about how select companies, large and small, public and private, all around the world, are tackling these problems in a new and positive way and how leaders, managers, entrepreneurs, and everyday employees are speeding up progress and effecting social change.

Leading For a Better Future

Millennials and Gen Z will comprise over half the workforce in a few years. Many of them have been schooled in sustainability and shared value in their MBA and undergraduate programs, participated in green teams and service-learning assignments on campus, and take jobs (and leave them) based on a company's purpose and social performance. They will query you during interviews: Is the operation really green? Are raw materials or supplies being sourced ethically? Are the products produced and services provided harmful, neutral, or helpful to the planet? Is what you do useful to society? How so?

Cone's surveys report that 83 percent of Millennials say they would be more loyal to a company that helps them contribute to social and environmental issues, and 88 percent say their job is more fulfilling when they are provided opportunities to make a positive impact on social and environmental issues. "For Millennials, it's not enough to simply work for a company that's doing good," says a Cone executive, "This generation wants to get their hands dirty—providing ideas, suggesting improvements and participating in efforts on the ground. Companies that give Millennials opportunities to get involved will be rewarded with a more engaged and invested workforce."[17]

Gen Z employees and consumers are "digital natives" and far more racially and ethnically diverse than prior generations. Some one in six Gen Z adults in the US are LGBTQ. Over one in seven worldwide have joined in protests aimed to "make a difference" on social issues. To many of them, what companies have accomplished to date on sustainability and shared value is not sufficient. They aspire to "change the system" and they want to produce "social impact." And they think of themselves as changemakers. Are you ready to lead them?

In this book, you'll meet social impact investors (a $2.1 trillion industry) who support B Corps, social businesses, and other enterprises that aspire to profitably produce benefits for society. Smart companies are themselves operating as impact investors by funding social entrepreneurs to source new ideas and by hosting contests, maker spaces, labs, incubators, and "action tanks" where employees (and customers) can, individually or in teams, develop socially beneficial ideas and translate them into plans and proto-types. We will look at corporate social innovation through which compa-nies, their employee "intrapreneurs", and other partners develop products that take pollution and carbon out of the air, fortify foods with healthier nutrients, increase access to banking, technology, and education, and open new markets in poor inner cities, among underserved populations, and in rural areas untouched by modern commerce.[18]

Social change is being sped up by the Fourth Industrial Revolution where the Internet of Things (IoT), artificial intelligence (AI), autonomous vehicles, robots, drones, 3D printing, cloud computing, nanotechnology, are all open-ing up a brave new world where machines can think and do tasks heretofore accomplished by people.[19] Biotech is already producing wonder drugs (e.g., the coronavirus vaccine) and can be used to fight disease, improve health, increase crop yields, reduce hunger, lessen industrial waste, and even clean the air of pollution and greenhouse gas (CO_2) emissions. Some 3.8 billion people have a smartphone today. Will all of this technology help to solve our problems and open up a brighter future? It may but it also promises to disrupt industries, displace workers, lead to more personal surveillance, and exacerbate social inequities. Are you ready for this future?

Rest assured, this is *not* a book about "altruism" in business or about companies that generally "do well by doing good." It speaks to specific, real challenges companies face, how they turn problems into opportunities, and what actions they take that produce tangible and intangible benefits for the firm, its multiple stakeholders, and the world we live in.

Our intent is to get you to think more creatively about your business and your role in it, and more broadly about yourself as an investor, consumer, and citizen of society and the planet. We've studied hundreds of companies world-wide and met with countless managers, marketers, entrepreneurs, and work-ers to learn what they are thinking and to see what they are doing to make a better world. These companies don't operate with a "secret sauce," and none has a foolproof recipe that others can follow. Managers in these firms are not a "special breed." They face the same day-to-day demands you do of produc-ing growth, delivering results, developing people, and innovating to meet marketplace needs and beat competitors. What distinguishes them is not that they care about the world we live in, but that they have reimagined how to do business with that aspiration at their core.

What's Inside?

This book is organized in two parts. Part I is about Where We Are Now, Where We Are Going, and How to Get There. It provides an overview of the sustainability journey to date and why business is stepping into a new role to lead social change. It includes a close look at how companies we have studied and worked with—Novo Nordisk, Ben & Jerry's, Interface Carpets, Nike, and Unilever, among others—took up the mantle of being agents of change. It concludes with some guidance for you on "how to" change your organization to change the world—whether as a startup, an established business transforming itself, a company being changed from the "bottom up," or one continuously adapting to the future.

Part II addresses How to Lead Social Change. Successive chapters speak to the challenges to be faced in leading your business in this "next" wave of social change. You will be invited to "look in the mirror" and rate your own company's progress (short questionnaire in each chapter). Hopefully, you'll record some real accomplishments, but you'll likely also see areas where your performance is NOT GOOD ENOUGH. To stimulate and guide you, each chapter presents ideas, examples, and even inspiration to draw from in moving your organization forward on Purpose, Prosperity, People, Products, and Planet, and engaging with others to effect Systemic Social Change.

Buckle up: the journey ahead isn't easy and once you've started on it, there's no turning back.

PART ONE

Where We Are Now, Where We Are Going, and How To Get There

01

Sustainability:
The End of the Beginning

For several decades, we have tracked the journey toward sustainability for companies around the world. Early on we observed how a set of eco- and socially conscious trailblazers—Ben & Jerry's and Patagonia in the US, the UK-based Body Shop, India's Jaipur Rugs, and Brazil's Natura, among others—embraced greening and sought, from the get-go, to use their products and profits to improve conditions in society. They set an example that social businesses emulate to this day. Their influence is seen in both mid-size players like buy-one-donate-one TOMs shoes, Warby Parker eyewear, and the social media platform Hootsuite as well as in smaller shops such as Oakland's educational toymaker GoldieBlox, Madrid's clothing recycler Ecoalf, a London consultancy, The Social Change Agency, that helps its clients get going on crowdfunding, and CarePro in Japan that provides on-the-spot health checks in train stations and shopping centers.

In 2007, we chronicled how big companies got on this track. In *Beyond Good Company*, we reported that mainstream business worldwide had accepted the idea that "business as usual" was no longer viable. CEOs understood that society expected more responsible conduct and that their operating environment had changed.[1] Activists and investors were holding them to account for their business "externalities": pollution, waste, harmful additives, unsafe products, exploitation of people and land in global supply chains, false or misleading marketing, and "bad" behavior generally. Complex social issues—rising rates of obesity, youth unemployment, a digital divide, and declining trust in business—posed new challenges and threats. A top-down mandate emerged: clean up our operations and dress up our image with philanthropy. And a new agenda was set: minimize our negative impact on people and the planet, mitigate risks to our business and brands, and protect our reputation, all guided by this cautionary ethic: "Do less harm."

We also saw some leading-edge businesses taking a more affirmative approach and framing their strategies in terms of sustainability and a brand-driven approach to corporate social responsibility (CSR). To gauge their progress, we introduced a model of the sequential "stages" that most companies go through as they progress toward more sustainable and responsible ways of doing business. Some firms, like Nike and Shell, were thrust into this journey by public protests and shaming over their abuse of human rights and the environment. Others, like British Telecom, La Farge, Microsoft, PepsiCo, NEC, and even Walmart "woke up" and began making solid, incremental progress. And a few, such as Danone, Novo Nordisk, and Unilever—the "best of the good"—sped through the stages by repurposing themselves to "make a better world" through their businesses.

A few years ago, we started another deep dive into business around the world. A sea change was underway. Big companies were conducting regular assessments of social, political, and ecological issues to identify those that were "material" to their business—in terms of costs, growth, and risks. Leading firms were "internalizing" their impacts on society and had plans and programs to address them. Some had embraced the idea that business should be measured against a "Triple Bottom Line" (TBL) and began accounting for their economic, social, and environmental performance.[2] Many issued annual sustainability reports that touted, alongside data on profits and earnings-per-share, how they were greening their factories and offices, protecting the people and land in their overseas supply chains, and addressing social issues through CSR. (In increasing numbers, these reports are audited by independent parties.)

To manage this makeover, companies tasked their human resource group, consumer affairs office, investor relations people, supply chains functions, and departments concerned with CSR, sustainability, and public affairs with monitoring the firm's impacts and mitigating potential harms. Each of these functions keeps a checklist of dos-and-don'ts, makes sure the business is in compliance with laws and policies, and, most important, protects the firm from adverse publicity or, in business-speak, "reputational threats."

What has all this progress given us? More Responsible Conduct. Seemingly More Accountable Companies. And Less Harm to People, Societies, and the Planet. All good, but is this Good Enough?

The Company Footprint: Manage Risks, Do Less Harm

When the idea of sustainability first caught on in business, so did the need to attend to your company's *footprint*. Initially, the footprint referred to the environmental impact that a business has on society from its carbon emissions, energy use, waste production, pollutants, and such. Later, it was applied to a company's negative impact on society—such as unhealthy food, unsafe products, unfair employment practices, and other unsavory business doings. In response, food producers and franchisers reduced their use of "bad" ingredients and turned to more environmentally friendly packaging. We see the impact today as soaps, perfumes, and hair sprays are stripped of unhealthy chemical additives—to do less harm.

Former CEO of fast-food chain Wendy's, Emil J. Brolick, tweeted: "We want to get to the point where nothing on our labels looks like it came from a chemistry book."[3] His comments came after another fast-food competitor, Subway, said it would remove the chemical azodicarbonamide from its bread. Why remove it? Well, food blogger Vani Hari, who runs the website FoodBabe.com, gained 75,000 signatures to a petition asking to ban the chemical which is also found in shoe rubber and yoga mats.

Recent years have seen many companies *stop* doing bad things. CVS pharmacies stopped selling cigarettes. Walmart and Dick's Sporting Goods stopped selling assault-style weapons. Restaurants stopped using plastic straws. Hotels, with a guest's approval, stopped washing bedsheets and towels every day. Major retailers certify that their overseas suppliers are *not* exploiting labor, polluting the environment, or taking bribes. Google announced that it will stop selling ads using your personally identifiable information from web browsers. In his annual letters to investors, Larry Fink, influential CEO of BlackRock, has urged businesses to stop focusing on financial performance alone and take social and environmental concerns more seriously. This is a big leap from decades ago when, as one CEO joked with us, "we used to laugh and say we were good environmental stewards. We paid our fines on time."

The point here is that a company's oversized footprint on the environment is bad. Everybody wants less of it! Cone Communications' annual survey of consumers finds that nearly one in three "regularly or always" considers the environmental impact of their purchasing decisions and that nearly 90 percent expect companies to address the full environmental impact of a product over its lifecycle, from its manufacture, to use, to disposal.[4] Top companies have, as a result, made CO_2 reduction and eco-efficient production key priorities. This is not due to corporate beneficence. Green is gold! Companies save money by reducing waste, using less energy, and conserving water. And even when they have to put in new technology or processes to "green" things up, the payback is still significant.[5]

How about a company's footprint in society? No employee should suffer at the hands of an abusive boss or work for an exploitative company. The spillover in higher blood pressure, drinking, drug abuse, and family problems can be staggering. No customer should be scammed or discover they purchased unsafe or defective goods. No investor should be lied to or cheated. And no community wants a bad company in its neighborhood. It is widely known that consumers, investors, and the public at large will punish "bad" company behavior—by bad-mouthing the business, giving it a thumbs down, and sometimes going so far as to join social media campaigns and boycotts. Even Milton Friedman, we believe, would argue that company actions taken to forestall such problems are in the best interests of investors.

So we're all for reducing the harms of the company footprint as concerns the ecology of the planet and the health of its inhabitants. But this approach has been mostly motivated by risk management. Attention to their footprint has seen companies focus on *minimizing* impacts, *mitigating* risks, *protecting* reputation, and "doing less bad." Operating in this mode makes managers reactive rather than proactive, dutiful rather than creative, and cautious rather than courageous.

Look at the consequences: John Elkington, the "Godfather of Sustainability" and originator of the Triple Bottom Line concept 25 years ago, has issued a "recall" on the TBL. He has "given up" on this "report card" because it has been "captured and diluted by accountants" and reduced to "box ticking" in corporate annual reports.[6] Like so many endeavors, it seems the sustainability movement has been damned by its first principle. With all of this focus on risk management and harm reduction, as one wag put it, the company footprint is now "stuck in the mud."

Doing Better: Sharing Value and Serving Stakeholders

Scan business periodicals, search the web, look at company websites and annual reports and you'll see heartfelt stories, evocative pictures and videos, and even some credible evidence that companies are doing good deeds. A few years ago, *Fortune* began to publish an annual list of big corporations that "Change the World" through their good works. Look closer, however, and you will find that most do-good initiatives are funded and managed by a corporate foundation or CSR function. In other words, charity. Now the idea that business should "give back" some of its profits to society is laudable. It is a hallmark in US business history and good for communities. Many US companies are generous with their philanthropy, work hand in hand with nonprofits to serve society, and even provide "paid time" for employees to give voluntary service under the corporate banner. These practices are spreading around the business world today, to companies on every continent.

A familiar and, to our eyes, tiresome critique is that CSR is just greenwashing, designed to deflect attention from what's really going on in companies. But a stronger challenge is that these CSR-type activities are typically "bolted on" rather than "built in" to the business. They are "nice" to do but are simply not planned, managed, measured, and held to account like business activities connected to the P&L statement and managers' performance reviews.

Bridging this gap, Michael Porter and Mark Kramer proposed in 2006 that companies key their philanthropy to the interests of stakeholders and the firm's brand ("Strategic Philanthropy") and in 2011 made a business case for "shared value" whereby companies could find business opportunities in social and environmental problems and devise business models that benefit both business and society.[7] The *Harvard Business Review* heralded this as "the next evolution of capitalism."

Our recent scan of businesses around the world confirms that many companies have evolved. Jeffrey Hollender, the green founder of Seventh Generation, prefaced this point in *What Matters Most: How a small group of pioneers is teaching social responsibility to big business, and why big business is listening.*[8] Big companies first responded by acquiring socially responsible brands. The Body Shop was bought by L'Oréal, Tom's of Maine by Colgate-Palmolive, Stonyfield Farm by Groupe Danone, Burt's Bees by Clorox, and confectioner Green & Black's by Cadbury Schweppes. Unilever acquired Ben & Jerry's and later Seventh Generation. Then leading companies took steps to clean up their existing product portfolios and develop new healthy, eco-friendly, and socially conscious offerings and brands.

PepsiCo took up this challenge when Indra K. Nooyi was named CEO of the company and connected purpose to profit. She described her aspiration in this way: "Performance with purpose is what I'd like PepsiCo to stand for... We have a profound role to play in society, and we have to make sure that we are constructive members of society." On a corporate level, PepsiCo brought its purpose into focus with its decision to sell off fast-food franchises KFC, Taco Bell, and Pizza Hut (the "bad stuff"), and then acquire Tropicana, Gatorade, and Quaker Oats (the "good stuff"). These moves positioned the company to offer healthier food choices for consumers. In turn, Frito Lay reduced saturated fats and sodium and eliminated trans fats in its offerings, and joined the multi-company Roundtable on Sustainable Palm Oil (RSPO) to source 100 percent certified sustainable palm oil.

PepsiCo then formed a Global Nutrition Group, comprising R&D, innovation, marketing, product development, procurement, and supply chain, to develop more nutritious foods and beverages, or what it termed "good-for-you" products. PepsiCo's good-for-you offerings include snack recipes with lentils and rice, yogurt, hummus, and baked grains plus a juice, Tropicana Farmstand, that provides one serving of fruit and one serving of vegetables in each eight-ounce glass. What has happened to its "fun-for-you" products—like Pepsi Cola? The company reports that its sugar- and salt-laden products shrunk to 12 percent of its revenues, while nutrition brands, low-calorie beverages, and healthier snacks grew to roughly 45 percent.

Nowadays "purpose" is the watchword in business circles. Consumer companies have turned to purpose-driven branding and marketing. B2B companies use purpose to differentiate themselves from competitors. Employers pitch purpose to their Millennial and incoming Gen Z employees. And countless management gurus promise business leaders that purpose produces significant profits. It surely can, but for whom: shareholders?

We got a fresh answer when US CEOs of the Business Roundtable declared, "Americans deserve an economy that allows each person to succeed through hard work and creativity and to lead a life of meaning and dignity" and were joined by the World Economic Forum in favor of stakeholder capitalism. But here's the rub: 84 percent of Americans believe that companies "often hide behind public declarations of support for stakeholders but don't walk the walk."[9] It is easy enough to see why so many view this purpose pledge, given past history and performance, as corporate PR, gaslighting, or worse, "putting lipstick on a pig."

Winners Take All, an insider's book by Anand Giridharadas about the big business leaders who meet at the World Economic Forum at Davos, sign on to Business Roundtable's purpose pledge, and herald their company's CSR and sustainability credentials, calls it all "an elite charade." These business titans, says one reviewer, purport "to change the world while also profiting from the status quo," and goes on, "Theirs is conservatism camouflaged in radical adjectives; change you can't believe in."[10]

The Next Step: Leading Social Change

How about creating change people can believe in? We are at the "end of the beginning" of this current wave of sustainability. One of the early movers into the next wave is Unilever, a global maker of food, beverages, and home and personal goods. Listen to Paul Polman's beliefs as he took over leadership of the company:

> Professor Michael Porter's shared value theory proposes aligning a company's purpose with meaningful contributions to society. My philosophy goes a step further: it's not enough to say you contribute to a better world. The world is at a point where you have to solve the issues and reverse what is happening… Instead of finding ways to use society and the environment to be successful, companies must contribute to society and the environment in order to sustain success.[11]

Unilever's Sustainable Living Plan was launched "to decouple our growth from our environmental footprint, while increasing our positive social impact," Polman explains:

> We set some big—uncomfortable—targets to keep us focused and build trust. This included 100 percent sustainable sourcing; improving the health and hygiene of over a billion people; enhancing livelihoods and accelerating gender equality throughout our value chain; and moving to zero waste. With a global deficit in trust, transparency and accountability were vital to building confidence in our strategy.

One of us worked closely with Unilever on this journey and we will delve into its efforts throughout this book. What's behind its agenda? Polman states it plainly: "Companies that want to be around long-term must have a positive impact on society and the planet. Being less negative simply isn't good enough anymore."

Forces For Change

What is driving companies to shift gears from sustainability to leading social change? Social and political issues unimagined even a decade ago; different societal expectations and demography; hopeful new ideas and innovations; and a collective realization that solving our problems requires collaboration between government, civil society, and business—including its employees, customers, suppliers, and investors. On our recent visits to companies, we saw social change sweeping into the mindsets and practices of managers and innovators throughout the world. Traditionally, business has been a bystander in response to turbulence in society. Now three-fourths of people globally expect CEOs to lead social change rather than wait for government intervention.[12] What at the key forces at work?

1 **Societal challenges are blinking red on the radar screen.** Activists, for sure, but also employees, customers, and other stakeholders expect companies today to speak out and take action on climate change, racial and economic equity, #MeToo, minimum wage and corporate tax rates, and, in the United States, matters like voting rights, immigration, criminal justice reform, and gun control. Edelman's Trust Barometer finds that over nine in ten employees, in a sample of over 34,000 surveyed in 28 countries, want their CEOs to "speak out" on social issues. Surveys also find that 62 percent of consumers want companies to stand up for the issues they are passionate about and seven in ten believe companies have an obligation to take actions to improve issues that may not be relevant to everyday business operations.[13]

2 **Traditional company responses to these challenges are not sufficient.** Sustainable business practices seek to *maintain* living systems without further degrading them. Changemaking companies are turning to regenerative practices that aim to *restore* and even *enhance* the world we live in. We shall see how through biomimicry, carbon capture technologies, and nature-based solutions, companies are moving to net-zero CO_2 emissions and helping to bring back biodiversity. As for social issues, companies traditionally addressed societal challenges through charitable giving and CSR initiatives. Their move to shared value sounds nice, but it licenses a company to care about society only when it is in their self-interest. This doesn't do very much to reconnect business to society, reduce mistrust, or redress the rich–poor gap as such. The corporation remains at the center of this Copernican universe, and the other planets merely align around its gravitational profit-making pull.

3 **Connecting to society is a crucial company competency.** John Browne, former CEO of BP, contends that the ability to "engage radically" with society is the new frontier of competitive advantage for business. He writes, "The connected firms of the future will push the boundaries of human possibilities in their quest to contribute."[14] Along these lines, we have made a case for "shared values" (adding an 's' to shared value)

which requires that corporate aspirations for profits and efficiency be considered alongside social progress and equity. This shifts the center of gravity from self-interest to collective interest and creates a gravitational "field" where all stakeholders understand and appreciate the essential and necessary contributions of other parties.[15]

4 **Technology is changing everything.** Tech products and services with benefits to people, business, and society are proliferating. Consumers today have smart phones with a camera, email, and chat functions; myriad social media sites to make friends and share stories, pictures, and videos; and streaming services packed with information, entertainment, and "edutainment." There are countless apps to aid in travel, monitor your physical activity, health, and heart, get spiritual counsel and social support, and, of course, spend your money. Businesses manage their supply chains via the Internet of Things, store data in the cloud and secure it with blockchain technology, use "big data" to understand customers, deploy select products through 3D printing, and run their meetings virtually. As for biotech, there is CRISPR, which can be used to edit genes and is already making an impact in biomedical research, clinics, and agriculture. A "tech for good" movement is promoting "the intentional design, development and use of digital technologies to address social challenges." What could this movement mean for your business?

5 **Employees are geared up for social change.** There is a growing movement of young people taking creative action under the banners of social innovation and entrepreneurship. Take Babson College (where we are research fellows). The college historically groomed budding business entrepreneurs. Today its inventive and idealistic students work in the school's social innovation lab to devise life-changing apps, formulate healthy food recipes, develop energy-saving technologies, and incubate business ideas aimed at social good. You'll find similar labs at Harvard, Stanford, MIT, and Oxford, on campuses in Singapore, Munich, Sao Paulo, and Beijing, throughout Latin America and Africa and most everywhere else. Where do they go after they graduate? Some start or join social enterprises or B Corps. But many more join companies and look for opportunities to produce social innovations and operate as social intrapreneurs.

6 **Social issues are business opportunities.** Management sage Peter Drucker once opined, "Every single social and global issue of our day is a business opportunity in disguise." In this light, companies are devising strategies and business models to solve societal problems. Their motivation is not altruism.

A 2020 survey of executives finds that over nine in ten believe that addressing social issues and helping to solve societal problems generates increased customer loyalty, aids in employee recruitment and retention, and differentiates their company from its competitors. A great majority (83 percent) said that it also results in better financial performance.[16]

No doubt solutions to our societal problems will depend on leadership and cooperation from government, civil society, business, and each of us. But many executives believe that business, with its speed, scale, and acumen, has a leading role to play in addressing society's pressing issues—immediate ones like recovery from the coronavirus pandemic and its economic fallout, and going forward, climate change, social and economic inequities, and gaps in education and healthcare. Where could the push for business to take a leading role in social change take your company?

02

Social Change: The Start of Something New

Social change reflects transformations in societal mindsets, attitudes, and behaviors, in norms and relationships, in structures and institutions, and ultimately in the prevailing "order." It progresses positively as visionary voices point to a better way, new ideas and innovations emerge, education and aspiration levels rise, and a new generation grows to adulthood full of promise. But social change seems to cycle forward and back as economies boom and bust, birthrates rise and fall, future horizons grow and shrink, and liberal/conservative political ideologies and their appeal wax and wane. Stability is the norm when the existing order seems to be working. The pace of change accelerates with new cultural inputs and social movements and amidst and in the aftermath of wars, plagues, and disasters—natural and manmade.

Business has traditionally had an uneasy outlook on getting involved in social change. Companies have been advised to be bold and courageous in the midst of social change, but as often to be cautious and calculative. Some slogans urge business leaders to surf the waves of social change or be swamped by them, but others counsel them to stay the course as the storm will pass. In making their shift from risk management to creating social value, we see leading businesses taking on a bold new role: an Agent of Change.

One such change agent is Danish pharmaceutical Novo Nordisk. Consider how it takes leadership, creates solutions, and drives change on one of today's most pressing issues.

Leading Social Change: Novo Nordisk

Diabetes is a disease that can either be inherited (type I diabetes) or induced through obesity and other lifestyle factors (type II diabetes), and it poses major health risks for a growing percentage of the world's population, particularly in its type II preventable form. Today one in every eleven persons worldwide suffers from diabetes and, unless something changes, this will grow to one in nine by 2045. This led Novo Nordisk to devise a three-prong strategy to, as the company defined it, "drive change to defeat diabetes" by: 1) Preventing the rise of type II diabetes and obesity; 2) Providing access to affordable care for vulnerable patients in every country; and 3) Driving innovation to improve lives.

Address a Pressing Need. Big pharmaceuticals' business model is based on developing blockbuster drugs that generate at least $1 billion/year in sales. Their R&D is expensive, but their drugs are costly and pharma earns bigger profits than almost every other industry. Novo Nordisk makes insulin as well as diabetes treatment systems (smart insulin pens). And it's a highly profitable business. But that's not good enough for Novo. Its business model involves raising awareness, educating the public about diabetes, working with national and international health systems to treat diabetes, and making its therapies more accessible and affordable. In January 2021, for instance, it announced a cut in the ceiling price of human insulin from $4 to $3 per vial in 76 low- and middle-income countries. That's what it takes to fulfill its guiding purpose to "Defeat Diabetes."

Take Leadership. Public health statisticians estimate that 415 million people worldwide have diabetes but have never been diagnosed and don't know what ails them. Reaching well beyond pharma's traditional mission, Novo sought to change that. First, it created and then invited competitors to join the World Diabetes Foundation (WDF). Novo and the WDF then partnered with the International Diabetes Foundation (IDF) to introduce a resolution to the UN General Assembly to make 14 November an annual World Diabetes Day (only the second health issue, after HIV-AIDS, that the UN has acknowledged in this way). Next, it launched a "Changing Diabetes" World Tour where a bus, staffed by company personnel, nurses, and other health professionals, toured five continents disseminating information on the prevention and treatment of diabetes. The tour team met with more than 58,000 people, and generated media coverage reaching nearly 460 million people worldwide with messages about diabetes. Novo also launched an initiative to bring attention to the problems faced by young diabetics

("Young Voices") and a campaign that provides diabetes education along with free beauty makeovers, diet tips, and peer conversation forums for poor women living with diabetes.

Create Solutions. Novo turned to corporate social innovation to develop integrated diabetes care for the poor. In rural India, for instance, health workers, doctors, and pharmacists were formed into a network and trained to bring diabetes testing and medicines to patients' doorsteps. As of now, over 750,000 people have been reached; 4,000 doctors and paramedics have been trained; and some 100 community diabetes centers have been established. In Nigeria, Novo constructed one-stop-shop diabetes kiosks (to eliminate price markups by pharmacists) and formed a private–public partnership with a hospital in Lagos State to establish a diabetes care center. It recently announced that it would offer insulin free of charge to children in Nigeria as well as Ghana.

Drive Change. To scale its efforts, Novo was a leading voice in formulating and communicating the UN's Sustainable Development Goals (SDGs). SDG No. 3, which calls for a community to "Ensure healthy lives and promote well-being for all at all ages," has specific objectives related to non-communicable diseases (including diabetes). To drive systemic change, Novo is a founding partner of the Cities Changing Diabetes initiative—a cross-disciplinary, cross-sector collaboration to respond to the dramatic rise in urban diabetes across the world. The partnership leverages Novo's expertise in treating diabetes to map and analyze root causes of urban diabetes and identify and scale up solutions to ensure healthy lives and promote well-being in cities. In Rome, one in four children and teens are either overweight or obese. The Rome partnership mapped out 74 walking routes throughout the city and developed an app to motivate and guide young people of every age to get moving. In Johannesburg, the statistics on youth obesity are even more concerning. The Johannesburg partnership set up a program in schools that includes nutrition education, peer support groups, and "performances" where kids learn to cook healthier meals. Over 30 other cities on every continent are involved in the Cities Changing Diabetes partnership.

Why is Novo Nordisk instigating social change? Susanne Stormer, Novo's VP of Corporate Sustainability, explains the motivations in this way: "It seems to me that the role of business in society has changed in the last generation. We as companies need to recognize that we are important to the community not just because we provide economic activity, but also because of the influence we can have." She adds, "When companies are driven by a social purpose, they usually have a clear view of how they can help the people they serve."

Stepping back from this example, you can see that there is no "market requirement" for Novo Nordisk to produce a "public good" like defeating diabetes around the world. But does a business have a public responsibility? Should it create value for society? Typically these kinds of questions are addressed in an ethics course in business schools and forgotten in the day-to-day maelstrom of commerce. But they are being raised afresh amidst social unrest, health pandemics, and worldwide concerns about inequality and climate change.

The Case For Social Value Creation

When companies strive to "solve the problems of people and planet profitably," they draw on the talents of their employees, leverage their philanthropic monies, and deploy the assets of the core business to create social value. But what is social value? To be honest, it's not a familiar business term and not typically covered in a business finance course.

In the world of nonprofit organizations and social entrepreneurs, social value refers to the "non-financial" benefits that social projects, programs, and organizations produce, especially for the "well-being of individuals, communities, and the environment." As Gregory Dees amplifies it, social value is "about inclusion and access... respect and the openness of institutions... history, knowledge, a sense of heritage and cultural identity. Its value is not reducible to economic or socio-economic terms... it has intrinsic value."[1]

But we challenge this narrow construction and have documented social value in endeavors that yield both intrinsic *and* extrinsic (e.g., economic and socio-economic) benefits. These include job creation, community economic development, and other initiatives that expand prosperity; education, training, and development efforts that prepare people for employment or gain them upward mobility; commercial ventures that increase access to banking, technology, and healthcare; and, yes, products and services that make you smarter, healthier, happier, safer, or more self-confident, creative, and productive. In our framing, *social value encompasses the financial and non-financial benefits that companies produce that enhance the physical, psychological, social, and economic well-being of people and society, the health of the planet, and the future of humankind.*

The Value of Intangibles. Social value is often subjective, can mean different things to different people, and like other "soft" variables, is hard to quantify and measure. Traditionally, businesspeople run their companies to produce value that is well-defined, objective, and measured in the "hard" terms of costs, prices, and profits. But here, too, things are changing. Business now recognizes that "intangibles" can have tangible and significant economic value.

Consider the fact that 10,000 publicly traded companies in the world have a market capitalization of more than $200 million and revenues of at least $100 million. Together they generate $40 trillion in revenues and have $74 trillion of enterprise value. Yet only 30 percent of their market value is represented by assets on their balance sheet. The other 70 percent consists of "intangible value"—subjective estimates of their worth by market investors. Look at the S&P 500, the big global companies. In 1975, intangible value accounted for 17 percent of their market valuation; today it's nearly 90 percent.

Now some of this intangible value reflects a company's intellectual property—patents, trademarks, copyrights, and such. But the lion's share is based in a company's reputation, its relationships with customers, employees, suppliers, and other stakeholders, confidence in its management, and, dare we say it, its perceived social value to society. So when you create social value, and your stakeholders and the public give you a thumbs up, your brand value goes up too. Judy Samuelson, author of *The Six New Rules of Business*, says it plainly: "Reputation, trust, and other intangibles drive business value."[2]

Markets for Virtue. As a business leader, you have choices to make: who to hire, how much to invest in your people, where to locate your offices, facilities, and maybe your retail shops, what products and services to make and how to make them, how to position them in the marketplace and what to charge for them, and so on. Typically, these decisions are made based on markets and economic criteria. How does social value figure in?

Economist Joseph Schumpeter was the first among his peers to highlight the import of social value in shaping markets—back in 1909! Listen to his foundational principle: "It is society—and not the individual—which sets a value on things."[3] While from Adam Smith onward the individual rational actor has been the model for most economists, Schumpeter understood that markets are shaped by social influences. People are influenced by what they see respected others think and do, by what is deemed valuable in their neighborhoods, social groups, communities, and in public opinion, and even by shared values about what is right, just, and good.

We have seen for the past several decades these influences converge into what some call "markets for virtue."[4] These markets today include green, healthy, and socially conscious consumers looking for the right products that fit their lifestyle and values; investors who put their funds into companies creating social impact; and employees who want to work for and give their best efforts to companies that are socially responsible. As we shall see, these are not just "niche" markets based in North America and Western Europe. They are big and growing and found all around the world.

That's the theory of the case for creating social value—what does it look in practice? Shinola employs laid-off auto workers and young, mostly Black and ethnic minorities to make watches and leather goods in a reclaimed factory in inner-city Detroit. Jaipur Rugs engages a network of 40,000 artisans in more than 700 villages in India who, in their homes, weave rugs and pillowcases with exotic designs and colors that can be found in high-end stores throughout the world. Leading e-tailers offer their customers a curated selection of sustainably sourced and produced coffee, tea, lotions, potions, and other personal goods through subscription services. Eileen Fisher, Timberland, and Sweden's Nudie Jeans make products from recycled waste and work with consumers to give their used clothes, boots, and jeans a "second life." Meanwhile, in B2B markets, industrial giants "future proof" their business customers through "servitization" contracts where they "lease" customers machinery or equipment, service the gear through a contract period, and then recycle and reuse it with another customer. Social value creation is not some distant next step in the marketplace: next is now.

The Evolution of Good Business: The Next Wave

The next wave in the evolution of good business is already taking shape. How does it differ from the sustainability wave?

- Companies will actively help to SOLVE SOCIETAL PROBLEMS.
- Attention will turn to EQUITY AND INCLUSION.
- Employees will DEVELOP as SOCIAL INNOVATORS to enable their organization to create a better future.
- Customers will be ACTIVATED and CO-CREATE products and services that solve their problems *and* those of society.
- Our collective ambition will be to RESTORE and REGENERATE the planet.

- Business, government, and civil society will work together to create SYSTEMIC SOCIAL CHANGE.

That's a lot. Let's see the logic behind these big moves.

Seek a Higher Purpose: Solve Social Problems. Is stakeholder capitalism the answer to all our problems? In *Grow the Pie: How great companies deliver both purpose and profit*, Alex Edmans makes an evidence-based business case that companies can get themselves out of the box of managing "trade-offs" between shareholders versus other stakeholders by growing revenue and giving more to all concerned.[5] It's an appealing win–win–win message for companies, shareowners, and other stakeholders but "pie-economics" doesn't speak to what business could do to tackle systemic racism and inequities, or to respond to the 50 percent of today's employees who find no meaning in their work, let alone the 200 million worldwide who want but can't find a job. Nor does it tell companies how to make good and healthy products more affordable or how they might help to reverse climate change.

Unilever's Paul Polman has an answer: "We are finding out quite rapidly that to be successful long term we have to ask: what do we actually give to society to make it better?" There is more to this than growing the pie. The question asks about whom you employ, how you operate, and what you produce—does it make society any better? Business leaders and entrepreneurs are banding together to make society better through "conscious capitalism." The emphasis in this new movement, started by Whole Foods' John Mackey and academic Raj Sisodia, is that companies need a "higher purpose" and more socially aware and attuned leaders, managers, and work cultures.[6] Along these lines, B Corps have joined in a worldwide community that "works toward reduced inequality, lower levels of poverty, a healthier environment, stronger communities, and the creation of more high-quality jobs with dignity and purpose."

Move to Equity and Inclusive Prosperity. Let's be honest, business has not to date shared value equitably. From 1975 to 2019, productivity increased 155 percent in the United States while wages rose roughly 12 percent overall and, inflation adjusted, actually declined for hourly and nonsupervisory salaried workers. Current pay gaps between employed men versus women persist in the US (16 percent), EU (16.2 percent), and Asia Pacific (14.8 percent). And wealth gaps have grown between rich and poor nations, and between majority versus minority populations within nations.[7]

CEOs who have awakened to "fairness" are taking steps to fix inequities. A salary audit at cloud computing company Salesforce revealed a statistically significant difference in pay between men and women. "It was everywhere," CEO Marc Benioff admitted in a *60 Minutes* interview. "It was through the whole company, every department, every division, every geography." The company responded by spending $3 million in 2016 to start to correct things and then another $3 million in 2017 to eliminate differences by gender, race, and ethnicity across the company. This propelled a clean-up of pay inequities in tech companies around the world. Good enough? Not for change-minded companies. They are taking strong steps to build a more multicultural and bias-free workplace. Starbucks, for instance, has pledged that BIPOC (Black, indigenous, people of color) employees will comprise 30 percent of its corporate workforce by 2025 and over 40 percent of its retail and manufacturing jobs. Its managers are schooled in how "unconscious bias" intrudes on their judgments about people and the company launched a series of internal "courageous conversations" among staff about social justice. Starbucks has begun to publish details on the racial, ethnic, and gender makeup of its workforce from top and bottom, and measure and reward its managers based on diversity hiring and advancement. It's astonishing what business can accomplish when it puts its mind to it and resources behind it. Business was a driving force in the legalization of gay marriage in the United States and elsewhere. As we will see, leading companies are now supporting the Black Lives Matter movement.

Engage Employees as Social Innovators. In our recent studies, we spotted a new kind of "developmental" contract between employers and their employees where a company aims to more fully develop and activate its employees to produce greater value for the business *and* society.[8] This includes work on greening the supply chain, reducing energy use and emissions, improving product stewardship, and in jobs involving fair trade or cause-related marketing, social auditing and reporting, stakeholder engagement, and so on. These activities constitute "good work" and provide the social significance predictive of higher levels of employee engagement

How about getting employees engaged in social change? Manuel Martinez, Manager of Open Innovations at Ferrovial, the Spanish multinational in the design, construction, and operation of urban infrastructure, has activated employees as intrapreneurs via a worldwide innovation contest. The program, titled "zuritanken" (which is a combination of the Swahili term "nzuri" meaning "good" and the Swedish term "tanken" or "idea"), invites zuritankers to offer solutions to challenges in each of the company's strategic business areas. The winning idea at an inaugural innovation contest, called "Floor Power—Not a Step Wasted," was a walkway that harnesses kinetic energy generated by footsteps and converts it into electricity. Today, you can find Floor Power at Heathrow Airport (which Ferrovial manages).

Ferrovial's innovation contest is held every two years and employees are invited to offer solutions to challenges proffered by each of the company's strategic business groups. Factors considered in evaluating their proposals are that the innovation be novel to the business, feasible in application, and have a high potential impact. The four zuritankers who devised the Power Floor at Heathrow were given top marks and the go-ahead to implement because it was, in the judge's terms, "a sustainable, efficient innovation that minimizes energy consumption, provides information on foot traffic at the airport, and improves passenger satisfaction by making them feel part of the infrastructure."

Co-Create with Customers. Nearly nine in ten consumers in the US and UK say they want brands to "help" them become more eco-friendly and socially conscious in their purchases and daily lives.[9] Companies have responded by being more transparent about their sourcing and ingredients, creating QR codes to connect customers to the farmers that grow their coffee beans or cotton fibers, and using product labels, websites, and social media posts to tell the sustainability "story" behind what their consumers eat, wear, and buy to furnish their homes. The social research and consulting firm GlobeScan has recently partnered with IKEA, PepsiCo, Visa, and the World Wildlife Fund, among others, to study consumers' "healthy and sustainable living habits" and develop insights to "facilitate consumer behavior change." We will see some of the findings and early actions taken further along in this book.

Socially innovative firms have made a ju-jitsu move and turned this around by asking consumers to help them to develop and market good stuff. LEGO got into this game early when its brand fans began to propose "idea sets" for the company and many LEGO users devised brick constructions that promote STEM learning for youth. Heineken's co-creation platform asked game lovers, beer drinkers, and eco-conscious consumers for ideas to make its packaging more sustainable. A German consumer proposed a device (now called the Heineken-o-Mat) that turns recycling into a game. Look today at Unilever's open innovation platform: ideas are pouring in on plant protein, positive nutrition, natural antioxidants, prebiotics and micro-biome (gut bacteria) control, regenerative packaging, and more.

Regenerate the Environment. Sustainability specialists in companies are shifting from "controlling costs" through product lifecycle management to "adding value" by adopting the principles of a circular economy. What does this look like? Ocean plastics are transformed into fabrics for clothing and furnishings; old tires are reused to make shoe soles and floor mats; wastewater is recycled into recipes for fertilizer; and carbon is captured from smokestacks and injected into cement mix (which also speeds up its curing). Around the world, agribusiness and food companies are helping farmers to revive the soil and rehabilitate natural habitats.

Ray Anderson transformed Interface carpets and his industry by dramatically reducing waste and water intake, ridding carpets of petroleum-based materials, and launching "Cool Carpets," which are "carbon neutral," put on the floor without glues, and completely recyclable. We'll look inside this transformation in the next chapter and at the company's current endeavors to be restorative. Listen to Ray's clarion call:

> I have challenged the people of Interface to make our company the first
> industrial company in the whole world to attain environmental sustainability,
> and then to become restorative. To me, to be restorative means to put back
> more than we take, and to do good to Earth, not just "no harm."

Collaborate to Effect Systemic Social Change. Over the past two decades, business collectively has been urged to step up and take over a larger role in improving society. Government attention to social needs in many lands has shrunk and the nonprofit sector has neither the means nor the scale needed to have a significant impact. Meanwhile, the intensity of social and environmental challenges has multiplied. Into this breach, leading NGOs have shifted from criticizing to partnering with companies and entire industries to protect human rights and natural resource stocks, promote sustainable farming and fair trade, and reduce poverty and other gaps between the haves and have-nots. Multi-business and multi-sector initiatives are in place to address climate change (alliances for carbon trading and energy conservation), natural resources (partnerships around sustainable fish, water, agriculture, and food), and people's lives and livelihoods (codes for supply-chain management and fair labor practices).

For companies, these early partnerships were mostly about risk management, with the added benefits that they leveled the playing field to ensure that "free riders" would not profit from exploiting people and the planet. Now we see a turn to forming partnerships to effect systemic social change. Cisco, IBM, Microsoft, Ferrovial, and other high-tech companies collaborated with NGOs and city officials to turn Barcelona, Spain into a "smart city." It features a parking system that guides drivers to available spots, LED lighting that adjusts to pedestrians and the weather, an air quality sensor network, smart waste bins that reduce odors, widespread public Wi-Fi, and digital democracy—including an open, digital marketplace that makes government procurement transparent and helps small companies compete, and an online platform that enables citizens to access city-wide data, make proposals for corrective measures and improvements, and even draft legislation.

Next big move: regenerative capitalism. This is the theme of John Elkington's *Green Swans*, where he reports that we're moving from an age of corporate responsibility to a time where "resilience will be on everyone's lips." He goes on, "How do we build resilience into our companies, our supply chains, our economies, our societies and communities and the biosphere? In the end, the only way to do that is through regeneration."[10] The aim is to create what he terms "system value." Examples: major automakers have committed to producing only electric cars in the near future and multi-sector partnerships are forming to deploy charging stations and add sensors to highways in preparation for driverless "autonomous" transport.

The Company Handprint: Create Social Value, Do More Good

Sustainability was symbolized by a footprint—with the message being to reduce your company's footprint and do less harm. How should we symbolize the message to increase your company's social impact—to create social value and do more good? We propose the company handprint (see box)! Here's a bit of backstory on where that idea and image came from.

WHAT IS YOUR COMPANY'S HANDPRINT?

When you visit caves first occupied during the Stone Age, observe boulders in the mountains of Australia or the US Southwest, or scramble up rocks in areas once inhabited by Bronze Age Norse or Celts, you will see handprints of our ancestors. Some are stenciled, some painted, and some chiseled into stone (petroglyphs). Paleoanthropologists assign different meanings to these handprints but concur that they evidence an assertion of human presence and identity. Extending this idea, a company's handprint not only identifies "who we are," it communicates what we stand for and our raison d'être (reason for being). A company purpose that stems from its identity and origins is more authentic and inspiring than slogans that are put together by PR firms and meant to be "catchy." Good companies want a strong and credible handprint and take seriously their commitments to maximize their positive impact on society.

Two decades ago Dow Chemical announced bold goals to improve its environmental performance. Stretch targets for reducing energy use and waste, and for eliminating leaks, spills, and injuries on the job, would demand a 90 percent improvement from baseline performance. No one thought it possible but Dow met its goals and more—and saved $5.5 billion from these improvements, based on an incremental investment of $1 billion. Next round, Neil Hawkins, then Dow's VP of Sustainability, proposed even harder to reach environmental impact reduction targets. But the reaction was ho-hum— "been there, done that." Colleagues challenged Neil: "If Dow is truly a leader in science and technology, why not apply that know-how to solve significant world challenges?" Why not indeed? Beyond reducing its impacts further, Dow would shoot for a five-fold increase in sales of products using "sustainable chemistry" (which maximizes energy and material efficiency and reduces environmental harm). And it would deliver three breakthroughs from its labs to solve world challenges.

As of this writing, Dow is running ahead of its sustainable chemistry sales target, has achieved its first three breakthroughs, and, as Hawkins characterizes it, delivered many more with "high-impact innovations in essential areas for society." In discussing this game change with Hawkins and another executive Bo Miller, we all agreed that the company had shifted its approach from reducing risks to seizing opportunities. Bo summed it up this way: "we are not just doing 'less bad'," he said, "we are doing 'more good'." Thus the idea of a company handprint was born

We then compared differences between a company's footprint and handprint (see Figure 2.1). Typically, companies talk about their footprint in terms of the natural environment. The handprint represents a company's impact on the ecology *and* society. Companies try to *minimize* their footprint and "do less bad." The handprint is about *maximizing* a company's social impact—enhancing employees' lives, repairing the environment, finding opportunities in response to social challenges, and "doing more good" for people and the planet. Companies "tick the box" and report on their environmental and social impact. By comparison, hands can reach out, feel, touch—and meet and mingle with other hands. Improved environmental performance can produce profits: Green is gold. A positive impact pays off, too, for both business and society.

To maximize your company's positive impact, rather than minimize its negative impact, calls for a paradigm shift. It means more than turning your focus away from quarterly profits and an exclusive emphasis on risk management. Companies have to repurpose themselves to produce social impact

FIGURE 2.1   Company Footprint versus Handprint

and effect social change. And if your firm means business about truly bene-fitting the world, then the way it does business will need to change, too.

So shift your focus from footprint to handprint, from managing risks to creating social value. Imagine using your company's talent and treasure to produce more "good"—to drive the business toward a nobler purpose of serving society, to promote more inclusive prosperity, to make products or deliver services that are truly beneficial for consumers, to help restore the planet's health, and to fulfill the aspirations of your employees who care about the world we live in. Sounds idealistic doesn't it? It is—and it can also be a profitable and rewarding way to run your business today.

It's All About the Business Case, Or Is It?

Many companies premise their social value creation activities on a "business case" for doing good. We worked with a research team from McKinsey & Co. to trace the logic from 1) social actions and investments to 2) the impact on the business to 3) the market's valuation of a firm (Figure 2.2).[11] There is a direct line of sight from producing healthier, socially useful, and environmentally friendly products and services to *revenue growth*. Socially purposeful hiring, innovations, and marketing can also enable your company to open new markets, develop more relevant products and services, differentiate from competitors, and build brand loyalty.

Reducing waste and using eco-efficient production methods yield cost savings even taking into account necessary investments. Other savings associated with purposeful business include lower recruiting and replacement costs (for employees and customers), less need for price promotions and discounting, and a chance to charge a price premium and be listed in social investment funds. Motivated people pay off in increased productivity—all of which can increase your company's *return on capital*.

Enhancing your supply chain, engaging your employees in community service, and making philanthropic investments not only have human and societal benefits, they also win public support and enhance your license to operate around the globe. As for *risk management*, they can provide a company with some "insurance" in case of public criticism—whether warranted or not. Consultation with and engagement of stakeholders also helps a company to uncover risks and gain buy-in to involvement in activities and communities where its motivations might otherwise be suspect.

FIGURE 2.2   Financial Returns from Social Value Creation

Social Value Creation	Business Impact	Market Value Driver
Employ underrepresented populations	Access to New Markets	Growth
Reach underserved consumers		
Social- and eco-conscious products	Brand Differentiation	
Social activism		
Social and eco-innovation	Public Support, Reputation	
Community investment/partnerships		
Waste and emissions reductions	Eco-Efficiency	Returns on Capital
Staff education, training, activation	Productivity	
Employee and customer engagement	Retention, Price Premium	
Supply chain enhancement	Fewer Disruptions	Risk Reduction
Philanthropy, volunteerism	License to Operate	
Stakeholder engagement	Uncover Risks/Increase Buy-In	
Social purpose	Public Approval	Management Quality
Social intrapreneurship	Develop Capabilities	
Social responsiveness, accountability	Strategic Management	

Finally, there are many indirect links between purpose and profits when a company adopts and fulfills a higher purpose, embraces equity and inclusive prosperity, activates its staff as social entrepreneurs, connects deeply to its customers, and regenerates the planet. All of these are signs of strategic foresight and of adaptable and "*high quality*" management. This especially increases a company's "intangible" worth to investors and the stock market.

Beyond the Business Case. As important as a sound business case is for investing in social value creation, it should not be the only reason to take action. In many companies, we've seen R&D and product development teams, marketers, and specialists in sustainability, CSR, HR, and public affairs grilled by executives: What is being proposed? Who specifically are we targeting? At what cost? And what return to us? Here are the downsides: When the sole or even primary motivation is to enhance your reputation or earn returns for the bottom line, choices about where and how to create social value can center on image-burnishing rather than impact, and turn into a self-serving public relations campaign. The business case methodology can also translate your company's relationship with society into a patchwork of initiatives, programs, and products—each cost/benefit calibrated but without a sense of how they hang together and what you are trying to accomplish overall. So let's shift the business case from "What's in it for Me?" to the added and most vital consideration, "What's in it for all of Us?"—and this includes not only customers, employees, and other stakeholders, but also society and our collective future.

Companies that lead, rather than lag, social change do not business case every action they take, contemplate the risk/rewards of everything they do, or discount intangibles like people's passion, ambition, and aspirations to make a better world when they make their investment decisions. On the contrary, we find that business leaders, managers, and individual contributors who fully live the twin ideas of creating social value and leading social change do so because of who they are, what they believe in, and the personal impact they want to have on their world.

Unilever's CEO Paul Polman exemplifies the point. Growing up in prosperity in the Netherlands, he saw himself and his countrymen as "winning the lottery ticket of life." But what about those born in poorer lands or circumstances—those left behind? As we shall see, he vowed to "fight" for them, to make his company a "driver of change," and to help create what he sees as a more inclusive type of capitalism. Do such noble motivations pay off in profits? If translated smartly into programs, products, and services, likely so but… no guarantees. Of course, you can wait and watch others move forward until you see a solid business case and "proof points" for taking action. Or you can take a leap of faith, enter uncharted territory, and blaze a new trail.

You may wish it were otherwise, but a leap of faith may be more of a necessity looking ahead. As many have characterized it, we are living in a VUCA world—of Volatility, Uncertainty, Complexity, and Ambiguity— where the only certainty is constant change.

Churning Seas of Social Change

We all know that the seas of social change are churning again. In addition to the ravages of hospitalization and death for millions, the Covid-19 pandemic brought societal inequities into sharp relief. While most high-wage workers could shelter in place and work remotely from their homes, lower-wage workers faced a double jeopardy: disproportionate numbers of them were laid off and those who kept working in healthcare, social services, and other "essential" businesses, were more apt to be exposed to the virus. Black and Hispanic workers (and their communities) in the United States suffered higher rates of infection and death as a function of exposure and underlying health disparities. As health official Dr. Fauci put it, the virus shined "a very bright light on some of the real weaknesses and foibles in our society."[12]

At the same time, business stepped up to the challenge. Dyson, the UK company known for its vacuum cleaners, partnered with Ford and General Electric to produce ventilators. Lacrossewear, a sports apparel company, repurposed the microsuede fabric used in its performance shorts to create masks. For every customer purchase, a mask was donated to frontline workers via a buy-one donate-one campaign. Alibaba, Jack Ma's e-commerce firm, launched the Global MediXchange for Combating Covid-19, an online platform to help doctors around the world share expertise and best practices to fight the pandemic. Draganfly, a manufacturer of unmanned and remotely piloted drones, joined with Vital Intelligence, a healthcare data services and deep learning company, to use existing camera networks and drones to monitor and detect infectious and respiratory conditions around the world.

Pharma sped development of messenger RNA vaccines to inoculate the world and Merck, who failed to develop its own vaccine, jumped in to mass-manufacture one made by Johnson & Johnson. Recall how doctors, nurses, ambulance drivers, orderlies, and staff selflessly served the sick, devised new treatment protocols, and held up cellphones so the dying could have their last words with family. Here's the takeaway: we can do really good things when called upon.

Some projected the pandemic would focus business back on profit making and away from doing good. Yet studies find that in 2020 and 2021 companies with better ESG profiles outperformed their peers. There was also a mega-surge in Green Bonds and social impact investing and applications for B Corps multiplied. In Edelman's 12-country study, 55 percent of the public said that brands and companies responded more quickly and effectively than their government.[13] What's next? Some 93 percent globally say that the pandemic has intensified their focus on climate change. Cyrus Taraporevala, CEO of State Street, framed our next challenge aptly: "Covid was the pop quiz for existential crisis, and climate change is the final exam."[14] An existential question for you: does business have the will and wherewithal to do its part?

Meanwhile, employee activism is on the rise in business. A few years ago, the CEOs of Fox News, Roger Ailes, and of Uber, Travis Kalanick, got marched out of their jobs for being sexual predators. In November 2018, more than 20,000 Google employees "walked out" to protest the way their company had been handling sexual harassment claims. Google listened to them and changed its policies to allow employees to go public with harassment claims against other Google employees in a court of law, instead of going through a private arbitration process. #MeToo.

In June 2020, after George Floyd's death at the knee of a policeman, Starbucks prohibited its employees from wearing #BlackLivesMatter gear— for fear that it might incite violence in its stores. Calvin Bensen, a 22-year-old barista from Atlanta, told the media that Starbucks' response was "disappointing in ways I can't express in words. It is silencing and Starbucks is complicit. Now more than ever, Starbucks needs to stand with us."[15] The coffee maker brought its staff together to dialogue in an open forum and then designed t-shirts for its baristas "to demonstrate our allyship and show we stand together in unity." The shirts depicted protest signs saying "Speak Up" and "Time for Change," and one featured a raised black fist announcing "It's not a moment, it's a movement."

If you think this kind of social activism and the call to action on climate is more than a moment, and might be a movement, then it is time to connect your company's purpose to the high-minded aspirations of your employees and customers. They are calling on you!

FIGURE 2.3   Dimensions of the Company Handprint

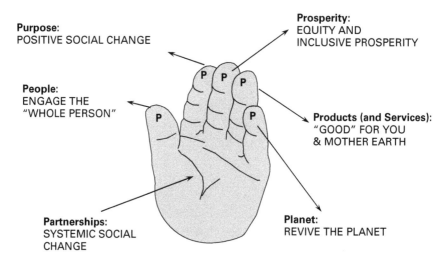

So here's an invitation to learn from changemakers and be one yourself. To stimulate and guide you, the next chapter looks at the journeys of good companies we have studied that moved successfully through the old wave of profit maximizing and the new wave of sustainability and into the churning seas of the next wave of social change. Each chapter in Part II then presents ideas, examples, and even inspiration to draw from in moving forward on Purpose, Prosperity, Products, Planet, and People, and in developing Partnerships for systemic social change (see Figure 2.3).

03

Business as an Agent of Change: Four Icons

The idea that business can be an agent of change in society has many precedents. History is replete with business leaders and companies that changed the world (mostly) for the better: Any roster would feature Thomas Edison (GE and electric lighting), Henry Ford (his namesake mass-market automobile), and Alexander Graham Bell (AT&T and the telephone) from the United States. Worldwide you would include Messrs. Harrod and Selfridge (retailing), Louis Vuitton and Guccio Gucci (branded goods), Henri Nestlé and the Mars family (confections), Akio Morita and Masaru Ibuka (SONY consumer electronics), Jamsetji Tata (India's first conglomerate), and Mmes. Estée Lauder and Mary Kay Ash (cosmetics and their marketing). Also prominent are the likes of Walt Disney, Ted Turner, Rupert Murdock, and Oprah Winfrey (entertainment and media), Ray Croc (McDonald's), Sam Walton (Walmart), Ingvar Kamprad (IKEA), Bill Gates (Microsoft), Steve Jobs (Apple), Jeff Bezos (Amazon), Jack Ma (Alibaba), Elon Musk (Tesla), and many more.

Now can you name a company that is changing the world by offering products or services that are socially conscious and environmentally friendly? By promoting equity and inclusive prosperity or by treating its employees with uncommon dignity and respect? If you are scratching your head, please know that nine years ago, some 45 percent of the world's public couldn't come up with the name of a single one.[1] By now, almost everyone can—and most can cite multiple exemplars. Things change.

In this spirit, we share with you brief stories of select companies that we have worked with or studied that have been agents of social change. Each of them—Ben & Jerry's, Interface Carpets, Nike, and Unilever—faced the challenges of doing good business amidst the old wave of profit maximizing and were industry leaders in the move toward social responsibility and sustainability. And they are reinventing themselves in this next wave of creating social value.[2]

As you read along, look for how these companies operated as agents of change and what they shared in common:

- The Trailblazers (Ben & Jerry; Interface) envisioned the future and built their companies to help create it. The Transformers (Nike; Unilever) picked up on "early signals" of social change, adapted smartly, and set a lead that others would rush to follow. Each of them placed "big bets" on where society and the market were going and bet right.

- They led change with a deep sense of purpose (North Star) and a guidance system tuned to their values and moral compass. They walked their talk.

- They used an informed and disciplined process for leading their companies forward. They studied what was and might be happening next in the world around them; engaged stakeholders, experts, and thought leaders for ideas and feedback; hosted deep, reflective, and personal conversations in-house about "who we are" and "who we want to be"; educated and mobilized their employees; and ran experiments, learned fast, and kept innovating.

Note that as trailblazers or transformers, these companies were seen as "outliers"—novelties, curiosities, or "one-offs"—in their industries. But because of the foresight of their founders, or prescience of their leaders and managers, they became "first movers" in successive waves of social change.

A New Kind of Capitalism: Ben & Jerry's

Baby boomers came of age in the US in the late 1960s and 70s amidst anti-Vietnam war and Apartheid protests and the Civil and Women's Rights movement. Students in France took to the streets in the summer of 1968, culminating in a nation-wide strike. Activists in England and throughout Europe joined the fray. Everywhere the "establishment" was under attack and a youthful counterculture was taking shape expressed in new forms of dress, music, and interests ("sex, drugs, and rock and rock").

It was in this whirlpool of social change that eco- and socially conscious pioneers—Patagonia (1973), the UK's Body Shop (1976), and Ben & Jerry's (1978)—established a new kind of business. Yvon Chouinard, the mountaineer who founded Patagonia, made environmentally friendly clothing and outdoor gear and pledged 1 percent of his company's total revenue (not profits!) to the preservation and restoration of the natural environment. Anita Roddick and her Body Shop pioneered the introduction of green products into the health and personal care marketplace. Aiming her global sourcing at "trade, not aid," she went to Amazonia to acquire natural oils and witnessed massive deforestation. Soon thereafter the Body Shop launched a public education campaign to save the rainforests. Listen to her "business as unusual" philosophy: "Business has to be a force for social change." How about Ben & Jerry's?

Ben Cohen and Jerry Greenfield were childhood friends, dropped out of college in the late '60s, and together opened a small ice-cream shop in Burlington, Vermont in 1978 with scant know-how (they learned ice-cream making though a $5 correspondence course) and less capital (they started with $12,000—a third of it borrowed). When Mirvis began working with Ben & Jerry's in the mid-1980s, the company's guiding purposes were to "have fun" (Jerry) and "give back to the community" (Ben) and, oh yes, make the world's best ice cream. B&J gained legions of fans over the next years through its ice-cream add-ins (huge chocolate chunks, cherries, pretzels, and later cookie dough), off-the-wall brands (Cherry Garcia, Chunky Monkey), and creative campaigns to support social change.

These two "real guys" were activists. Early on, Pillsbury, the food giant known for its oversize mascot, the Pillsbury doughboy, and owner of the ice-cream brand Häagen-Dazs (named for two places on a map of Denmark that sounded "foreign" and "luxurious"), put pressure on grocers to keep B&J off their shelves. Jerry led a one-person protest against this anti-competitive practice by picketing Pillsbury's corporate headquarters carrying a placard that read "What's the Doughboy Afraid Of?" The resulting publicity opened the market and pushed B&J into nationwide distribution.

Linked Prosperity. Ben had a change agenda, and it was "Not Corporate America." As board member Jeff Furman described it, B&J wanted "to make a difference in the world... to plant seeds of new and different possibilities of looking at our culture." On the financial side, the company raised capital by selling its stock to Vermonters at the nominal price of $1 per share. It paid local farmers a guaranteed premium for supplying cream (to support them during market downturns), devoted 7.5 percent of its pretax profits to charity, and established a 5-to-1 salary ratio between the CEO and lowest-earning worker (later raised to 17 to 1 when the company hired a CEO from outside its ranks). It also gave same-sex partners equal access to the benefits of married couples, such as health insurance and parental leave, long before this was even discussable in corporate America. All of this was guided by the company's commitment to "linked prosperity—for everyone that's connected to our business: suppliers, employees, farmers, franchisees, customers, and neighbors alike."

In its early days, B&J gave away ice cream to worthy charities. Then a deeper ambition emerged. As Ben put it, "I think philanthropy is great. But there is a limit to how much you can just give away. If you integrate social concerns into day-to-day profitmaking, there's no limit to how much you can do." But the company hit a roadblock in the late 1980s, when it launched its "1% for Peace" campaign, which set a goal to redirect one percent of the US national defense budget to fund peace-promoting activities and projects. Ben then proposed to launch an ice-cream Peace Pop that would spin off its proceeds to the 1% for Peace campaign. Conflicts arose within the company over the aims and intent of the campaign, whether the messaging was too "anti-military" and not enough "pro-peace" and, as the rollout was planned, how it squared with the US launch of the Gulf War in 1991.

Three-Part Mission. Through a series of retreats, first with board members and then management, all B&J leaders spoke to their personal views of what the company was all about.[3] Employees chimed in at all-staff meetings. There was within B&J misgivings over the ice-cream maker's activist versus commercial emphasis. One influential board member, Henry Morgan, then drafted a "three-part" statement that highlighted the firm's economic, social, and quality missions—all to be considered equally (a harbinger of the triple bottom line). It was debated vigorously by board members and managers and adopted as the company's mission statement. To communicate it to employees and the public, B&J launched a series of programs featuring a mix of education and fun. These covered the social mission (a talk by Anita Roddick), quality (a talk by Mr. Clean! and the launch of a cleanliness campaign), and finance (a visit to a company where every employee gets a P&L statement every day), plus home-grown skits, songs, and such— including Jerry wielding a sledgehammer to break a concrete brick over Ben's belly at the company's annual meeting, and then-CEO Chico Lager donning a skin-diving suit and diving into a pond of recycled ice cream to prove its safety and his own mettle.[4]

Peace Pops were thereupon launched, albeit with more positive messaging, and the company's three-part mission was expressed over the following years symbolically and in actions such as erecting a large picture of the planet at the entrance to corporate headquarters (a top tourist attraction in Vermont); sourcing chocolate brownies from Greyston Bakery in Yonkers, NY, made by the "chronically unemployed"—ex-convicts, former drug abusers, and disadvantaged youth—whom Greyston hires and trains in business and social skills; setting up ice-cream partner shops in Harlem and Baltimore to employ the disadvantaged and handicapped; and driving B&J's mobile-home "cowmobile" around the nation featuring ice-cream giveaways and promoting dialogue about "no growth hormones" in cattle production.

In the late 1990s, amidst the shareholder's rights movement, B&J faced its Rubicon: a new CEO was brought in to cut costs, amp up profits, and prepare the company for sale. In April 2000, B&J was acquired Unilever for $326 million, to the disappointment of Ben and Jerry and despair of their legion of brand fans. Would they see their company's culture and values squandered (see box)?

BEN AND JERRY: SIDELINED, THEN A COMEBACK!

When Unilever acquired B&J, it installed its own CEO and would not allow a $5 million fund established to incubate new businesses with a social agenda to carry the Ben & Jerry's name. Threatening to leave the company he co-founded, Ben declared:

> The only way the social mission of Ben & Jerry's and the heart and soul of the company will be maintained is to have a CEO running the company who has a deep understanding of our values-led social business philosophy, who had experience with the company and with how that worked in practice.

Our research into the aftermath of the acquisition found that Unilever had trouble digesting B&J and its progressive practices.[5] Production was assigned to one part of the parent company and marketing to another. Key staff left, cause-related product concepts were put on hold, and customer complaints multiplied. Then Walt Freese (2005), a non-Unilever exec with experience leading social businesses, became CEO (Chief Euphoria Officer) and sought to resurrect the founding values of the company. He reengaged Ben and Jerry personally in social campaigns and the company introduced new "Ben & Jerry's-like" product concepts such as the Stephen Colbert "AmeriCone Dream" and "Hubby, Hubby," supporting gay marriage. Ben and Jerry once again spoke out for social change (allying with the Occupy Wall Street movement and Black Lives Matter). With the support of Paul Polman, B&J's manufacturing and marketing functions were reunited and B&J became the first subsidiary of a publicly traded company to be named a B Corp.

Climbing Mt. Sustainability: Interface Carpets

Ray Anderson started Interface Carpets in LaGrange, Georgia in 1973 by bringing the European innovation of carpet tiles into the US market. The story he tells is that up to age 60, as CEO of the world's largest commercial carpet maker, "I never gave one thought to what we took from or did to the earth, except to be sure we obeyed all laws and regulations."[6] When pressed in the mid-1990s to provide interested customers with Interface's environmental goals, he found he had nothing to say. Then a saleswoman in the company sent him Paul Hawken's book on industry's harms to the environment, *The Ecology of Commerce*, and he had an epiphany. "Hawken's message was a spear in my chest," Anderson reports, "I was totally oblivious to the natural world and how dependent we were [on it]... I was convicted right there as a plunderer of the earth."[7]

We met Ray at that time and two students, Mona Amadeo and Guy Vaccaro, tracked what happened after his proverbial spearing.[8] Anderson first began to "read voraciously." He pored over Rachel Carson's 1962 book, *Silent Spring*, which highlighted the deleterious effects of DDT pesticides on insects, birds, and agriculture. He learned that behind the social, environmental, and political shifts that began in the 1960s was a broader shift in thinking itself—what futurist Willis Harman called a "global mind change."[9] Central questions about nature and the role of human power and purpose were thrown open to inquiry. Scientists found out that the forces of nature were far less predictable and controllable than imagined and that efforts to manage the natural world often yielded unintended and undesirable consequences. Lessons from the "new physics" showed that system dynamics were nonlinear and circular and that industrial models of growth and control ran counter to the natural course of life. The take–make–waste model was not sustainable. Industry needed the 3Rs: recycle–reuse–reduce.

Committed to bringing this thinking into his company, Anderson assembled an advisory team that included Paul Hawken, Amory Lovins, and Hunter Lovins (co-authors of *Natural Capitalism*), plus Janine Benyus (author of *Biomimicry*), Bill Browning (of the Rocky Mountain Institute), Daniel Quinn (author of *Ishmael*), Jonathon Porritt (Forum for the Future—UK), John Picard (E2 Consulting), and Walter Stahel (Product-Life Institute—Geneva). Dubbed the "Dream Team," these advisors, along with an internal team, began to sketch out a practical action agenda. Let's follow the story as our grad students described it.

Planning the Climb. The Dream Team understood the scale of the challenge. Said Anderson, "This is a mountain higher than Everest; we named it Mount Sustainability. It was probably a year or two before we had the seven faces defined and I can remember being in small groups of people at a blackboard drawing circles and linkages," adding, "This way of thinking about it and presenting it evolved." The brainstorming exercises yielded seven interconnections between the company, its supplier and consumer markets, communities and the natural world. The climb was defined on each face of Mt. Sustainability: 1) zero waste; 2) benign emissions; 3) renewable energy; 4) closing production loops; 5) resource-efficient transportation; 6) sensitize stakeholders; and 7) redesign commerce.

Anderson's initial call to action was met with skepticism in the company. One recalled, "Ray has been the visionary always. It's a big idea every month. After this one, I honestly heard people say, with love and affection for their mythical hero, that at 60 years old he had finally cracked. He had gone around the bend." On this point, Anderson remarked, "It took about 50 speeches by me before we really got a lot of buy-in from our people. The toughest challenge was really to be sure that we stayed on the drum beat, the consistent, persistent message. This is where we've been, this is where we're going, and we have got to do this."

Starting Out. Teams throughout the company, in manufacturing locations on four continents, began to work on hundreds of projects and deploy new technologies to take the company up those seven faces toward sustainability. The Natural Step, a nonprofit founded in Sweden in 1989 by Swedish scientist, Karl-Henrik Robèrt, was hired to help facilitate a "sensitivity hookup" with staff. As one internal change agent described it, "we went on to educate employees and to build awareness. We also went to sensitizing stakeholders. Okay, let's talk about what we're doing. Let's make sure that all of our stakeholders from our vendors to our customers to our community know what we're doing."

Anderson stressed to us the import of the Dream Team in the company: "Engineers would follow Amory Lovins around the factory. Amory would stop and get the nameplate date off of a motor and punch into his calculator and tell you what that motor was costing you." He added, "When (Bill) Browning talks about Green Building our people listen. Those influences reach all down into and through the company."

The Ascent. On this climb Anderson transformed his entire industry by using recycled plastics and polymers, rather than petroleum-based materials, for carpet backing; that way, carpets can be recycled and produce less waste. Interface made ingenious use of principles of biomimicry in carpet design. Interface mimicked nature by producing carpet tiles with natural leaf patterns that could be laid out on the floor in any order—just like leaves falling in the forest—with no time or materials wasted lining the carpet tiles up and matching seams. And, with nature in mind, the company also used biomimicry to invent a way to tape the tiles together, like a spider web, rather than glue them to the floor surface—protecting both the people laying the carpet and the environment from toxicity. One result was "Cool Carpets," which are manufactured without petroleum, put on the floor without glues, and are completely recyclable.

To the Summit. Taking its zero-waste mission to its full ecosystem, Interface reclaimed tons of abandoned commercial fishing nets—which kill fish trapped in them and pollute the oceans and beaches—and transformed them into carpet yarn. That yarn features in a new product line with 81 percent total recycled content, and an industry-first 100 percent recycled nylon face fiber. Ray passed on in 2011 but the ascent continues. In January 2019, the company achieved a milestone: every flooring product that Interface sells — carpet tile, LVT and rubber sheets and tiles—is now carbon neutral across its full lifecycle. It is now leading "Climate Take Back"—a movement to reverse global warming by developing processes and products that create a positive impact on the world, with a goal to become carbon-negative by 2040.

Transformation: Nike

Nike moved into sustainability by sprints and stumbles—racing forward, falling down, then racing again. The company was positioned, from its founding in 1964, as a trailblazer in burgeoning markets for athletic shoes and gear, sports and leisurewear, and then trendy fast fashion. Listen to Nike founder Bill Bowerman's statement on the market: "If you have a body, you are an athlete." Nike poured its resources into marketing while its manufacturing was outsourced first to Japan, then to South Korea and Taiwan, and then to Vietnam and Indonesia, wherever the cheapest labor could be found. Through celebrity jock endorsements, from runner Steve Prefontaine, to basketball's Michael Jordan, to golfer Tiger Woods, Nike (with its swoosh) became an iconic global brand. Then it tripped and fell.

The fall began in the 1990s when as Nike's fortunes grew its sociopolitical troubles began to mount. An article in *Harper's* magazine by labor activist Jeff Ballinger contrasted the piddling pay of an Indonesian contract laborer (19 cents per hour) with Jordan's mega-million-dollar endorsement contract.[10] The comic strip *Doonesbury* lampooned the company and documentary filmmaker Michael Moore caught then-CEO Phil Knight flatfooted, justifying the employment of 14-year-olds. In 1998, the story hit the mainstream with a *Time* magazine article on the "Sneaker Gulag." It contained the account of Nguyen Thi Thu, a 23-year-old girl who was trimming shoe soles in a Nike supplier plant in Vietnam when a co-worker's machine broke, spraying metal parts across the factory and into her heart.[11] Over the following years, Nike's reputation, sales, and market value plummeted. How would it respond?

From Reactive to Proactive. In its first transition, Nike moved from denying any responsibility ("We don't make the shoes") to establishing basic labor codes for suppliers and employing outside firms to audit compliance. Next it strengthened its compliance function and created a team of senior managers to assess why labor problems persisted. This team not only looked at the overall supply chain but also at Nike's own business practices. It documented how just-in-time procurement methods, internal cost allocation rules, and production incentive schemes encouraged suppliers to pressure their workers and avoid overtime. These practices were fixed—at some cost and amidst grumbling.

Setting Industry-Wide Standards. In its strategic phase, Nike went for an industry-wide fix that evened the competitive playing field. The company joined with other shoe and apparel makers, NGOs, and select retailers in groups such as the Fair Labor Association (in the United States) and Ethical Trading Initiative (in the United Kingdom) to ensure broader-based buy-in to, and compliance with, labor and trading codes. In another move, Nike became the first in its industry to voluntarily disclose the names and locations of the more than 700 active contract factories that made Nike-branded products worldwide.

Identifying Meta-Trends. Recognizing the need to keep in touch with its world and stay abreast of trends, Nike built an in-house social research function and was one of the first big companies to regularly engage with its immediate stakeholders—retailers, consumers, suppliers, employees—as well as more distal ones—environmentalists, activists and NGOs, academics and thought leaders, as well as industry critics. As a result of these inputs Nike prepares a map of the "meta-trends" in society and analyzes ones that most relate to its business (what auditors say are material to a company's financial condition and operational performance). In recent ones, Nike puts energy use, water adequacy, and climate change on the high-risk side. In the opportunity space are the public's increasing ease of access to health and fitness information, women's involvement in sports, and the growing market potential in the Southern Hemisphere.

Sustainable Processes and Products. The game changed when Nike shifted from playing defense to offense, as insiders put it, and introduced sustainability into its operating processes and products. We observed an inflection point in 2009 when the corporate responsibility function in Nike was redefined as the Sustainable Business and Innovation Team (SB&I) under the leadership of Hannah Jones. Made up of about 140 people, the SB&I team leads sustainability strategy development throughout Nike and provides content expertise and consulting to product teams companywide. Revving its innovation engine, Nike embraced "considered design" practices to create products with more environmentally friendly materials and fewer toxins and waste. Eco-innovations like recyclable shoe design and Nike's Reuse-a-Shoe campaign (where used shoes are recycled into running tracks) are among its ways to manage its footprint.

The company has since become a pioneer in sustainable infrastructure. At a massive distribution center in Europe, nearly all incoming shipments of shoes arrive by canal instead of on trucks, and the whole center runs on renewable energy. Six giant wind turbines produce as much power as 5,000 houses use; rooftop solar panels cover an area the size of three soccer fields. A thermal energy system stores warm water in the summer to use for heat in the winter, and flips when the seasons change. By 2025, Nike plans to run on 100 percent renewable energy.

Changing Sports Worldwide. In line with its core purpose, "to bring inspiration and innovation to every athlete in the world," Nike is now creating social change. It has, for example, digitized its relationship with its customers. Leveraging data collected by the Nike Run Club app, which runners use to track their time, distance and pace data, Nike introduced Nike On Demand. The platform paired Nike experts, coaches and trainers with runners looking to train for a goal or to stick to a training regimen over WhatsApp. In 2019, Nike acquired Invertex, an Israeli fashion-tech startup specializing in three-dimensional modeling and deep learning technology. Invertex's foot-scanning technology enables users to map every curve of their foot on a proprietary ScanMat to find the shoes that will fit them best. As the technology matures, customers will be able to achieve an in-store fit without having to leave home.

Women account for less than a quarter of Nike's sales. To engage them in sports, Nike's considered design team developed a Motion Adapt Bra made from special fabric that is soft and flexible during low-impact activity but becomes more supportive as activity gets more intense. Another changemaking innovation: the world's first Pro Hijab for Muslim women designed to "make sports a more inclusive space." Nike's newest celebrity endorsers are a multicultural mix of women: tennis star Serena Williams, gymnast Simone Biles, fencer Ibtihaj Muhammad, snowboarder Chloe Kim, and members of the US Women's National Soccer Team.

In its outreach to the poor in the global south, Nike organized the First Women's National "Slumsoccer" Championship in India and similar contests in over 40 countries. And, in response to activism in the US and among its clientele, the company took a risk, and scored a huge win, with its 30th anniversary "Just Do It" campaign, fronted by the politically polarizing quarterback Colin Kaepernick, who gained notoriety by kneeling down at professional football games during the national anthem, in protest of racial inequities.

Rebirth: Makeover of Unilever

Unilever's historic commitment to society traces to its founder, William Hesketh Lever, who in the late 1800s proclaimed his company's purpose: "To make cleanliness commonplace, to lessen work for women, to foster health and contribute to personal attractiveness, that life may be more enjoyable and rewarding for the people who use our products." Lever grew up in the Victorian era and was schooled in Disraeli's writings, which described the difference between rich and poor in England as "two nations between whom there is no contact and no sympathy; we are as ignorant of each other's feelings as if we were dwellers in different zones or different planets." He was determined to make washing soap available and affordable to the working class, who had never had access to quality hygiene products. Lifebuoy was its name. He also created a company village, Port Sunlight, that offered housing to workers at reasonable rents and introduced the then-unheard-of eight-hour workday, sickness benefits, holiday pay, and pensions for both male and female employees.

Over the next century, however, this uplifting model was diluted by hundreds of acquisitions and a succession of CEOs who neither preserved the company's caring culture, nor lived out its founding values. Under the full lash of shareholder capitalism in the early 2000s, the company had undergone several restructurings and extensive downsizing, and slimmed its product lines to select global brands and a few national gems. But complaints were growing that the company could not "shrink its way to prosperity."

Then-CEO Patrick Cescau oversaw the acquisition of US-based Best Foods (home to Wishbone salad dressings and Hellmann's mayonnaise) and the purchases of Slim-Fast and Ben & Jerry's. His mandate was to improve the balance sheet and move Unilever on a path of profitable growth. Yet Cescau knew that Unilever was under pressure to expand and integrate its social and environmental agenda. Louis "Tex" Gunning, then a Unilever business group president in Asia and vocal advocate of sustainability, assembled and led the multilevel and multidisciplinary study team (including Mirvis).[12] Over the course of one month, this team, racing from executive offices to videoconferences, interviewed nearly all of Unilever's top executives, many of its business leaders and marketers around the world, and staff specialists in finance, human resources, logistics, and such, plus outside experts and members of the board of directors. The team also benchmarked the practices of other firms in Unilever's industries, studied best practices worldwide, and scanned findings from surveys of business leaders, consumers, and CSR and sustainability experts.

Over 200 executives reviewed the findings, discussed and analyzed the parallel problems of obesity and malnutrition, the company's impact on air and water, and the like. This stimulated heated debate about the moral responsibilities of corporations versus the moral hazard posed by using shareholders' monies to address the world's problems. Then one executive made this breakthrough comment about Unilever taking a purposefully positive role in society: "It's who we are. And the way we do business... It's in our genes."

Addressing Society's Problems. One of the first orders of business for Unilever was to be more proactive on issues around nutrition. Obesity is widespread in the United States and Europe and growing in India, China, and elsewhere. Accordingly, 25,000 Unilever recipes were put through a nutrition profile model and reformulated to reduce trans-fat, saturated fats, sugar, and salts. In addition, the company began to put a "Healthy Choices" logo on products to help consumers identify foods that have limited amounts of bad ingredients.

Next it shifted its focus toward the growing trend of healthy and sustainable consumption. On the beverage side, the company introduced new tea products that featured antioxidant benefits and at the same time dramatically reduced the sugar content of iced tea. It also introduced a smoothie beverage made from concentrated vegetables and fruit juices. Unilever then began to source its fish from sustainable fisheries and worked with the Marine Stewardship Council to certify its claims. In addition, it had the Rainforest Alliance certify the sustainability of its tea plantations and products (e.g., Lipton).

How about the problem of "undernutrition" in poor parts of the world? New strategies included the sale of iodized salt in India and parts of Africa, which addresses a dietary deficiency common among the poor, and a campaign for handwashing where its Lifebuoy soap can reduce diarrheal disease. In each instance, the company devised new local supply chains to make products more affordable and developed distribution channels that used underprivileged women as village-level entrepreneurs. In partnership with UNICEF, Gunning helped to launch a "kid's nutrition" campaign that included original research on the impact of saturated fats on children's physical and mental performance, conferences on improving youth eating patterns and preferences, and development of healthy breakfast foods aimed at fortifying the diet of poor kids.

Finally, Unilever added social messaging to its upmarket global brands. It launched, for example, an "inner beauty" campaign for Dove Soap. Company research found that just 12 percent of women are very satisfied with their physical attractiveness; 68 percent strongly agree that the media sets an unrealistic standard of beauty; and 75 percent wish the media did a better job of portraying the diversity of women's physical attractiveness, including size and shape, across all ages. Dove's public message about inner beauty was conveyed in advertisements showing "real women have curves" and a film that shows how fashion model images are distorted to conform to an idealized but unattainable type. This message was carried into schools around the world in a program to promote young women's self-esteem.

Taking Sustainability to Society. The journey picked up pace with the appointment of new CEO Paul Polman in 2009, which set Unilever on its way toward a full-scale makeover. One of Polman's first acts was to stop reporting quarterly results to turn managers' attentions to longer-term value creation. As he put it, "You cannot solve issues like poverty or climate change or food security with the myopic focus on quarterly reporting." He also warned investors that "we were going to run the business for the longer term. We were going to invest in capital spending. We were going to invest in training and development. We were going to invest in new IT systems. And we were going to invest back in our brand spending."

With over 400 brands, Unilever reaches one in every three people on the planet. Its sustainable living plans engaged them directly. As a brand marketer frames its aim: "Raising awareness is 'not enough'," (we) are trying to "change consumer behavior" by providing them "inspiration" and "practical solutions." As a leading maker of soaps, Unilever teamed up with Walmart in a promotional campaign to encourage consumers to reduce energy use when showering ("Turn off the tap"). In a market test, sachets of Unilever's Suave shampoo and conditioner informed Walmart customers that families could "save up to $100 and 3,200 gallons of water per year by turning off the water when you shampoo and condition." Next step? Unilever rolled out a "dry" shampoo—no water use necessary.

It also amped up its digital and social media communications with consumers. Websites dedicated to personal care for the skin and hair illustrated the environmental and social benefits of Unilever's goods and encouraged consumers to rate them, write reviews, and submit ideas for product improvements. User-generated text, video and images appeared in social media conversations, digital advertisements, and product packaging. Meanwhile, the company required all of its suppliers to eliminate deforestation and improve livelihoods in their operations, and Unilever's overall impact on society—warts and all— was measured in managers' scorecards and reported to the public. The result: Unilever has been named for six consecutive years as the top company in Globescan's survey of 1,000 sustainability experts around the world.

A Force for Good. By mid-year 2017, Unilever had, under Polman's leadership since 2009, increased its share price five-fold (from 10.99 to 51.37). But that's not what animated him or his company—as he said, "I'm not just working for them (shareholders)." In an interview with our colleague Andy Hoffman and two Michigan MBAs, Polman wondered aloud, "What's the game we're playing here? For whom are we playing it?" His answer: "At the end of the day, you need to ask what matters. What drives you, what should drive you, is humanity." He went on, "We can only make humanity function if we respect each other and are able to live with each other and have the… common values of dignity and respect, of equity."[13]

In his tenure, Unilever bought over 70 companies and Polman put the founders together in a Founders Circle. He reports on what they taught him:

> They were more entrepreneurial. They hated our bureaucracy. They came with suggestions that would have never come from an established system… It makes you feel uncomfortable and you go faster… I got a lot of change from, let's say, Ben and Jerry doing things and then people said, "Well, why don't you do this corporately, if Ben & Jerry's can do it?" I wasn't working day and night for Ben and Jerry… [but] they certainly moved my level of consciousness up.

As of now, eight of those acquired Unilever companies have been certified as B Corps.

Unilever also continues to forge partnerships to care for the world. In the areas of sustainable agriculture, water, and fishing, the firm is the founding force or a leading member of global, multi-company forums that develop policies, share best practices, or monitor results in these natural resource areas. In addition, it participates in partnerships, alongside other firms, government agencies, and NGOs concerned with social issues involving nutrition, health, hygiene, dental care, and the plight of the poor.

BATTLE FOR THE SOUL OF CAPITALISM

In 2017, it looked as though Polman's good work might be undone when Kraft Heinz launched a $143 billion hostile takeover bid for Unilever. To the dismay of Wall Street, Unilever rejected the bid. On the surface this was a clash of competing models of making money—Unilever's focus on long-term value creation versus Kraft Heinz's emphasis on constant cost cutting. Speaking to the broader implications, experts termed it a "battle for the soul of capitalism."

History has proven the wisdom of Unilever's rejection of the bid. In the next two years, Kraft Heinz's share price would drop by 70 percent and Unilever's would increase roughly by 50 percent. As Polman reflected on this, he said, "Some people think greed is good. But over and over it's proven that ultimately generosity is better." Since then, other companies have ceased quarterly reporting, the CEOs of top companies have spoken out on social issues and in favor of stakeholder capitalism, and Polman's idea that business can be a Force for Good has gained a following.

In early 2019, Polman stepped down as head of Unilever and launched IMAGINE, an "activist corporation" that works with companies and industries to achieve the 2030 Sustainable Development Goals. In a recent speech to top executives, he laid out the key challenge ahead:

> Capitalism, which has been responsible for the growth and prosperity that has done so much to enhance our lives, is a damaged ideology and needs to be reinvented for the 21st century. Business needs to reinvent capitalism. We need to build a new model of inclusive and sustainable capitalism.[14]

How do you build this new model? Now that you've seen how Ben & Jerry's, Interface, Nike, and Unilever did it, the next chapter presents some ideas and guidance on how you can start up, develop, or change your company to change the world.

04

How to Change Your Company to Change the World

We've just seen four examples of companies that changed their ways to change the world. They all operated in the era of profit maximizing, surfed smartly into sustainability and to meeting the needs of multiple stakeholders, and are now at the forefront of a movement where business leads social change. Their experience (and others') offers guidance and lessons to prepare you and your company to move forward into this frontier.

This chapter speaks to key considerations in how to start up, develop or change your business that might apply to you and your company, depending on your current situation, what needs to change, and how much change is required. Here's what we will cover:

1 **How you approach change.** We've seen companies take two different approaches to change:

   o **Design and develop it**—Entrepreneurs (like Ben & Jerry's) or companies entering into uncharted territory (like Interface) have a vision of where they are headed but typically have to experiment, improvise, and make things up as they go along.

   o **Transform it**—Established companies (like Nike and Unilever), by comparison, typically rely on a change process where they study the situation, formulate plans, and mobilize people for change. The "old" way must be transformed to the "new" way.

2 **The scope and scale of change** can range from targeted actions to changes in the core business, the full value chain, the business ecosystem, and beyond to multi-party systemic social change.

3 **Innovation and continuous change** has companies continuing to innovate with new programs and products in response to emerging issues and enhance existing efforts in light of social change.

Design and Develop It: The Entrepreneurial Model

If you are just starting your business, how to get it going might seem straight-forward. Come up with a great idea, map out your thinking on, say, the business model canvas, develop a business plan, put together an appealing storyline, then pitch it to potential investors at a "shark tank," and, if the stars are aligned, you'll get funding and be off and running. One of us (Googins) teaches and works with socially and ecologically minded entre-preneurs whom, he advises, also have to put together a "social value proposition" for their products or services, pinpoint both their direct customers and ultimate beneficiaries of their doings, and show how they plan to deliver and measure social impact. He also has them explain how they will invest their profits to do further good.

While detailed business plans are helpful and may be essential to securing capital, our colleague and former President at Babson, Len Schlesinger, contends that for entrepreneurs "action trumps everything."[1] "There's a whole way of thinking... that doesn't include... an 85-page business plan and 12-year forecast spreadsheet," he explains. At its core is a model of Entrepreneurial Thought & Action® (ET&A). It favors "smart" action over detailed planning, moving quickly from the whiteboard to the real world, trying different things out, failing fast, and learning continuously.

Act, Learn, Build (Repeat). This was Ben and Jerry's (B&J) approach to building their business. They had early successes by intuitively taking smart action and moving fast with ice-cream add-ins and funky brands. Then they hit a wall with Peace Pops and the 1% for Peace campaign. Before the launch, there were issues with the intent and messaging that had to be aired out and worked through with the board and B&J employees. Then there were quality problems, as making ice cream on a stick is more complicated than in pint cartons. Marketing and distribution issues loomed. It turned out that Peace Pops were an "impulse" buy that sold well at convenience stores but not so much in groceries where it was pricey compared to compet-itors and not altogether appealing to soccer moms shopping for their kids. Lessons learned? "We learned that a product doesn't sell just because you're trying to do good in the world," said Jerry. "You still have to have healthy distribution, a good marketing strategy, and price the product properly."[2]

Flash forward to today and British retailer Lush is now at the forefront of social change. Founded as a supplier to the Body Shop, Lush features health and beauty products that are handmade and 100 percent vegetarian. Over the years, founders Liz Weir, Mark Constantine, Mo Constantine,

Rowena Bird and Helen Ambrosen evolved the business from being a supplier to a mail order company to a brick-and-mortar retailer to a digitally driven brand. Along the way, there were missteps and bankruptcy (of mail order Cosmetics to Go) that were overcome through dogged determination and serendipity (a visit to a London delicatessen inspired the use of fresh ingredients in its cosmetics). Throughout, Lush has tried to be both "fun" (staff regularly detonate "bath bombs" in basins throughout its stores) and "serious" (with social campaigns on animal testing, transgender equality, etc.).

Lush is now sold in "naked stores" where no product packaging is visible. Instead customers scoop out lotions and potions from bins into recyclable containers—like at an ice cream shop or deli. Labels? Customers can find a full list of ingredients and guidelines for product use by scanning the product bin's smart code with the Lush Lens App. Like other trailblazers, Lush spends nothing on advertising and uses its strong social media presence on Instagram and Facebook to build buzz about its products and doings. It has relied on user-generated content to transform it customers into an engaged community of brand advocates.

Lush regularly takes a stand, through its practices and social campaigns, as a leader in the fight against animal testing and injustices in the world. In 2018, however, it got caught up in the social media flap #SpyCops. According to news accounts, undercover police were "spying" on leftist groups, including animal rights activists, and there were accusations that some of the police had been sleeping with informants.[3] On 31 May 2018, store fronts of Lush stores in the UK were made to look like a crime scene, with faux police tape that read "Police Have Crossed the Line." Its Facebook page, website, and Twitter handle were filled with explanations of why Lush was speaking out and why this kind of policing had to stop. But not everyone supported the protest. British authorities saw it as an "anti-police" message and #FlushLush tweets called for a boycott of the company. Lush then explained, "This is not an anti-state/anti-police campaign. We are aware that the police forces of the UK are doing an increasingly difficult and dangerous job whilst having their funding slashed." One month later, the Lush "anti-spy cops" campaign ceased.

What did Lush learn from its foray into "uncharted waters"? To think through its campaigns and get full staff and store support before launching them. Chief Digital Officer Jack Constantine noted, "Everybody is going to make mistakes. Your standards and transparency, they're key." This was not the end of activism for Lush, who spoke out on #BlackLivesMatters in the United States.

Grow the Business Purposefully. As an entrepreneurial venture grows, there will be gaps in its infrastructure and capabilities. B&J's, for example, announced its environmental credentials early on by feeding ice-cream overflow to pigs near its headquarters. A heavy fine and adverse publicity over untreated wastewater led the firm to redesign water quality control and construct a treatment greenhouse. But it was not until Gail Mayville, secretary to the CEO, led a self-initiated program in recycling and formed employee green teams in plants that B&J could truly walk its talk.

Interface also found its way forward experientially. As one engineer put it, "We were feeling our way every step of the way." The emergent process gradually yielded a series of small wins that helped to bring the overall effort into focus and built momentum for change. "We could start to see progress," recalled a manager. "The minute that you start to see progress you start to get enthusiastic. Then you realize baby steps are taking you a long way."

This importance of building your business purposefully applies not only to small startup businesses, but also to giant ones that take shape via mergers and acquisitions. The Japanese company LIXIL was created in 2011 through the merger of five building materials companies and has since acquired American Standard and GROHE. The purpose of this newly formed business seemed motivating and clear: "to make better homes a reality for everyone, everywhere." But Jin Montesano, Head of Public Affairs, had her doubts about that. "What about the 2.3 billion people in the developing world who have no access to modern toilets?" she asked herself. Now, typically, public affairs executives lobby governments and shield their companies from risks and problems. Jin had other ideas and boldly assembled a team of engineers into a business unit to design SATO low-water-use toilets that are affordable, easy to install, have an innovative trap door technology that eliminates odors, and a self-sealing toilet pan that keeps flies and insects away. Nearly 2 million bright blue SATO toilets are in use today, improving the sanitation of over 9 million people in developing nations.

Entrepreneurship in Big Business. Our Babson colleague Cheryl Kiser, co-author of *Creating Social Value: A guide for leaders and change makers*, makes the point that ET&A can also be applied to change-making within large companies.[4] Changemakers in a business unit in Verizon, for instance, took an entrepreneurial approach to making mobile devices more accessible to people with disabilities. Campbell's used ET&A to develop its line of healthy soups. So the entrepreneurial model can apply to starting and growing your own social business and to developing socially oriented programs and products in a big firm. But how do you transform a large company, with years of history and a more set-in-stone organization culture?

Transform It: How to Remake Your Company

Established companies confronted with a need to change face two different kinds of problem. Some are *technical* problems that are relatively easy to identify and analyze, have clear causes and logical solutions, and can be solved by existing expertise and authority in your company. These kinds of problems are amenable to "change management" which, while not simple or painless to implement, is no doubt familiar to you. Time frame: weeks or a few months. Others are *wicked* problems that are complex and ill-defined, have multiple causes and no one "right" solution, and whose resolution requires the input and buy-in of different interests, some of whom may operate beyond your company's boundaries.[5] Tackling these kinds of problems calls for "organization transformation" and often involves system-wide change. Time frame: several years or more.

There are many models that feature 3, 5, 9 or even more "steps" to take in transforming your business. This gives the impression that the process is linear and sequential and can be logically planned and smoothly executed step by step. We've described how Interface, Nike, and Unilever remade their companies on the edge of social change. While their change processes read as linear, in fact they often had managers step forward then back, plan on the fly, constantly improvise, solve a problem in a way that created new ones, with plenty of missteps and foul-ups. Those of you who have been involved in system-wide change know how this story goes.

There is no single path from A→B in transformational change. Instead the route to change requires adaptation and rerouting. Using a rock-climbing metaphor, corporate responsibility manager Laurie Regelbrugge, who led the makeover of a company's engagements with stakeholders and then with society, describes the use of "handholds" in making change:

> In scaling a wall of rock, a rock climber must find and make effective use of the meager or substantial handholds along that wall. Some handholds that seem promising may ultimately lead the climber to a dead end, while others allow the person to reach the desired destination. Different climbers, presented with the same rock face, may choose a different set of handholds and, therefore, follow a slightly different path. The key is that there are often many options, and climbers choose certain holds for reasons having to do with their skills, experience, what results they can anticipate, and the plan they have for scaling the rock face.

Every company has to find its own handholds on a transformational journey. What can we learn from firms that sailed into the sustainability wave successfully and are today leading social change? The list below outlines some of common features of their transformations that may be relevant to your situation and up the odds of success:

1 **Face the Future.** Sense trends and patterns of social change; look for opportunities, not just threats.

2 **Study the Situation.** Investigate (hands-on) changing market and societal conditions; tough-love critique of your own assumptions, practices, and values.

3 **Develop the Big Idea.** Formulate a positive vision of where your company is going; intellectually convincing and emotionally appealing.

4 **Make Change Participatory and Inclusive.** Involve multiple levels of your company and stakeholders in the change process; expert input and guidance when needed.

5 **Mobilize People and Your Organization for Change.** Use change champions, teams, and employees to design actions, develop prototypes, launch experiments, and run with change initiatives.

6 **Learn Continuously.** Check progress, fix problems, make course corrections, and finetune solutions.

7 **Inform and Educate.** Campaigns to prepare both your organization and stakeholders for the launch of new initiatives.

8 **Lead Change.** Lead from the top, bottom-up, and middle-out; distributed leadership.

Face the Future. Nothing wakes up an organization to change more so than a crisis—whether it is a perceived one, like Ray Anderson feeling a spear in the chest, or a real threat, like the cover story on its "Sneaker Gulag" that confronted Nike. It is more difficult to see and come to grips with slow-moving changes in the market or society that might impinge on your business. Even with their risk management systems, companies are not typically alert to ambiguous warning signals or ones that aren't blinking red. And when a threat or opportunity is spotted, there are often divisions in an executive team between those who sense a need for action versus those who are in denial about what is happening, comfortable with the status quo, and/ or threatened by the implications of change.

Early movers into the waves of social change have educated intuitions about what is coming and deploy boundary spanners to spot trends, talk with experts and innovators on the leading edge, and engage in "future casting" to think through the change implications. This has companies creating scenarios about the future, as Royal Dutch Shell does regularly, or getting a large number of people together in a future search conference. When Interface launched its "Take Back Climate" agenda in 2019, for instance, it was based on future projections that even reaching its moonshot goal of zero emissions would not sufficiently address the climate crisis. It then created a prototype of a carbon-capturing carpet tile.

Study the Situation. How do you come to grips with a wicked problem? Best practices include intelligence gathering about the situation at hand, deep dialogue among change actors about its meaning and implications, and periodically stepping back from the fray to see the big picture—"a view from the balcony"—which enables you to better identify the many forces at work and their potential interactions. Other essentials are personal reflection and even soul-searching. The solutions to wicked social problems often require changing attitudes and behaviors of all involved in a situation, including your own.

It is commonplace for big companies to hire a consulting firm or think tank to conduct market studies, interview staff, review company practices, and prepare a report on "what needs to change." Note, by comparison, that Unilever engaged a full portfolio of executives, managers, and staff specialists in a "self-study" of changes in society and their marketplace. That helps to create ownership over the findings. Still, they have to be debated and digested. As managers at Unilever dialogued about their study's findings, they observed that the company had a plethora of sustainable initiatives but no consistent strategic thrust behind them. "Too many unaligned programs and messages," reported one leader. "Social responsibility has not been 'interiorized' in the company," said another. The conclusion was clear: "We need a change from 'corporate initiatives' to 'business initiatives'." They also knew that employees, worn out from constant restructuring, were hungry for more meaning and inspiration in their work—something that a fresh social agenda might provide.

Develop the Big Idea. We've seen the big ideas that guided the transformations of Interface (Mt. Sustainability) and Unilever (Sustainable Living). Jim Collins and Jerry Porras document how top companies use a BHAG—"big hairy audacious goal"—to stimulate "out of the box" thinking and make their vision emotionally energizing.[6] Remember Dow's original BHAG, to reduce emissions by 90 percent, and then its even bigger and hairier one to "solve world challenges."

There's always a risk that a big idea, when translated into a statement of purpose or vision, will be seen as empty words. You might recall British Petroleum's pledge to move "beyond petroleum" decades ago? What it lacked was the institutional will and managerial acumen to translate its commitments into action. High-minded pronouncements need to be translated into a strategic direction and logical map of how a company moves from its current reality to a desired future state. We've seen this in Interface's climb of Mt. Sustainability: seven different faces to ascend, with specific goals, frameworks, tools, and people involved in each of them.

Make Change Participatory and Inclusive. Transformational change is a team sport that involves 1) relevant stakeholders, including employees, suppliers, operators, distributors, and even customers through a company's value chain; 2) content experts, process facilitators, and other parties that can inform and speed progress; and when circumstances warrant, 3) partnering with an NGO, government agency, and other businesses. Many companies smartly engage employees, stakeholders, and partners early on to get them involved in studying the situation and developing the big idea. Their involvement is essential later on when it comes to implementing ideas and practices that create social value.

Nike, for instance, took a big step forward in addressing factory conditions overseas when it started working directly with factory owners and workers to come up with solutions. As part of its full makeover, Nike consulted with NGOs and other companies to guide the cleanup of its supply chain and later joined the Sustainable Apparel Coalition to develop the Higg Index, a suite of tools that standardizes value chain sustainability measurement for all industry participants.

Mobilize People and the Organization for Change. Thinking about transforming your company? Is your intent to:

1 Further green your operations and supply chain?
2 Become more transparent and accountable?
3 Design and develop more socially relevant products or services?
4 Activate your employees as social intrapreneurs?
5 Step up your social advocacy? or
6 ALL OF THE ABOVE?

Companies that do "all of the above" need to develop new policies and programs, design new work methods and processes, train operators and support staff, set up appropriate measurement, information, and control systems, and all the while keep the business running! Whew. Transformation is not for the faint of heart.

Successful change at this scale involves change champions, teams, and individual employees taking smart action. You'll see in the next chapters examples of how companies devise prototypes of new process and product designs, pilot programs to test new ideas, secure small wins to gather momentum and confidence, and then make big things happen. The human side of change also needs constant attention. When a company shifts its mindset and ways of doing business, the whys and wherefores need constant communication (accompanied by some persuasion and arm twisting), and attention must be giving to coaching managers and to developing new score-cards and reward systems to support and reinforce behavioral change.

Learn Continuously. Sometimes there are slip-ups. We saw that with B&J's Peace Pops. Interface had its problems, too. It developed a woven floor covering without nylon fiber that was greener than what existed but failed because of performance problems. An early attempt to use bio-based yarns also flopped due to their lack of durability. A recycling project using dissolution technology proved too expensive and actually did more environmental harm than good. So it typically goes. Continuous assessment, after-action reviews, and course corrections are needed on this journey. As an exec at Interface puts it, "Setbacks are par for the course. We've learned how to embrace these experiments to apply what we've learned to design the next solution."

Inform and Educate. To prepare his people for change, Unilever's Tex Gunning led managers and young leaders from 17 national companies in Asia-Pacific on a series of "learning journeys" to raise their consciousness about social, economic, and environmental issues and the needs of their countrymen. They traveled to locales of historic and cultural relevance, hiked through mountains and deserts, met with school children, indigenous peoples, everyday consumers and the poor, learned from leaders in business, government, and community organizations, and talked deeply with one another about their personal and business purposes. This deep engagement with society touched many of Unilever's Asian leaders personally. Said one:

> The communities we visited reminded me of an "itch" that has been bugging me for the longest time, that is, to give my time and effort to a cause which is

beyond myself (and even beyond my family). I have been blessed so much in this life that the least I can do is to help my fellow men. I need to act now.

It was also a source of inspiration for community-based business initiatives and a testing ground for new product and market development ideas under the company's base-of-the-pyramid business strategy and CSR-relevant brands. Many of those who participated in these journeys in turn led them for their next layers of management and everyday employees, ultimately engaging over 26,000 employees in consciousness raising about the world around them.[7]

Lead Change. There is a vast literature on leading organizational transformation with appropriate references to vision, inspiration, big-picture thinking, and role-modeling. When changemaking is on your agenda, we urge you to refresh your thinking on transformational leadership, reflect on your prior change experiences (favorable and not), talk to others who have led changes of the type you are contemplating, get expert help where warranted, and take a disciplined approach to the work. But note this: leading change is not a solo activity. Ronald Heifetz and colleagues make the point that "adaptive" leadership is not about having all the answers and driving change from on high.[8] Instead, it involves experimenting, discovering new knowledge, and making numerous changes throughout your company that require distributed leadership—top-down, bottom-up, and middle-out.

Does Change Have to Start at the Top?

This idea that change has to start at the top is common wisdom. Listen to this line manager at Interface: "I was as cynical as anyone but I began to see that Ray was serious about this, that people who were close to him were serious about it, and that somehow we were going to make it happen." But maybe you're not a CEO, a top executive like Tex Gunning in Unilever, or a sustainability lead like Hannah Jones at Nike. You can still take action and lead your company toward doing good business. Scientists who study complex systems discovered the "butterfly effect" to explain how one small occurrence (a butterfly flapping its wings) can translate into something greater (sunny skies or a violent storm) later on.[9] What actions might you take to be the "wings of the butterfly" that instigates a wholesale change in your business?

Inspired by a 2011 article in *The Economist* about impact investing, two young employees at investment bank BlackRock, Zaneta Koplewicz and Rob Morris (28 and 26 at the time), created a voluntary working group to study the market. They brought their proposal to CEO Larry Fink who, coincidentally, was facing an increasing number of queries from institutional and private investors about the firm's social investing profile and how it took account of ESG factors in its portfolio. As one insider recalled it, "Increasing numbers of consumers were socially conscious, so were more employees, especially the Millennials, and so were more investors. To that point, we had been reactive. Larry asked, 'Could we become proactive? Should we?'"

A first task was to build out impact investing in the strategic product development group. A good start, but this was not intended to be just a "niche" business. In short order, innovation in BlackRock went viral. Over 100 employee SWAT teams, representing the various business lines, sales, product and client engagement groups, began to propose and incubate new ideas on the social investment front. BlackRock adopted proprietary ESG investment screens, risk analytics, and a "lean data" approach to assessing the social impact of companies. Funds were set up for social investing pertaining to carbon emissions, water use, poverty, and various "people issues."

As these diverse activities gained momentum, Fink hosted a "strategic summit" where employees across the various SWAT teams shared "best practices" and lessons learned from their efforts to date. Shortly thereafter, Deborah Winshel was hired as Global Head of Impact Investing and today, BlackRock has some $2.2 trillion under management, with products ranging from sustainable exchange-traded funds (ESG ETFs) to green bonds. This is change that started from the "bottom" up. But wherever it starts and whatever emerges, it then needs to pulse into the core business, your company's value chain, and ultimately reach your markets and society.

Build Change Out: Scale and Scope

PepsiCo began to change its business when Indra K. Nooyi took charge and decided, "We needed to change the way we made money—not just give away some of the money we earned."[10] We noted how PepsiCo sold off and acquired businesses and promised to deliver "performance with purpose."

But then marketing got ahead of the company's ability to deliver. You may recall the social media "cola war" between Pepsi and Coke at the 2010 football Super Bowl game. Coke's gridiron campaign invited social mediaphiles to "open happiness" and pledged $1 to the Boys and Girls Clubs of America for each person who previewed its Super Bowl ads on its "live positively" Facebook page. Pepsi, in a countermeasure, announced that instead of spending $20 million on Super Bowl ads, it would donate those funds to people who had "refreshing ideas to change the world." Applicants could make their pitch on its "refresh everything" website and the public could vote on their ideas.

Both campaigns came under fire from critics and on social media. What were the complaints? Cause marketing has to be authentic and reflect the true identity and culture of a company. There is no doubt that the Boys and Girls Clubs and the many projects proposed to Pepsi are "worthy causes." But if you ask conscious consumers which issues matter to them about soft drinks, topics like "junk food," "obesity," "advertising in schools," and "water use" pop out. In 2010, Pepsi (and Coke) were simply not yet ready to address those issues seriously and, to many eyes, continue to skirt around some of them. How then do you build out change in your business to credibly effect social change?

Figure 4.1 illustrates the scale (size) and scope (reach) of potential changes in your company. Let's look at each change target to guide your own thinking in these regards.

FIGURE 4.1   Scale and Scope of Change

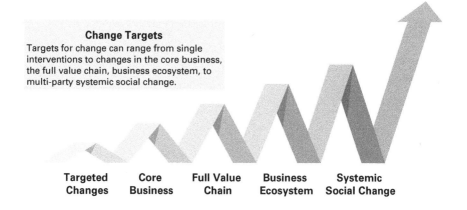

Change Targets
Targets for change can range from single interventions to changes in the core business, the full value chain, business ecosystem, to multi-party systemic social change.

Targeted Changes   Core Business   Full Value Chain   Business Ecosystem   Systemic Social Change

Targeted Changes. Companies that strive to lead social change launch new initiatives, projects, programs and products or revise existing ones through targeted actions. Here you often need "buy-in" from senior management, financial and technical resources, and skills in project and change management. The intent is not to transform the whole business but rather to address specific problems or opportunities relating to the interests of your employees, customers, or other stakeholders. Targeted change can create tangible and social value for the business and society. Consider a sampling of the types of innovations and changes we will look at in Part II of this volume:

- Over 30 companies we studied created global pro bono programs where employees volunteer for service assignments to nonprofits, social enterprises, government agencies, and small businesses to build their capacities to solve problems and create social change.

- Many companies in our research launched new initiatives on inclusion and social justice and some overhauled their compensation system to ensure pay equity.

- Select firms engaged existing R&D and product development teams to fortify foods, search for alternatives to plastic in packaging, or devise "tech for good" apps. Marketing and tech teams innovated in service of transparency and digital engagement of customers.

- Other firms built green roofs over their facilities, produced eco-friendly products, or enlisted their employees in various company and often community-based green projects.

Changes in the Core Business. Lots more is involved when you build out change in your core business. Here we studied companies changing policies, governance, accountability and reporting systems; devising new strategies and practices that affected multiple functions in the business; creating new production systems and organizational units or rearranging existing ones; or taking steps to increase the numbers of women and "underrepresented" populations in their staffing and managerial ranks. Typically one or more members of senior management "owns" these undertakings, the investments in resources and time are more extensive than a targeted change, and the change process is more elaborate and demanding.

But this is not necessarily so if you design your core business to do good from the start. Take the case of an entrepreneur we met, Sharleen Ernster, who left the mainline fashion industry to launch We Are HAH, a small California company that aims to make sustainable fashion "sexy" ("It's Hot-as-Hell to Care about Mother Earth"). HAH's eco-friendly lingerie and swimwear is alluring but, as she pledges, "suitable for my daughters." One factor that differentiates We Are HAH is its use of digital rather than traditional screen or rotary printing. Digital printing uses 95 percent less water than traditional methods and reduces the use of toxic dyestuff. It is also "waste friendly" in that the company prints fabric on demand and thus sends much less wasted fabric to landfills. It's a great choice for a startup, as a company can start taking low-quantity, on-demand orders without the high set-up costs of screen printing. Ernster fashions herself as an innovator and changemaker. Her #StartSomewhere social media campaign uses peer storytelling to stimulate others to "change the narrative around business."

On a larger scale, to deliver profits with purpose, PepsiCo formed a Global Nutrition Group to develop more nutritious snacks and beverages. When Dr. Mehmood Khan, a medical doctor, took the reins as PepsiCo Chief Scientific Officer, he noted that the company "had a lot of talent" but it was not "cross-pollinating." When he started, 100 percent of his leadership team were American, all men, and all had backgrounds in food engineering and technology. Seven years on and one-half of his direct reports were women, half were non-American, and many came from beauty care and the life sciences as well as foods. This diversity of talent led to innovations for consumers interested in "good for you" products.

Changes in the Full Value Stream. As PepsiCo built out its new product lines, change extended upstream into sourcing and its supply chains and downstream through marketing, retailing, and into consumers' throats and stomachs. Further acquisitions and some selective divestitures followed. Looking over the full value stream, there are entrepreneurs who build out their business with a socially conscious business model and large firms that undertake a full transformation of their business. Let's start with an entrepreneur.

Ejido Verde is a Mexican pine resin supply company that works in a partnership with rural communities that harvest resin. The company provides zero-interest loans of $4,800 per hectare to communities in exchange for the communities providing land and labor to harvest pine resin. The community assigns land rights and responsibilities to individual families. When the trees start producing resin at year 10, resin tappers then repay the loan with 10–15 percent of their resin and Ejido Verde buys the remaining resin at a fair market price from years 11 to 20. After that, the tappers own 100 percent of their resin. Ejido Verde's reforestation model is designed to maximize long-term resin yields without harming the trees while improving soil health, restoring watersheds, and expanding wildlife habitat.

As for big company makeovers, we've seen Nike transform its supply chain, R&D, marketing, and customer engagement strategies. Summing up the company's journey, Hannah Jones reported on its key features:

> We have a new vision; we've redefined goals in Nike terms—"there is no finish line." It requires innovation in our design process, our production, our sourcing, our tools and metrics, and our whole team structure. Fortunately, innovation is in our cultural DNA and provides a strong foundation. Even so, embedding sustainability thinking in our strategy and then educating every person and evolving the process in the company is a challenge that takes time, continual reassessment, and unerring commitment.

"It's not about a few people making sustainable products," adds Nike Considered Design GM, Lorrie Vogel. "It's about making sure that every person in the system adopts a different world view, sense of purpose and approach to their job."[11]

Changes in the Business Ecosystem. Many companies we have studied have made investments and undertaken changes that affect the business ecosystem. These range from a company's philanthropic spending for education and community infrastructure to larger-scale partnerships to address social issues. JPMorgan Chase, for instance, has been making big investments in Detroit, Michigan. It started with a $100 million commitment to the city in 2014 and then the bank sent in employee volunteers in the form of its pro bono Detroit Service Corps. The first pro bono teams partnered with four local not-for-profit organizations to support neighborhood and workforce development. By now, nearly 100 employees have helped 21 Detroit organizations to improve their capabilities and strengthen community outreach. Financial support and employee assistance from Morgan Chase has enabled these local organizations to provide training and career education to nearly 15,000 Detroiters and technical assistance to 18,000 entrepreneurs and small businesses, yielding more than 700 new jobs. Recently, JPMorgan Chase expanded its local service corps and grants to Chicago, New York, London, Paris, and Hong Kong.

We also saw companies function like social venture capitalists and run workshops and labs for external social entrepreneurs where their employees provide mentoring, business guidance, and technical assistance. Sometimes these engagements develop into partnerships between firms and social enterprises. Leona Tan, head of the Development Bank of Singapore's (DBS) Foundation, adapted the bank's platforms to assist commercial startups to the social sector. The first stage of support has DBS employees serve as advisers to social startups and the Foundation offers them pilot/prototype grants. In the second stage, for enterprises two to five years old, there are employee-run incubators, innovation tool kits and case studies, and a full ecosystem of DBS mentors who can provide counsel on every aspect of growing an organization. The third stage of support is for scaling the enterprise. At this phase social enterprises have access to a full suite of DBS banking services which, according to Leona, are provided "virtually free." Beyond the social benefits, Singaporean startups are exposed to banking culture and DBS staff gain from the cultural exchange on how startups innovate and grow.

Reams have been written about the individual and collective lobbying of US businesses against progressive social change. This includes fighting against consumer rights, minimum wage increases, climate solutions, and, of course, business tax increases. There is also a growing "lobbying for good" movement. Business for Innovative Climate and Energy Policy (BICEP) is a coalition of leading businesses including Nike, Levi Strauss, and Starbucks that lobbies in favor of sustainable climate and energy policy. The Business Coalition for the Equality Act has grown to include more than 400 major US corporations calling for passage of the Equality Act—federal legislation that would modernize the nation's civil rights laws by including explicit protections for LGBTQ people, as well as improve protections for women, people of color, and people of all faiths. Such moves take a company well beyond its fenceline and to the forefront of social change.

Systemic Social Change. At this scale and scope, companies work together and often with governments, NGOs, and other interests to lead systemic change efforts—not just to advocate and lobby for them. Activities here have historically ranged from early-stage consciousness raising efforts to multi-party collaboration to ensure ethical trade, certify organic produce, protect forests and wildlife habitat, and so on.[12] In the emerging wave of social change, collaborative action aims to promote racial justice, combat climate change, and tackle the world's most pressing problems.

Over the years, we have seen progressive businesses come together in Britain's Business in the Community, the US-based Businesses for Social Responsibility, CSR Europe, the Asian Forum for CSR, the United Nations'

Global Compact, and more recently the Shared Value Initiative and Conscious Capitalism movement. These are great venues for sharing experiences and gauging progress. Joining in them gets you on the playing field.

We noted how Nike joined the Fair Labor Association (in the United States) and Ethical Trading Initiative (in the United Kingdom) in 1999. Its aims were to get every industry player into fair and ethical sourcing and establish a level playing field. The Fair Labor Association has a code of conduct, oversees third-party compliance assessments of companies, and posts the results of factory audits on its website. Meanwhile, the Ethical Trading Initiative now has over 90 member companies and its code of conduct protects over 15 million workers worldwide. Some nine in ten companies have improved their ethical trade performance since joining. We will look at various of these coalitions involved in purpose, prosperity, people, products, and the planet.

Now we see companies coming together with government and NGOs in "action tanks" to collectively effect social change. Business for Inclusive Growth (B4IG) is a new partnership between the Organisation for Economic Co-operation and Development and corporations from across the globe that aims for action. On a smaller scale, 10 companies have joined a *Call to Action: Better business through better wages*, to develop and propagate their experiences building living wage business models in challenging arenas like agriculture and clothing. Unilever is a founding member of both groups and has promised all of its supply chain a "living wage" by the year 2030. This initiative will significantly boost the pay of millions of employees working in its 65,000 direct suppliers in 190 countries.

In Part II we will see how companies build in or build out the scale and scope of change in their purpose and in their efforts toward more inclusive prosperity, developing and activating their people, delivering products and services, and regenerating the planet. A final chapter covers systemic social change. Before you move there, let's look at innovation and the need for continuous change.

Continuous Change

The change practices and targets presented are relevant whether you are starting or growing your small good business, or redesigning and remaking it in light of social change. After you have developed or changed your business are you finished? Hardly so in the world of continuous change. Top companies continue to innovate and fine-tune existing initiatives.

New Ideas from "Outside-In." In *Think Outside the Building: How advanced leaders can change the world one smart innovation at a time*, Rosabeth Moss Kanter makes the point that innovation can be stifled when companies stick to their current approach and "fail to see the wider world outside." In our studies, we found companies turning to open innovation models to source fresh ideas, bringing innovation "outside-in" from social entrepreneurs, partnering with other businesses in collaborative innovation, and adapting innovations created in the developing world to meet needs in their home markets (reverse innovation). Fresh ideas are needed to address novel problems. Studies find that even when company leaders sense dramatic changes in their business context, they tend to respond with what Donald Sull calls "active inertia." Stuck in the modes of thinking and working that brought success in the past, they keep on doing what they have been doing, just harder and faster, in hopes that that will do the trick. Most times it does not and it's a prime reason why, as Sull puts it, "good businesses go bad."[13]

Collaborative innovation is especially important for entrepreneurs aspiring to change the world. The social business d.light aims to improve the lives of the two billion people in the developing world that live without access to reliable energy. The company offers affordable solar energy solutions for households and small businesses that are transforming the way people all over the world use and pay for energy. Shell provided early financial support for d.light and technical assistance addressing key challenges in designing LED lighting modules and lithium batteries. The company also has a channel partnership with Unilever whereby d.light sells solar home systems to Unilever, who place them in the small-scale retail shops that stock their products. Latest move: the company partnered with the Australian Government Department of Foreign Affairs and Trade, off-grid energy company Sola PayGo, and payment service provider Bmobile to bring solar solutions to over 2,500 remote households in Papua New Guinea.

Social Innovation in Business. Mark Thain, an accountant turned intrapreneur, is founder of the Barclays Social Innovation Facility, an internal accelerator for the development of commercial solutions to social and environmental challenges. Employees within Barclays participate in a three-day intrapreneur lab where their ideas are developed and they gain a deeper understanding of what it takes to launch innovations within the company. For the next three months, they get support from internal mentors and then pitch their innovations to senior execs. Innovations launched include a credit card aimed at Millennials that "rounds up" the charge at the bank's expense and donates the added funds to social purposes, loans with reduced credit charges for consumers who otherwise wouldn't qualify for such rates, and a suite of impact investing products.

In service of the business ecosystem, the Barclays accelerator is also open for other companies. It hosts an innovation accelerator, a 13-week program for fintech startups, run in partnership with Techstars. More than 300 companies from almost 50 countries worldwide applied for one of the 11 places on the program. The winning ideas range from an alternative to payday loans, to a next-generation credit scoring system, to a peer-to-peer funding platform for real estate. "It is time to redefine financial services," said Michael Harte, Barclays' Chief Operations and Technology Officer:

> We're seeking to connect the world's most active innovators to each other, to corporates, and to resources and support networks. By accelerating the development of groundbreaking products and services, we know that we can help to keep Barclays at the cutting edge of financial services, all while helping to revolutionize the industry.

Sustained Social Impact. One company we've studied, Danone, has been a pioneer in corporate social innovation. In 1972, CEO Antoine Riboud repurposed his business with a dual commitment to business success and social progress. Forty-plus years later, the Paris-based business with brands such as Activia, Evian, and Dannon yogurt, issued a manifesto for an "Alimentation Revolution" that commits the company to the "quest to find better health through better food and beverage for the greatest number." To activate this quest and make it an ongoing part of the business, Danone employees are engaged in social innovation projects of their own design and many small-scale "lab to land" projects to protect and restore the planet.

We discovered one lab team in France that reduced methane emissions by feeding cows with flaxseed. This not only had a beneficial environmental impact (reducing methane and thus CO_2 emissions), it also improved the milk's nutritional quality. Another lab's team experimented with removing the wrapping paper around its yogurt containers. While this reduced packaging waste, consumers worried about a loss of product safety and quality. The team went back to work to develop a bio-sourced plastic wrapper that ultimately reduced costs and environmental impact. Yet another lab team, based in the UK, proposed the simple idea of "co-distributing" Danone products together with products from other makers in shipments to customers. The retailer ARLA participated in the pilot projects and now co-distribution is used in many countries.

Each of these social innovation projects began with a challenge posed to employees. As a Danoner described it, "These types of crazy projects force us to forget everything we know, and to start from scratch, and that is an enormous source of innovation."[14] To promote corporate-wide learning, an annual meeting of Danone's Social Innovation Lab brings together employees from different country business units to share their innovative ideas and best practices on both social (say, cooperative farming arrangements or serving poor customers) and environmental issues (say, how to measure impacts or water use). Participants learn from successful models, analyze unprofitable ventures, and propose new ideas in brainstorming sessions in a variety of workshops. A recent lab included a review of over 70 social innovation projects including Danone's work with SAP to develop carbon emission metrics, its social business partnership with Grameen to scale a yogurt business in Bangladesh, and its many projects with community groups supported via the Danone Ecosystem Fund.

To further institutionalize the idea of continuous social change, Danone indexes one-third of managers' bonuses to achieving social impact and provides direct recognition from top management to Danone intrapreneurs who deliver business results and social progress. The Social Innovation Lab has of late expanded its ranks beyond Danone to include participants from relevant nonprofits, as well as academics, social entrepreneurs, and sustainability experts. Listen to the words of one of these outside participants: "Did Danone give me a glimpse of what a world could look like where big businesses went beyond CSR and put social impact at the heart of what they do? And should I be thinking how to work with other businesses to help them to do the same?"[15]

Are you ready to move beyond CSR, sustainability, shared value, and all the other good things companies are doing today? Are you game to move into tomorrow, to go for social impact, and to turn more of your attention and resources to leading social change? Part II shows you how.

PART TWO

Creating Social Value: Your Company's Handprint

05

Put Social Purpose First

When impact investor James Rhee joined Ashley Stewart's board in 2013, the company was broke. He recalled:

> We were operating out of an insect-infested warehouse in Secaucus (New Jersey). On the surface of it, you say, "That's the brand," but if you peel back the onion... I thought that the brand stood for a lot of great things... community, and self-esteem, and respect... It was one of the strongest women's brands I'd ever seen.

Rhee didn't want to see the company die. "There was a force making it live," he said, "and that was passion, that was friendship. Those are the things that really spoke to me as a human being more than as an investor."[1]

So Rhee left the board to become CEO of Ashley Stewart. To many eyes this seemed a setup to a culture clash. What could Rhee, a venture capitalist and son of Korean immigrants, bring to the mostly female and Black staff except harsh cost-cutting and culturally clueless top-down leadership? At his first town hall, Rhee told the staff that he was unsure if Ashley Stewart had a future, but he was determined to save the company. He led with his own version of the golden rule: "You will have to be kind," he explained. "Kindness, empathy... these things are transcendent to diversity and inclusion." It resonated with employees, one of whom reminded him that "Everyone has to be kind!"

Ashley Stewart was driven by a social purpose at its startup in 1991. Its intent was to get fashionable plus-size clothing primarily to Black and minority women through retail stores in inner-cities in the United States. Over the next two decades, it expanded from a single shop in NYC to over 380 stores in 100 cities. Rather than run advertising campaigns, Ashley Stewart hosted community-based fashion shows and was lauded for hiring women then on welfare to staff its stores. All good, but here's the problem: the company had not been driven very well. It was sold off several times to private equity investors and twice lurched into bankruptcy.

The strategic actions taken by Rhee ranged from closing 100 stores and retrofitting the company for e-commerce, to transforming Ashley Stewart's website and supply chain. The company's purposeful message to its customers was, "I see you, I hear you, and I will serve you." This resonated especially with Black women consumers who are traditionally underserved by marketers. And it built on the company's heritage. "Ashley Stewart was often the first store willing to extend credit to some of these women," says Rhee. "It was about more than a purchase of a dress that made her feel beautiful. She was treated with respect."[2]

Within a few years, the company turned a profit—after two decades of losses—and began to work with a new generation of Black and socially conscious designers. With its focus on digital marketing and social connection, Ashely Stewart helped to create a community of customers who participate in image-boosting contests and provide social support for one another. Its #Momspiration event invited women to upload photos and stories of their mothers or other women who played important roles in their lives. A #SheDidThat campaign encouraged them to post photos of themselves and many added captions with phrases such as "She Slayed" and "She Persisted." The retailer gave away shopping sprees to the winners of each contest.

"Our whole goal in being a social commerce brand is we're looking to give voice to women across America," says Andrea Berner, Senior Vice President of Ashley Stewart. "This social engagement platform allows women to have a voice and to speak it loud."[3] Hear this message posted by one "Ashley Stewart Woman": "Empowered women empower women. Let's uplift each other and not bring each other down."

What's a Business For?

Corporate thought leader Charles Handy asks, "What's a business for?" Most people reply with this top-of-mind answer: "To make money!" To this he counters, "The purpose of a business… is not to make a profit, full stop. It is to make a profit so that the business can do something more or better. That 'something' becomes the real justification for the business…."[4]

Many entrepreneurs today start with a purpose to deliver something more and better. Clothing retailer Life is Good says it simply: "To spread the power of optimism." Natural food purveyor Kashi harbors a "Dream of a world where everyone embraces natural health." Trillium Asset Management promises investors that its funds will deliver "positive impact, long-term value, and 'social dividends'." But a sense of purpose isn't just for B Corps or companies that cater to socially conscious consumers and investors. Several big mainstream companies have repurposed themselves in positive ways. IBM is working toward a "Smarter Planet," Ikea pledges to be "People & Planet Positive," and Mars, which makes everything from candy to cat food, proclaims, "The world we want tomorrow starts with how we do business today."

At first blush such proclamations can sound vague, puffed up, or simply BS. But as Rosabeth Moss Kanter finds in her studies, "Great companies think differently" about this.[5] Their sense of purpose is deeply informed by an understanding of and responsiveness to the needs of the world around them. So, take a look at your company's handprint and ask: *Are you in business to create positive social change?*

A strong and uplifting purpose gives employees a sense of direction and meaning in their jobs. It also tells customers, suppliers, investors, competitors, and the public at large: this is why we exist and what we are in business for. But then you have to deliver on your purpose—authentically, fully, transparently, and reliably. This chapter starts with some background on the whats and whys of purpose and focuses squarely on what purpose means in companies that aim to lead social change. It then looks at how to create (or recreate) a sense of purpose in your company, build it out with employees, bake it into the business, and ultimately take purpose to your customers and society.

The Purpose of Purpose

Over the past 30 years, leading companies have formulated visions, crafted mission statements, defined their values, and cultivated their organizational cultures. Why all the hullabaloo over declaring their purpose? A case can be made that "purpose" adds a missing piece to a company's governing ideas—it speaks to why yours exists, your "reason for being." How does it fit into the guidance system of a business (see Figure 5.1)?

- **Vision** tells people "Where" a company aspires to be. It articulates a desired future and in its detailing paints a compelling picture of where a company is going.

- **Mission** tells people "What" a company is doing and has on offer. It sets out goals and can chart out the path toward realizing a company's vision.

- **Values** concern "How" a company does things. It expresses a philosophy of how things ought to be done and how employees, customers, and other stakeholders are to be treated.

- **Culture** expresses "Who" we are as a company and connects values to norms of behavior inside a business and in its dealing with customers and business partners.

- **Purpose** addresses "Why" a company exists and ideally serves to align vision, mission, values, and culture.

Now don't get hung up on distinctions between these terms. They can overlap and in practice interconnect. Some companies have mission statements that speak to their purpose. Listen to the BBC's mission, "To enrich people's lives with programmes and services that inform, educate and entertain." Likewise, vision statements can reflect purpose and passion: high-tech

FIGURE 5.1   Your Company's Guidance Systems

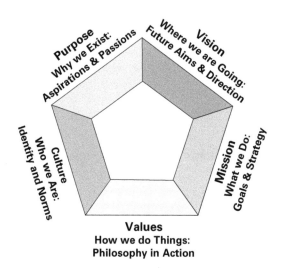

Cisco's vision is "Changing the way we work, live, play, and learn." Whatever you label these proclamations in your company, it is important that your business addresses the question, "Why do we exist?" Simon Sinek's *Start With Why* popularized the idea that thoughts about "what" are processed in the outer section of the human brain (neocortex) which handles analytic thinking and language. By contrast, thoughts about "how" and especially "why" are processed in the middle section of the brain (limbic system) which guides behavior, decisions, and feelings.[6]

Marketers have turned all of this into the mantra: "People don't buy *what* you do, they buy *why* you do it." And managers have been advised that while vision, mission, and values can *drive* you, purpose can *guide* you. But before you proclaim your purpose and hire a PR firm to design the campaign, understand that the public is wary of "purpose washing" and expectations about that "something" that guides your business are affected by massive social change.

Business Purpose and Social Change

Business historians have studied company statements about their purpose.[7] The first generation of statements were appealing slogans like Disney's "To make people happy" or General Electric's "We bring good things to life," meant chiefly for advertising and company placards. Then companies began to speak directly to their customers. McDonald's said it this way: "To be our customers' favorite place and way to eat and drink," and Wal-Mart put it plainly: "We save people money so they can live better."

With the move to serving shareholders, messaging on company purpose took on new dimensions. For instance, Limited Brands (who then owned Victoria's Secret, Pink, and Bath & Body Works) said it was "committed to building a family of the world's best fashion brands offering captivating customer experiences that drive long-term loyalty and deliver sustained growth for our shareholders." In turn, Disney's purpose morphed into business speak: "To be one of the world's leading producers and providers of entertainment and information, using its portfolio of brands to differentiate its content, services and consumer products." Today we hear statements that speak of sustainability and shared value. Dupont proclaims its purpose this way: "To create shareholder and societal value while reducing the environmental footprint along the value chains in which we operate."

Companies that go further and aspire to lead social change face a future of heightened expectations and more demanding constituencies. Here is what's ahead.

People Want to Work for, Invest in, and Buy Goods and Services from a Company with a Compelling "Social Purpose." Good products, profits, and employment practices are "table stakes"—they get you into the good business game but don't enable you to win against forward-thinking competitors. What do we mean by a social purpose? Listen to one uplifting definition: "A business with a social purpose is a company whose enduring reason for being is to create a better world. It is an engine for good, creating societal benefits by the very act of conducting business. Its growth is a positive force in society."[8]

Surveys show that large majorities of the world's public hold business fully responsible for ensuring product safety, providing fair wages to employees, not harming the environment, maintaining a responsible supply chain, and the like—all within a company's operating arena. But large numbers also expect companies to provide long-term financial stability for employees, to support communities and charities, to help reduce the rich-poor gap, and to solve social and environmental problems.[9]

What social purpose connects your business to issues of concern to society? Many companies stress their green credentials and others their charitable giving, commitment to diversity, community development work, and so on. All of this is laudable but it doesn't necessarily address "why" they are in business or translate into a social value proposition for their brands. Who gets this right? Take Patagonia, whose clothing is made of organic cotton or recycled fibers, sourced only from suppliers that meet its strict environmental and labor codes of conduct, and has taken a lead in the reusable clothing movement. After it pledged 1 percent of its total revenue to the preservation and restoration of the natural environment, it enlisted other small, environmentally intensive firms like builders, contractors, and construction supply companies, plus big ones like Hyatt International, to make this same pledge. Here's how Patagonia expresses its social purpose: "Build the best product; cause no unnecessary harm; use business to inspire; and implement solutions to the environmental crisis."

Your Social Purpose has to be Authentic and Embedded in your Business. Studies find a daunting "purpose gap" in business today.[10] Plenty of executives say it is important for their company to have a guiding sense of purpose, but most have not incorporated purpose into their strategy, goals, and measurement systems. This gap turns off employees, customers, and social media critics who regularly call out companies for disingenuousness and hypocrisy.

Who "walks their talk"? We have seen how Novo Nordisk has taken its aims to "Defeat Diabetes" into society. To express its core purpose inside, the company formulated its Novo Nordisk Way of Management (NNWoM) that covers corporate values, principles of management, and key commitments, including pledges that its products and services make a "significant difference in improving the way people live and work" and that its "activities, practices and deliverables are perceived to be economically viable, environmentally sound, and socially fair." Every employee is expected to spend at least one day a year with someone connected to diabetes—a patient, a caretaker, or a healthcare professional—and then to suggest improvements for how the company does business. To ensure performance to the highest standards, employees are involved in documenting and improving the company's triple bottom line performance. A group of 30 to 40 non-executive "facilitators," drawn from employee ranks, meets with every work unit and every employee, over a three-year cycle, to ensure that actions and decisions live up to the promise of the NNWoM.

People Want to Believe and be Engaged in Your Purpose—From Tell Me to Show Me to Activate Me. PR campaigns with uplifting slogans and evocative videos get your message out are but a first step in taking your purpose into the world. People need more to believe in you. B Corps use their certification to show they are committed to being a socially purposeful company. If that is not in your game plan, certification of your practices and products by credible social, environmental, and labor accreditation bodies is a step forward to credibility. Connecting your purpose to clear targets on, say, net-zero emissions or specific diversity and inclusion goals, puts you on record with your intentions. Tying this all into an integrative framework, such as the SDGs and/or the Global Reporting Initiative (GRI), signals seriousness of purpose and enables people to compare and gauge your performance versus others in your industry and geography. And a public accounting of your purposeful activities and results, ideally by an independent third party, provides proof points of your achievements and requires an explanation of gaps. Job done? Not so fast. In a social media world, people also want to talk with you about your social purpose, challenge, criticize and praise you when warranted, and get involved in your doings.

The Public Wants Companies to Speak Out on Social Issues. Should your company engage with controversial social issues in society? We noted how Nike dove into the churning seas of social change in 2018 when its ads featured the former National Football League player Colin Kaepernick, who became a center of controversy when he knelt during the national anthem at games to draw attention to police brutality against minorities in the United States. Nike's campaign drew both praise and criticism—many consumers lauded the company on social media, while some posted videos in which they lit their Nike shoes on fire.

Who could have imagined, amidst the Black Lives Matter protests in 2020, that Jamie Dimon, CEO of the US's largest bank JPMorgan Chase, wearing shorts, sneakers, and a mask, would, in the spirit of Kaepernick, "take a knee" alongside employees at a bank branch. In turn, NASCAR banned the confederate flag from its auto races; Quaker Oats shut down its Aunt Jemima breakfast food brand; Adidas committed to filling 30 percent of its new positions with Black or Latin workers; Google pledged that it would have at least 30 percent minority representation on its executive team by 2025; and Netflix announced it would put 2 percent of its cash holdings into financial institutions that "directly support Black communities in the US."

While speaking out and taking action have their perils, surveys find the 62 percent of consumers want companies to stand up for the issues they are passionate about. Nearly four in ten employees (38 percent) say that they themselves have spoken up to support or criticize their employers' actions over a controversial issue in society. Who do these activists speak to? The most common targets of their messages are other employees and top leaders in their organization, but one in three also hope to get the attention of the general public.[11]

Social Purpose: Promise and Pitfalls. Larry Fink, founder and CEO of BlackRock, has called his peers to action: "Society is demanding that companies, both public and private, serve a social purpose. To prosper over time, every company must not only deliver financial performance, but also show how it makes a positive contribution to society." Sounds good, doesn't it? But while most executives buy into this idea and say it is important to their employees (89 percent) and customers (80 percent), they drop the ball when it comes to articulating and delivering on it. A study by Gallup, for instance, found that less than half of employees worldwide know what their organization stands for and what makes it different.[12]

What's behind this "say–do" purpose gap? One factor cited by managers we talked to is that short-term profit pressures prevent them from thinking about and managing the business for a higher purpose. A second is that while many companies proudly and authentically define their purpose in terms of, say, their products or quality or being #1 in their industry, they simply haven't connected their business to a larger social purpose of benefiting society. And a third is that even when they do connect their purpose to society, it is mostly "lip service."

Purpose pronouncements issued from top management don't ring true to line managers and everyday employees who have had no voice in them and see contradictions in their day-to-day work. Talk about social purpose also seems hollow in companies whose performance scorecards and reward systems are tuned exclusively to productivity and profits. Meanwhile, activists, consumers, and the public are on alert to what critics call the "purpose scam." Look at what happened to Chevron (see box). And then take a look in the mirror by completing a survey about your company's purpose.

A PURPOSE SCAM

A few years ago, Chevron launched its "We Agree" campaign with the slogan, "It's Time Oil Companies Get Behind the Development of Renewable Energy." A series of print and online ads, and 30-second YouTube videos, were posted with purposeful messages about how oil companies should be green, support small businesses and communities, and put profits to good use, all affirmed by Chevron's statement "We Agree" in bold type. The problem? Chevron had sold off or closed most of its renewable business units and was embroiled in lawsuits that Texaco, which it had acquired, had dumped more than 18 billion gallons of toxic wastewater into the Ecuadorian Amazon rainforest, leaving local people suffering from an epidemic of cancers, miscarriages and birth defects.

In today's cynical and social media-saturated environment, whenever your company touts its good intentions, you better have the bona fides to back them up. Chevron's "We Agree" campaign was targeted by the activist group the Yes Men, which teamed up with the Rainforest Action Network and Amazon Watch to erect a fake website proclaiming that Chevron "agrees" oil companies should "fix the problems they create" and "clean up their messes." These protest groups then announced a contest for print, web, and tv ads satirizing Chevron's greenwashing. Hundreds of submissions were posted online and pasted up in cities nationwide. One contestant's advert read, "Chevron must think we're stupid!"

STRESS TEST: RATE YOUR COMPANY'S PURPOSE

Changemaking begins with facing reality. How about your company: Does it have a clear and noble social purpose? Does top management "walk the talk"? Does your company really deliver on its social purpose? Rate your organization in terms of its purpose.

CHECKLIST 5.1

Purpose: Is your company in business to create positive social good?

To what extent....   1 = Not at all   5 = To a great extent

	1	2	3	4	5
1. Does your company have a clear statement of its social purpose—its intent to make a better world?	☐	☐	☐	☐	☐
2. Does top management regularly communicate about the social purpose of your company?	☐	☐	☐	☐	☐
3. Do managers in your company "walk the talk" when it comes to social purpose?	☐	☐	☐	☐	☐
4. Are employees recognized and rewarded for contributing to your company's social purpose?	☐	☐	☐	☐	☐
5. Does your company "speak out" on important issues in society?	☐	☐	☐	☐	☐
6. Does your company truly deliver on its social purpose?	☐	☐	☐	☐	☐

Now add up the answers to these six questions: if you score 25 or more, your company has a strong social purpose and delivers on it. If 12 to 24, it's time to turn up the throttle. If lower, either clam up or roll up your sleeves. Here are some ideas and guidance on how to bring social purpose into being in your business.

Three Dimensions of Social Purpose

The Social Purpose Institute makes a case that there are three dimensions to social purpose in a business. What does this mean for your company?

Define your Company's Reason for Being. Every company has, in principle, a reason for its existence. As you think about your company, are you clear about why you exist, what you stand for, and what you are all about? Defining your purpose like "Be the best in the eyes of our customers, employees and investors" doesn't suffice. That could apply to most any business and certainly doesn't differentiate you from competitors. British fast-fashion company ASOS states its purpose aggressively: "To become the number 1 fashion destination for 20-somethings globally." That might motivate top managers and investors, but how about line staff and customers? Compare it to H&M's purpose: "To drive long-lasting positive change and improve living conditions by investing in people, communities and innovative ideas." While that statement doesn't exactly give execs a clear strategic direction, it does afford them criteria for making purposeful strategic choices—such as recent moves away from the wasteful consumption and earth-destroying world of fast fashion! It also gives employees a reason to join and for customers to buy from H&M.

Ideally your company's purpose speaks to why you are in business, differentiates you in the marketplace, is appealing to your multiple stakeholders, and helps you to decide what to do more of, less of, and differently as you run the business. But a social purpose goes further: it also addresses what need you fill in society and why the world should care about you.

Identify your Company's Social Ambitions. Shortly after launching its "Sustainable Living Plan," Unilever recognized that consumers were less interested in the company's plans and targets and more interested in how their lives would be affected and what Unilever's products could do for them. Accordingly, its purpose pledge was personalized: "To make sustainable living commonplace." Studies find that over six in ten of today's consumers want to buy from a company whose purpose is personally relevant, aligns with their values, and inspires them.[13]

We challenged you at the outset: consumers worldwide today want brands that both "solve my problems" *and* help to "solve society's problems." So as you think about your company's purpose, additional questions are on the table: "How do we contribute to the greater good? What social ills, injustices, or wrongs are we trying to address or make right through our business? Why is the world a better place because of us?" These aren't easy questions to answer but your answers to them are an integral part of defining your company's social ambition.

Novo Nordisk's social ambition to "Defeat Diabetes" was translated into specific targets and tangible programs to effect social change among young diabetics, poor women, those lacking access to diagnostic and medical care, and cities throughout the world. Focused, relevant, bold, and actionable. Let us be clear: no one expects business to solve all the world's ills or for any company to tackle social problems beyond its scope and capabilities to make a difference. So don't try to "boil the ocean." The key to putting purpose into practice is to identify the "right" social problems your business can address—ones that constitute a "meaningful challenge."

Connect your Company's Purpose to Profit. As we detailed in Chapter 2, there are many links between purpose and profits. Consumers gravitate to companies that care. Over three-quarters of consumers have a stronger emotional connection to purpose-driven brands and feel these companies care about them and their families, more so than traditional brands. B2B businesses can also benefit from a strong social purpose—to enhance reputation, attract and retain employees, differentiate the business, and increase customer confidence.[14]

So, if your company already has a social purpose, give it a fresh look in light of these three dimensions. If it needs updating, if you do not have one, or if the one you have suffers from a purpose gap, then here is some guidance on what to do next.

How to Purpose or Repurpose Your Business

Purposing the business starts with clarity on who you are, what you believe, and what you want to achieve with your company—whether you are its founder, CEO, a top executive, or simply have a voice in its aims, direction, and future.

A Point of View. John Mackey, founder of Whole Foods, started his business in 1980 with a higher purpose: "With great courage, integrity and love—we embrace our responsibility to co-create a world where each of us, our communities and our planet can flourish. All the while, celebrating the sheer love and joy of food." He supported this ideal with a "Declaration of Interdependence" that treats Whole Foods' stakeholders as an interdependent "family." The company went public in 1992 in the era of shareholder capitalism and Mackey had to answer investors who favored Milton

Friedman's philosophy that profits come first. Listen to his point of view: "High profits are necessary to fuel our growth across the United States and the world. Just as people cannot live without eating, so a business cannot live without profits. But most people don't live to eat, and neither must a business live just to make profits."[15]

How do you purpose (or repurpose) a company that hasn't articulated its social purpose or has lost its way? We described earlier how Unilever repurposed itself through a company-wide self-study of changing market and societal conditions and tough-love critique of its own practices and values. This is a model of how to do it—you can't simply issue a purpose statement from on high and drive its adoption by fiat top-down. A participatory and inclusive process is needed. It takes sustained discussions: 1) inside the company with your board of directors, top team, and eventually all managers and employees; and 2) outside the company with customers, other stakeholders, and ultimately the world.

Top Team Dialogue. Imagine a dialogue with your leadership team that begins with the question: What is our purpose? We saw one such discussion shut down quickly when the CEO stated, "Make money for our shareholders, next question?" But even when the boss gravitates to a social purpose, there is a need for more talk. In another company, executives quickly concluded their purpose discussion with an agreement to "Save the Earth." Then a contrarian piped up, "For whom?" This led to a deeper conversation about how their sense of purpose actually connected to their products, employees, customers, and then how it fit with their executive compensation system!

In most organizations, members of the top team will have diverse ideas and may be initially uncomfortable even talking about the company's purpose. How do you instigate an open, frank, and free-wheeling discussion about "why we exist"? Executives at Thailand's Charoen Pokphand Group were cautious about discussing their conglomerates' purpose for fear of being out of step with their longtime Senior Chairman Dhanin Chearavanont and out of synch with other business unit CEOs. To foster openness and creativity, the Chairman asked each of them to write an "imaginary" story, dated 10 years forward, about how the company transformed itself and the world. After some initial skepticism, the executives scripted their stories and then read them aloud, one by one, to their colleagues. The collective storytelling helped the various business group presidents to find common purpose around, for instance, "providing food for both body and mind" and "health and well-being for all" and to call on the Group to "embrace change." Each of the business leaders then replicated this process in their units and it eventually cascaded through 200 subsidiaries in 21 countries.

Talk with (Not at) Employees. Most every company has a favored method for "checking in" with employees—including town halls, peer-to-peer discussions, "listening" sessions, and so forth. Any and all of these forums can be focused on a company's purpose but it is important that higher-ups speak *with* not *at* their employees. In our research in Africa, we came across a regional mobile telephone operator struggling to differentiate itself in a crowded market. A full-staff presentation by the boss on company purpose was met with near silence and subsequent small-group dialogues yielded only generic and banal slogans. Things livened up, however, when each of the 200 people in attendance drew a picture of their company's purpose and collectively discussed the symbolism and meaning of each of them.

Listen to Stakeholders. An important part of sharpening your sense of purpose is to consider carefully the customer and market segments that will be served by your purposes and, more broadly, what the world wants from you. Wal-Mart spent over a year talking with its suppliers and environmental and consumer experts before launching and branding its strategy to tackle climate change. To get face to face with stakeholders, one company we worked with had its executives live in customers' homes for three days to better understand their needs and how company products served their purposes. Another had employees work alongside business customers to gain a fuller perspective on their purposes as a supplier. A third had its corporate staff visit social service agencies, schools, and community groups to ask them how their company met their needs. In each of these assignments, company personnel were given a short training course on cultural awareness, interviewing, and observation and then operated as "business anthropologists" in their stakeholders' settings. In the first case, their findings fed into development of a purpose statement and in the other two they were part of a purpose audit.

Bake Purpose into Your Core Business

Once you've talked fully and developed (or redeveloped) your company's social purpose, it needs to be built out in your organization. What can we learn from companies that baked social purpose into their business from the get-go? Whole Foods, as an example, put its purpose into effect by supporting organic and natural food suppliers and making their goods more available to consumers. Its "Whole Trade Guarantee" ensures that producers from the developing world are paid equitably and roughly 25 percent of the produce sold at its stores comes from local farms. Employees earn above market wages and all salaries are made public so employees can judge for themselves whether they are paid fairly. And the company's business model of providing customers with knowledge about product ingredients and sourcing along with an engaging shopping experience has proven highly profitable. The main complaint: shopping at Whole Foods is expensive—its prices have been 10 to 20 percent higher than at other grocery shopping venues, earning the company the unflattering nickname "Whole Paycheck"!

Codify Purpose Inside. Now if you are repurposing an established business, you've got more work to do. One reason there is such a gap between top management's proclamations about corporate purpose and employees' head-scratching response is that middle management has no ownership of any purpose pledge and few incentives to put it into practice. This problem can infect even a seemingly purpose-driven company like Levi Strauss & Co. that has been a pioneer in doing business the right way, dating from its founding years and continuing through creating a path-breaking code of conduct for suppliers in 1991 and leadership on workplace diversity. Nevertheless, its "profits through principles" mantra had been reduced to a slogan and was not integrated into the company's management model or measurement systems. Theresa Fay-Bustillos, Vice President of Worldwide Community Affairs, was frustrated by this gap and set out to bridge it. Rather than propose something new, she focused instead on revising the company's LS&Co Way that addresses its purpose, values, and ethical standards.

THE LS&CO WAY

To bring purpose back into the business, Theresa Fay-Bustillos first spoke with each member of the company's leadership team to develop a baseline of understanding about the company's social purpose and clarify future expectations. As she described it, "It is about listening to the businesspeople talk, boiling it down, and then using their own language to sell it back to them." Fay-Bustillos then convened a cross-functional, multilevel working group, including some senior execs, to sharpen LS&Co's social ambitions. As a former community advocate, she understood the need to incorporate "fringe" stakeholders into corporate consultations. So she asked, "Who aren't we listening to?" One of the biggest problems she unearthed in consultations with local NGOs in overseas markets was that law enforcement was weak in several countries in which LS&Co had supplier plants. Accordingly, she helped managers amplify existing supply chain practices to ensure: 1) host government agencies had resources to enforce labor and environmental laws; 2) local NGOs had help to advocate for better conditions; and 3) local residents had access to micro-lending to create a more stable economic base.

Another focus was respect for LGBTQ rights. At Levi's stores you'll see "Open to all" signs at the entrance, and the company has visibly fought against "trans bans" and lobbied for non-discriminatory legislation in Congress and in states. How did this change-from-middle approach work? Fay-Bustillo reports:

> Most of our programs work in silos. We tried to integrate them more throughout the company, but it has to be an effort by people, not just by systems and processes. Employees play an important role in asking questions about our practices and in consistently reinforcing for executives that one of the top reasons people come to LS& Co is because they think we are a responsible company.

Purposeful Measurement, Accountability, and Rewards. There's an old adage that "if it is important, it is measured and if it is measured, it is important." We have seen throughout the sustainability wave that many companies adopted ESG metrics to measure their performance in these areas and report it to the public. Standardized frameworks in use are variously geared to investors (Sustainability Accounting Standards Board), stakeholders (The Global Reporting Initiative), and environmental interests (The Carbon Disclosure Project and the A4S—Accounting for Sustainability). With their embrace of a social purpose, companies are also using specialized metrics and assessments to gauge the impact of their purpose on 1) their own organization and 2) social change in the world.

Apple, for instance, revised its core purpose when CEO Tim Cook took charge: "At Apple, we believe technology should lift humanity and enrich people's lives in all the ways people want to experience it." To check its authenticity and credibility, it used an independent party to survey its own employees.[16] Large majorities found Apple's revised purpose to be clear, inspirational, and readily applicable in their workaday lives. Employees posted hundreds of examples of how they personally fulfilled Apple's lofty purpose in their jobs and many noted, too, that customers' appreciation of the company helped fuel their pride. But Apple scored lower on how well it had integrated its core purpose into the business and how important CSR and sustainability were to management. Under Cook's leadership, Apple incorporated ESG criteria into managers' performance appraisals and in 2021 into executive bonuses—amounting to plus/minus 10 percent.

The drive to effect social change has companies undertaking both enterprise-wide and program-specific assessments that measure their social impact. This has a company identify: 1) which stakeholders will be affected by their programs, 2) what will be the measurable effects of the program, and 3) what will be the wider benefits and long-term changes produced. Jason Saul measures the social value of corporate social investments via his company's Social Value Scorecard™.[17] Originally targeted at measuring the social impact of nonprofits and corporate philanthropy, such scorecards are now being used by food producers to assess the impact of their recipes on family diets and eating habits and by tech companies to see the impact of software programs and apps on students' STEM learning and subsequent career interests.

Connect Your Purpose to Customers and Society

After you articulate your purpose and assimilate it in your company, it's time to activate it in the marketplace. Product brand managers are well aware of the importance of educating and engaging customers about their socially conscious offerings and corporate brand managers need to align their company's vision, culture, and image to reach their stakeholders.[18] We'll talk more about all of this in Chapter 9 on products and services. But apart from products and proclamations, how else can companies take their social purpose to customers and to society?

Engage Customers with Your Social Purpose. On a research visit to Novo Nordisk in Copenhagen, we came across the Guldsmeden Hotel group, which has enlisted its patrons in its "Love food, hate waste" program. The central idea is that you can "nudge" people to change their behavior in subtle ways. Dining guests are greeted by signboards and napkins with uplifting messages about organic eating and positive living, along with this advice about the buffet: "Take all you can eat. Eat all that you take." All servings are set out on small plates. Wait staff talk with customers about food waste and environmental issues. Leftovers from, say, the breakfast buffet are used to make paninis for lunch or next morning's muesli. And any food that is left over is collected by recyclers to make biofuel. The results? Roughly 80 percent of customers "eat all they take" and Guldsmeden has reduced its food purchases by 15 percent. How might your company nudge its customers?

Bring Purpose to Society: 1-1-1 Philanthropy. Salesforce co-CEO Marc Benioff has said, "The business of business is improving the state of the world." To do its part, Salesforce has devised a "1-1-1" model whereby 1 percent of its stock is put into the corporate foundation; employees are paid to donate 1 percent of their time to activities that fit the philanthropic priorities of the company; and 1 percent of customer cloud computing subscriptions are donated to nonprofits to increase their operating effectiveness and enable them to focus more resources on their core mission. Suzanne DiBianca, head of the Salesforce Foundation, explained her philanthropic approach to us using a triangle. The peak is "strategic philanthropy" that represents spending on education and workforce development. The middle layer involves "technology sharing" where the firm's core assets are donated to nonprofits. The base is "citizen philanthropy" where employees get support to pursue social causes of concern to them, or community groups get small grants to address pressing needs—along with volunteer assistance from Salesforce employees. The 1-1-1 model has caught on. Over 8,500 companies in 100 countries (such as Box, Yelp, Docusign, Twilio, Harry's, and General Assembly) have embraced it. This accounts for more than $1 billion in volunteer hours, product licenses, pro bono resources and philanthropic funding.

Social Purpose in the Public Square. Many firms have policies that govern "political speech" (in words, dress, and deeds) and forbid any messages that might be deemed harassing, offensive, or threatening. But how about embracing today's employee activism and using it as an opportunity to forge common ground? This means hosting listening sessions, promoting internal dialogue, and, yes, giving employees a voice in how your company responds. The key here is authenticity: take a stand on issues that you, your board, and company leaders believe in. No faking it. But be open to what your employees, customers, and even your kids believe in. Here's the broader payoff: studies find that when a company's purpose is in synch with employees' sense of their personal purpose, employees are more loyal, engaged, and willing to advocate for their company, and they rate their company's impact on society more positively, too.[19]

Challenges on the Horizon

There you have it: a strong social purpose is a foundation for good business. But things can change. Let's look at two different factors that could upset your social purpose-driven model.

Mergers and Acquisitions. Recall that Unilever had a lot of trouble initially managing its acquisition of Ben & Jerry's and was itself hit by a takeover attempt by a profit-maximizing firm. There have been several studies on the impact on socially conscious firms that are acquired by corporate giants and they present a mixed picture.[20] For instance, the Body Shop's social agenda was watered down following its acquisition by L'Oréal, who ultimately sold off the business to Natura. On the upside, Burt's Bees R&D budget increased by 50 percent in Clorox's hands and tapping into the parent company's expertise enabled it to introduce a skin lotion that moisturizes for 24 hours. In turn, Clorox made sustainability improvements to 35 percent of its overall product portfolio.

On 16 January 2017, Amazon acquired Whole Foods for $13.7 billion—with some 30 percent of that price based on Whole Foods' current business and assets and 70 percent reflecting its future growth. To the surprise of many, Amazon has supercharged Whole Foods' purposeful aims by making its products more *accessible* and *affordable*. With the parent company's buying power, logistics expertise, and marketing muscle, Whole Foods has been leading social change by opening grocery stores in former "food deserts" in inner-city Detroit, Newark, New Orleans, Oakland, and Chicago where consumers have lacked access to high-quality foods and fresh produce. A community development expert highlights the overall impact: "Whole Foods going into different communities of color is a game change… (it) sends a different signal to the community and to the marketplace about what is possible."[21] And, with membership of Amazon Prime, customers everywhere can place grocery orders online and have them delivered within two hours for free (based on a certain minimum order) or pick them up packaged at a store.

How about those paycheck-eating prices? Market studies find that Whole Foods' prices overall have dropped relative to the competition since its acquisition (now 4 percent higher than at other grocers) and that its fresh produce is often cheaper. Prime subscribers also get big savings with promotions and sales and the grocer has come out with a line of "Sourced for Good" products that are certified by independent third parties and competitively priced. Mackey says the grocery chain is in a "virtuous circle" of cutting costs, lowering prices, and attracting more customers.

Message: whether you are a buyer or seller in this arena, the compatibility of the two companies' social purposes and cultures are key considerations.

Activist Investors. It's easy to get caught up in the energy and excitement of having a social purpose and expanding your social impact, but you still have to mind your core business. It is important to remember that you are a business that is effecting social change and must continue to earn a profit, meet your payroll, and exercise your fiduciary duties while doing so. In January 2021, the activist hedge fund Blue Bell Capital, with a 2 percent ownership stake in Danone, helped to engineer the departure of its chairman, Emmanuel Faber. The activists' rationale? Over the five prior years, Danone's share price had underperformed compared to its immediate peers Unilever and Nestlé. Danone is the world's largest B Corps but even with governance protections of its social purpose, the activist investors won out.

But this goes in both directions. In June 2021 the hedge fund Engine No. 1 successfully waged a campaign to install three directors on the board of Exxon with the goal of pushing the energy giant to reduce its carbon footprint. To pull this off, it gained the support of some of Exxon's biggest institutional investors, including BlackRock, Vanguard and State Street. As we have noted, the market price performance of companies with a demonstrable record of strong social and environmental performance has consistently surpassed those of mainstream peers. This is at the heart of a progressive movement arguing that companies and investors take a longer-term perspective. There is even a Long-Term Stock Exchange (LTSE) where you can trade shares in companies that are built to last. Its ambition is to create "a public market that reduces short-term pressures and encourages a steady cycle of innovation and investment in long-term value creation to benefit companies and their investors alike."[22]

Does a Social Purpose Work for Your Business? If your company is in healthcare or pharmaceuticals, food and beverages, hi-tech or telecommunications, education, energy (renewables), even banking or finance, you can readily build out a social purpose from your core business. If, by contrast, you're in tobacco, firearms, or an extractive industry, not so much. Obviously, your marketplace is a consideration. But note that social purpose is not just for B2C companies. A B2B benchmark is Japan's multi-business NEC, whose purpose is "orchestrating a better world." It has developed a social value creation theme for each of its disparate lines of business and its social report details, with evidence, stories, and instructive graphics, how NEC deploys AI, IoT, and 5G technology to, among other worthwhile purposes, create Safe Cities, a Super-Smart Japan, and myriad improvements in commercial operations and infrastructure.

To close, marketer Paul Klein offers this perspective on how social purpose connects to positive social change:

- The social purpose of a business is based on the belief that social change is good for business and business is good for social change.
- The social purpose of business speaks to the ends (social change) rather than the means (corporate social responsibility).
- The social purpose of a business is integrated with, and indivisible from, everything the business does to make money.
- The social purpose of a business should embody the purpose of its leadership and its leadership should embody the social purpose of the business.[23]

A social purpose also gives you a platform to address the other problems facing business in this incoming wave of social change. Let's see next how it can help you promote equity and more inclusive prosperity.

06

Create Equity and Inclusive Prosperity

Jack Stack creates and shares prosperity through his business. Founder and CEO of Missouri's Springfield Remanufacturing, Stack in 1983 revived a dying business sold off by International Harvester and over the next four decades acquired 60 companies and created thousands of jobs. Remanufacturing is, as he describes it, a "tough, loud, dirty business." His company takes worn-out engines from cars, trucks, and bulldozers, and rebuilds them or salvages the parts for resale. It's a $450 million business today. What's the secret of his success?

When a team from Ben & Jerry's had a benchmarking visit with Jack, he gave us a crisp answer: "We're 100 percent employee owned and everybody's got a stake in the outcome." All employees, he explained, are educated about the company's P&L statement and learn how their productivity directly contributes to it. Each has an individual scorecard on daily performance and its impact on earnings, and work teams meet regularly to analyze trends, study variances, and take needed corrective action. More productivity translates into bigger paychecks. Many of Jack's peers cautioned him that line operators could never understand the "math" of running a business or track how sales, the supply chain, or inventory figured into profitability. Nonsense, he told them, operators follow sports teams and know all the statistics that go into winning and losing. His education program taught them finance in a business game format and they can fully monitor how they and the company are performing through "open-book management."

Jack's lessons, featured in his books *The Great Game of Business* and *A Stake in the Outcome*, have gained a following. Not far away from Jack's company's headquarters in Missouri we came across Askinosie Chocolate, a bean-to-bar chocolate maker that sources 100 percent of its cocoa beans directly from farmers. Lawyer-turned-confectioner Shawn Askinosie epitomizes the next generation of good business trailblazers. He extended the "stake in the outcome" business model to his cocoa suppliers on three continents. Askinosie shows farmers his company's financial statements and, in the host's native language, details the full costs through the value chain—from farming to picking, processing, packaging, and sale—and how much they can earn by supplying his firm. He typically pays the farmers a fair market price on the front end but then shares profits with them after chocolate made from their beans is sold. He puts it this way:

> I believe the social purpose of Askinosie Chocolate is to not only compensate our farmers fairly and treat them like the business partners they are, but to connect those farmers with our customers to build relationships of mutual understanding and appreciation, which makes our chocolate better and our business better.[1]

Is the "System" Biased?

The world had its first International Equal Pay Day in September 2020. There wasn't much to celebrate. Top corporate executives in the United States have seen their pay grow by more than 1,000 percent over the past 40 years, nearly 100 times the rate of average workers. Median FTSE 100 CEO pay was 120 times the average UK worker as compared to 47 times the average 20 years ago. In the United States, women who were full-time, year-round employees made 82 cents for every dollar men made in 2020. The pay gap is even more pronounced for Latina and Black women, and the overall pay gap between White versus Black men in the US seems to be widening. When comparing workers of similar age, education and experience doing the same kind of work, these gaps shrink, but studies show that women and minorities have less access to good-paying jobs.[2] Is capitalism the culprit?

Economists contend that business is a primary driver of prosperity.[3] A company pays wages and benefits to its workers and managers, makes capital investments, compensates its suppliers, provides products and services for customers, generates profits for investors, and pays taxes to the government. Businesses contribute to community economic development by creating job opportunities, improving infrastructure, and attracting other businesses, all of which increase living standards and enhance quality of life. On a broader scale, companies make things or provide services that increase the productivity and creativity of their customers—consumers and other businesses—that in turn creates more jobs and prosperity. Innovation, far more so than financial investment, is the main contributor to economic growth and helps to make societies healthier, smarter, safer, and more prosperous.

While all this sounds rosy, consider what the world's public today says about equity and prosperity:

- Nearly three-in-four people worldwide (74 percent) feel a sense of injustice ("The system is biased against regular people and in favor of the rich and powerful").
- A minority of people in the US (43 percent), Australia (32 percent), Italy (29 percent), UK (27 percent), Germany (23 percent), France (19 percent), and Japan (15 percent) believe that they and their families will be better off in the next five years.
- Some 74 percent worldwide express strong desires for change ("We need forceful reformers in positions of power to bring about much-needed change").[4]

These dispiriting views implicate economic systems, national policy, taxation rates, and global investment along with business priorities and spending. Our focus here is on what your company can do to create more equity and inclusive prosperity. You have choices about what kinds of jobs you create, how you pay people and ensure equity, and how much prosperity you deliver to communities and society. Consider this question about your handprint: *Does your company add to the world's prosperity and share value fairly?*

This chapter first looks at "current realities" about prosperity and inequities to highlight challenges facing business and what these mean for how companies spend their money when they aspire to lead social change. Then it examines what a company and its leaders can do to make themselves a force for fairness and more inclusive prosperity inside the business, throughout the supply chain, and in the community.

Business, Prosperity, and Social Change

We grew up and our parents worked in the so-called "Golden Age of Capitalism"—post-WWII through the 1970s.[5] Productivity increases were matched by hourly wage increases; payouts to shareholders were in line with pay increases to workers; and industry created high-wage jobs. Yes, there was pollution from factories and smog from gas-guzzling cars powered by leaded fuel; and inequities between men and women and Whites and minorities in employment markets and at work. But the US established legislation and agencies protective of the environment, occupational safety and health, consumer rights, and equal opportunity in the 1970s and similar initiatives were passed throughout nations in the European Common Market where high-tax welfare states enlarged and provided free and subsidized services and benefits as never before. Then things changed.

The move to shareholder capitalism in the 1980s, along with deindustrialization in the West, privatization of public services, globalization by business, and a shift in the political climate toward markets and away from government, all led to a massive increase in the wealth gap between nations— and within them. Sad to say but despite business's professed move to stakeholder capitalism and sharing value, that gap continues to grow. High-income households (the top 10 percent) in the OECD have seen their earnings from investments and wages skyrocket the past 25 years while the other 90 percent have seen their share of capital income unchanged and wages (adjusted for inflation) actually decline (see box below).

THE WEALTH GAP

The Rich Are Getting Richer.

Thomas Piketty's book *Capital in the Twenty-First Century* gave us empirical data spanning several hundred years that shows that the owners of capital accumulate wealth more quickly than those who provide labor, a phenomenon captured by the term "the rich get richer." According to IRS data, the top 1 percent of earners in saw their share of total US income increase from 10 percent in 1980 to upwards of 20 percent today. Americans in the top 1 percent today average over 39 times more income than the bottom 90 percent (and the top 0.1 percent earn over 196 times more than the bottom 90 percent!).[6] This is not just a US phenomenon. In the UK, the share of income going to the top 1 percent of richest households nearly tripled in the past four decades and the top 10 percent have 290 times more in total assets than those at the bottom.[7] Income inequality is not as pronounced in continental Europe, but differences in incomes between rich and poor EU countries are vast.

The Poor Are Doing Better but the Middle Class Is Shrinking.

The good news is that in China, India, and much of the global South low- and middle-income earnings have risen because of foreign investment and national development. But in the US and Europe, poverty rates are unchanged and the middle class is shrinking. A survey found that 40 percent of Americans would struggle to come up with $400 for an unexpected expense and 140 million people in the US are either poor or low-income.[8] Some 92 million people in the EU-27 are poor or low-income. Two daunting implications: fewer Millennials today are in the US middle class compared to when Baby Boomers were in their 20s and 30s and, in Europe, young people have replaced the elderly as the age group most in poverty.

Concerns about wealth and inequality have amassed into a wave and today a full nine in ten global CEOs say that global economic systems need to change and refocus on equitable growth. As one CEO put it, "Unleashed capitalism has created extreme poverty, terrible social conditions and a difficult situation for our planet. If we cannot manage a better social transition of the wealth, we will be in trouble."[9]

Executives offer many reasons why they simply cannot pay their people better, invest in long-term growth, and keep factories open, retrain employees, and create more equitable pay systems. They point variously to Wall Street, competitive pressures, talent markets, regulation, and other "realities" of running a profitable business. All are factors, but the evidence is clear that companies operating in the same or similar markets make different choices on how they spend their monies. Companies that aspire to lead social change have to address four challenges to create and share prosperity.

Society Needs More Good-Paying Jobs. Here's the current reality: companies that are growing, employ high-skill workers, and operate in red hot talent markets pay their employees better. Median salaries in tech firms like Google and Facebook, and in blue-chip consulting and finance companies, top the lists on employee compensation in recent years. What is happening otherwise? Researchers report that over two-thirds of the jobs created in the United States in the past few decades feature low wages and part-time work hours. In Europe, between 2000 and 2018 average real wages grew by only 0.9 percent per year and part-time work rose substantially in 22 of the 29 European countries.

But compare the pay practices of employee-oriented discounter Costco versus Wal-Mart's Sam's Club. Costco pays its US hourly workers on average over $24 per hour, not including overtime, while Sam's Club's average wage is about $13 an hour. Along the same lines, electronics retailer Best Buy offers a viable career path and development opportunities to its employees while its one-time competitor Circuit City (now out of business) routinely dismissed longer-tenured employees in lieu of giving them salary increases. How do jobs and pay in your company compare to others in your industry?

Demands for Pay Equity and Fairness are Growing. Many big company CEOs make in a single day what their everyday workers earn in an entire year. Defenders make the case that CEOs, like high earners in sports and entertainment, are "superstars" who lead winning (and profitable) teams. The evidence finds otherwise, however, as CEO pay (including stock options) is only marginally related to a company's annual bottom line and not at all to its longer-term stock performance.[10] Differences between CEO pay in the same industry can be eyepopping. Coca-Cola's stock price grew 24 percent in the past three years while PepsiCo's grew 37 percent. Last year the ratio at Coca-Cola between CEO pay and the median worker was 1657:1 versus 368:1 at PepsiCo. Guess which company got hit with an angry shareholder resolution on executive pay?

Pay inequity is a worldwide issue. For instance, almost eight out of ten British companies pay men more than women, while women are paid a fifth less than men on average. Workers of Pakistani or Bangladeshi heritage have the lowest average pay of any ethnic group, in the latter case earning 20.1 percent less than White British workers.[11] Studies find pay gaps between men versus women and majority versus minority populations worldwide. At the current rate of progress, the World Economic Forum estimates it will take 257 years to close the pay gap between men and women. What is your company doing on pay equity?

The World Is Calling for Philanthropy with Impact. Remember the pledge by Ben & Jerry's to give 7.5 percent of *pre-tax profits* to charity? The US corporate average giving in 2020 was miserly by comparison (0.91 percent). Patagonia gives 1 percent of its total *revenue* to good causes. The US average in 2020 was 10 times less (0.12 percent including cash and in-kind contributions). In the US, company charitable contributions are tax deductible and many large companies have foundations to handle their giving. In Europe and elsewhere in the world, tax deductions for company giving vary by country as do regulations on corporate foundations. Yet wherever your business is based, the days when a company could simply "write a check" and consider itself a good corporate citizen are long gone. Now philanthropy is all about achieving social impact.

Ford, GM, Chrysler, Toyota, and other auto suppliers contribute to Focus-Hope, a nonprofit based in Detroit, Mi., by helping to train, mentor, and provide internships for those looking to reskill or prepare themselves for jobs in industry. Focus-Hope has trained (or retrained) over 12,000 men and women (primarily African Americans) to become machinists, CADCAM operators, IT specialists, and systems engineers and partners with area universities that provide college degrees for trainees. It also runs a day-care center, a food bank, and community development programs—all in support of promoting economic development and racial justice in the Detroit area. Are you managing your philanthropic giving such that it helps to solve important economic, social, and environmental problems? Measuring the results? Are you giving your employees paid time and company resources to voluntarily serve society? More so than others in your industry?

The Global Wealth Gap Must Be Reduced. We've seen how Nike got called out for exploiting workers in its overseas supply chain, and cleaned up its act. Now its practices are certified by the Fair Labor Association (FLA) Workplace Code of Conduct. You'd think in this age of transparency, that almost any company that engages in predatory labor practices would be found out, excoriated on social media, and punished by consumers and the public. On the contrary—research by Oxfam finds that the majority of people employed in global supply chains that supply the world's clothing, goods, and food continue to work up to 13 hours a day and earn below the poverty line in their nations.[12] Who has it worst? The 190 million or so women who work in global supply chains. Does your company (or a third party) conduct "due diligence" on its suppliers and audit their performance on wages and human rights? Does it work with any certification bodies? Are you taking any steps to upgrade wages and working conditions in your global supply chain?

Nestlé has taken big steps to add economic and social value to peoples and nations where it sources its ingredients. Its former chairman and CEO Peter Brabeck-Letmathe stated, "We believe that the true test of a business is whether it creates value for society over the long term." Over the past 15 years the company has helped cocoa and dairy farmers in Africa and Latin America to adopt more productive and sustainable agricultural practices and promoted local cluster development among smallholders in villages in India and elsewhere that increases their access to capital and earning power. In the spirit of transparency, Nestlé also discloses the suppliers of 15 of its priority commodities and uses blockchain technology to enable consumers to track their food sourcing back to the farm. This makes its suppliers more accountable and puts a spotlight on the performance of its own procurement teams.

What Is Your Company's Economic Philosophy?

As you consider how your company contributes to prosperity, and might contribute more, an economic framework and guiding principles can help you frame your thinking, inform choices, and explain what you are doing to your board, management and employees, customers and other stakeholders, not to mention your bankers, friends, and family. What better place to start than with the concept of capital?

Multiple Forms of Capital. Business is traditionally managed through the logic and metrics of financial capital—equity, debt, and liquid working capital to fund its activities and pay its bills. These are the stuff of P&L statements, balance sheets, and cash flow reports. But there are also non-financial forms of capital that are relevant to business and integral to the wealth and well-being of individuals and societies and the state of the planet. These include:

- Human Capital—the value of the skills, knowledge, and experience possessed by an individual or population;
- Social Capital—the value of relationships among people who live and work in a particular society, and, in the business world, the value of relationships between a company and its constituents; and
- Natural Capital—the stock of renewable and non-renewable natural resources (e.g., plants, animals, air, water, soils, minerals) that combine to provide benefits to people.

Profit maximizing sees companies "extract" these forms of capital to increase financial returns. What kind of an economy would we have if companies instead "added to" these forms of capital? How can these new forms of capital be incorporated into the management and metrics of your business?

Economics of Mutuality. Mars is, and always has been, a principles-led business. The founder, who learned to hand-dip chocolate from his mother, was born in the US and his son, Forrest E. Mars, moved to the UK in the 1930s, setting up the business to "promote a mutuality of service and benefits among its consumers, distributors, competitors, suppliers, governments, employees and shareholders." This was a model of stakeholder capitalism—forged amidst the Great Depression and well before its time.

In 2006, questions were being raised about this model and its capacity to create shared prosperity. A major shareholder asked then-Chairman John Mars, "What is the right level of profit for the corporation?" Prompted by this, John wondered whether his company was taking too much profit in light of his belief that the "company's value chain is only as strong as its weakest link." He tasked Bruno Roche, former Chief Economist, with answering this question. An early conclusion was that traditional measures of business performance were inadequate. They failed to measure and take account of "holistic value creation for all stakeholders." As Roche reports it, "Our argument is that, essentially, profit is an outcome, not an objective.

The purpose of business therefore is not to make a profit but to develop profitable, scalable solutions to the problems of people on the planet."[13]

To find the right measures, Roche worked with the University of Oxford's Saïd Business School Professor Colin Mayer to devise an Economics of Mutuality (EoM) framework that incorporates human, social, and natural alongside financial capital. Their aim was to move business toward a "responsible and more complete form of capitalism that is fairer and performs better than the purely financial version operating today."[14] The EoM model has a company identify and measure its impact on human capital (people's competencies and well-being), social capital (trust, social cohesiveness, and capacity for collective action), and natural capital. This yields a performance scorecard with financial and non-financial results. Managers can set goals and devise KPIs for their human, social, and natural capital performance alongside financial objectives. Would the EoM work for your company?

Economy for the Common Good. Another group promoting more inclusive capitalism has a model of an economy for the common good. Created by Austrian Christian Felber, this network of over 2,000 small businesses as well as schools, cities, and community groups, uses a "common good balance sheet" to measure how their organization performs with its full range of stakeholders and includes indicators of human dignity, solidarity, and economic sustainability.[15] It goes a step further than EoM in its emphasis on workers' and other stakeholders' co-determination in company governance.

Many of these ideas were pioneered in Mondragon, an industrial cooperative with over 260 companies and subsidiaries, originally based in Spain's Basque Region but now reaching 35 countries. The federation brings in revenue of $14 billion and employs over 75,000 workers worldwide. Mondragon is, in its own words, "created by and for people." Among its governing principles: all employees have equal rights to vote and ownership; managing boards consist of a combination of employees from all levels of the organization; the highest-paid managers earn no more than six times the lowest-paid worker; distribution of 70 percent of profits after taxes with decision making taken through the General Assembly; no more than 20 percent of workers can be temporary contractors; and reallocating workers across cooperatives in the federation helps retain jobs and support the weakest performing businesses.

When we visited Mondragon in our recent research, we saw managers reallocating staff from a business in decline to growing ones and arranging for their necessary retraining and redeployment. It is hard to see this model of industrial cooperation fully making its way into mainstream business. But employee ownership is very much a consideration. The National Center for Employee Ownership (NCEO) estimates that approximately 32 million US employees participate in an employee ownership plan. Research finds that 100 percent employee-owned companies show consistent revenue and profit growth, report less staff turnover, and that both household net wealth (92 percent higher) and average income (33 percent higher) are greater for workers of employee-owned companies.[16]

With this backdrop, it is time to self-assess how your company spends its monies and what impact this has on prosperity.

STRESS TEST: RATE YOUR COMPANY ON INCLUSIVE PROSPERITY

Think about what your company does with profits, what jobs are created and how it pays people top to bottom, and how it invests in communities and social challenges—does your business truly contribute to prosperity and share value fairly?

CHECKLIST 6.1

Prosperity: Does your company add to the world's prosperity and share value fairly?

To what extent....   1 = Not at all   5 = To a great extent

	1	2	3	4	5
1. Does your company provide a fair and reasonable return to all of its stakeholders (e.g., investors, employees, suppliers, customers, and communities)?	☐	☐	☐	☐	☐
2. Does your company offer good jobs that provide decent wages and benefits?	☐	☐	☐	☐	☐
3. Is compensation fair from the top to bottom in your company?	☐	☐	☐	☐	☐
4. Does your company improve the economic health of communities where it does business?	☐	☐	☐	☐	☐

		1	2	3	4	5
5.	Does your company actively do business with women- and minority-owned companies?	☐	☐	☐	☐	☐
6.	Does your company invest in good causes (e.g., education, health, economic justice)?	☐	☐	☐	☐	☐

Now add up the answers to these six questions: if you score 25 or more, your organization creates prosperity and shares value fairly. If 12 to 24, not so much. If lower... your company needs to step up.

Moves Toward Inclusive Prosperity

How can a company contribute to more inclusive prosperity? It begins with making money. Seventh Generation is named in honor of the Iroquois belief that "in every decision, we must consider the impact of our decisions on the next seven generations." The company makes environmentally friendly cleaning, paper, and personal care products. Listen to what founder Jeffrey Hollander told us about the responsibilities of his business:

> Responsibility is about linking our company's financial success with its ability to effect the kind of societal change we want to see. It's our acknowledgment that if we don't make money (in an ethical and responsible way, of course), we won't be in business very long. And if we lose our business, we lose our power to effect change. So this principle is about keeping everyone focused on economics in addition to ecology and continually emphasizing the crucial balance that must be maintained between the two.

With its move into sustainability and into the next wave of leading social change, business has sought an alternative to the profit-maximizing model. Ben & Jerry's implemented a visionary model of linked prosperity decades ago and John Elkington proposed the triple bottom line. Principles of shared value were a further iteration. Stakeholder capitalism, the current approach, pushes business well beyond Milton Friedman's logic and shifts the location of the fence line between business and society to include every stakeholder in a company's ecosystem. Ed Freeman nudges this toward the handprint in an article entitled, "The social responsibility of business is to create value for stakeholders."[17] What's next?

There are some (including us) that foresee business taking responsibilities beyond its immediate stakeholders and extending its "duty of care" to society writ large and the planet. This shifts their wealth-creation function beyond just long-term value for their company to contributing to more inclusive prosperity in society. As one pragmatic executive put it, "We cannot be a sustainable company in an unsustainable society."

What's the logic behind this? Many reference the "contract" between a business, its constituents, and society. In the shareholder frame, à la Friedman, a company is obliged to comply with societal laws and regulations wherever it does its business but its legitimacy depends on the marketplace. In the stakeholder frame, à la Freeman, a company's license to operate depends on its ability to meet the expectations of these many diverse constituents. Where does the public's interest figure in? It is expressed in the "social contract" between business and society which concerns not only a firm's lawful and economic responsibilities but also its responsibilities vis à vis equity, justice, the health of the planet, and the prosperity of society overall. To be sure these claims on business can be legislated by society; they can also be embraced without legislation by companies that care about the world we live in.

Surveys show that large majorities of the world's public hold business fully responsible for ensuring product safety, providing fair wages to employees, not harming the environment, maintaining a responsible supply chain, and the like—all within a company's operating arena. But large numbers also expect companies to provide for long-term financial stability for employees, to support communities and charities, to help reduce the rich–poor gap, and to solve social problems.[18] This calls for societal impact and

FIGURE 6.1   The Next Operating Environment of Business

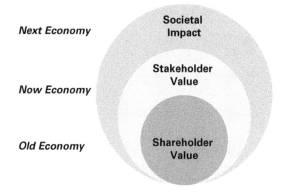

requires creating social value for society. Figure 6.1 depicts this next operating environment and what fulfilling its social contract means for a business. What are the implications for your company?

Make Your Company More Equitable

In this era of transparency and activism, many companies worldwide have increased entry-level and median pay significantly over the past few years. During the pandemic, large retailers and pharmacies increased hourly pay by $2 or more and enhanced paid leave for sickness. But the vast majority of low-wage workers are employed in small and mid-size businesses. Here you find less healthcare coverage and much less paid sick, vacation, and holiday leave. What can your company do to promote inclusive prosperity?

Create Good-Paying Jobs. There are many companies, large and small, that have good-paying jobs. Most "great places to work" pay competitive salaries to full-time employees, and offer a benefits package that includes health coverage, paid vacation, sick and parental leave, a company contribution to a pension or 401(k) account, training monies or tuition reimbursement, and typically an incentive scheme, bonus plan, and/or stock options.

How about Walmart—the 800lb gorilla of low-cost retail? When Greg Foran, then heading Walmart in the US, read Zeynep Ton's *The Good Jobs Strategy*, he said "Bingo"![19] Walmart upped its wages but in doing so the company also made changes in its operations and employment practices. Walmart rolled out a new induction process that includes training for new hires on customer service, merchandising, teamwork, and communication, and provided mentoring by experienced employees, plus it gave them a clear picture of career paths and what skills and experience are needed to advance. To increase efficiency, employees also got handheld computers to scan prices and check inventory. The kicker: Walmart employees are eligible for quarterly bonuses based on store performance.

Top employers are compensating part-time workers better, too. Home Depot, for example, offers its part-time employees tuition reimbursement, 401(k) matching, an employee stock purchase program, paid maternity and paternity leave, and dental and vision insurance. Starbucks has strong full- and part-time employee benefits. Every US employee working part- or full-time receives 100 percent tuition coverage for a first-time bachelor's degree through Arizona State University's online program.

How do employers in declining industries maintain good-paying jobs? Pridgeon and Clay (P&C), a Grand Rapids, Michigan auto supplier, was hit hard in the auto industry meltdown. But their focus on research and development, product innovation, and training positioned them for recovery. Rather than replace workers, they prepared and trained their existing workforce. They even instituted an in-house training program, which provided wage increases of more than 50 percent for entering the training and additional wage incentives for those that graduated. As a result, P&C rebounded far better than many, adding millions in revenue and growing their employee base from 400 to 650.

#fairpay, #equity. Is your CEO overpaid? Good luck with fixing that unless you are a board member or that CEO. On the broader front, three new ideas are in play: 1) base more of the CEO's pay on long-term rather than short-term market performance; 2) tie the CEO's pay to both financial and non-financial criteria (say, delivering on purpose, planet, products, and people!); and 3) give stakeholders a greater voice in company boards and compensation committee decisions.

How about fixing internal inequities? We've seen what Salesforce did. Another company that cleaned up its pay structure is PayPal. The company conducted an audit of its hourly and call center employees and found that 60 percent struggled to make ends meet and were living paycheck to paycheck, despite earning at or above market-level wages. Then it took action – raising wages, reducing healthcare costs, making all employees shareholders of PayPal, and launching financial literacy and planning courses for staff. To counter "unconscious bias" that can affect a manager's salary or promotion recommendations, PayPal now audits itself three times per year. We should add that over 50 percent of its employees who are VPs or higher are women or people of color, as are half of its board of directors.

Outsource or Insource? According to the Bureau of Economic Analysis, 10 million US jobs have been sent overseas since 2001. Millions of IT and back-office jobs have been "nearshored" from Western to Central and Eastern Europe. Companies like Nike, IBM, Apple, and most fast-fashion brands have had great financial success offshoring production and back-office work. But firms like Converse, Intel, Tesla, Skype, and higher-end fashion brands have also had success while keeping their production in domestic markets. Obviously many different factors go into decisions about outsourcing and offshoring, but experts contend that "cost savings" should not be your overriding consideration. How about creating jobs and economic opportunities for your local community? This is what Detroit watchmaker Shinola has done.

SHINOLA: "WHERE AMERICAN IS MADE"

In 2011, Tom Kartsostis launched Shinola, a high-end watch and leather goods company, in GM's abandoned Fisher Body warehouse in inner-city Detroit. "This company takes pride in the fact that it can provide hardworking Americans with the opportunity to have a career. Of all the things we make, American jobs might just be the thing we're most proud of," he says. Shinola imports watch works from Switzerland and then assembles and adorns them.

We visited Shinola's factory and saw aging employees who had been early retired or laid off by the automobile industry now mentoring young men and women, mostly Black and ethnic minorities, in high-skill jobs assembling watches or crafting leather bags and gear. "Not many people can say, 'I work for a watch company; I make watches'," says Shinola watch assembly team leader Te'nesha Martin. Before walking into the glassed-in watch assembly area, visitors must put on jackets, hair coverings and plastic booties—it's a "clean room" sans dust and debris. Listen to Indira Samuels about her work experience: "If you want the quality, you have to give your best. I appreciate that they're in Detroit and what they're doing for the community. It's something that's totally different."

Impact Philanthropy. B2B software maker SAP has opened up its vast ecosystem of employees, customers, and partners, as well as its small business management solutions and digital data platforms, to support social entrepreneurs. How does the program work? SAP runs an innovation accelerator for social entrepreneurs and teaches them design thinking, provides mentorship by SAP employees, gives them access to technology, and offers them access to impact investors provided through an Impact Capital network available to SAP's non-profit entrepreneur partners.

In addition, SAP runs contests to, among other things, apply information technology to automotive use in areas of urban mobility, traffic, fueling, parking, food delivery and such. A student submission from Clemson University's International Center for Automotive Research in South Carolina won in the parking category in one contest. Their application, ParkinGain, matches drivers with parking spots based on price, location, travel time, and distance to their final destination.

The Growing Gig Economy. Now consider your activity in the gig economy. Actually there are two different gig economies. One is composed of folks who drive for Uber or Lyft, make deliveries for Amazon Flex or Door Dash, sell their goods and services on Etsy or Fiverr, and all manner of freelancers. The other includes on-call, independent, and/or temporary workers, the so-called contingent workforce. As there is no "official" designation of gig workers, estimates are they comprise anywhere from 10–15 percent (contingent workers) to 35–40 percent (including multiple job holders and those with a "side hustle") of the US workforce.[20] But however you count and categorize those with "alternative work arrangements," this segment is expected to grow in the years ahead.

Touted benefits for gig workers include greater freedom and flexibility, and for freelancers the chance to be "your own boss." Downsides include social isolation and, for contingent workers, substandard pay and benefits, no pension, and scant job security. Should we include gig workers in a company's handprint? Surely so, and for three reasons. First, many companies employ contingent workers not only for added flexibility but especially because it saves them money—lots of it. How does your company treat and compensate its on-call, temporary and part-time workers? Second, many companies are outsourcing and offshoring jobs to gig economy workers—to handle customer calls and provide administrative support and web services— in lieu of creating more full-time jobs. Third, campaigners and regulators alike are urging companies (like Uber and other app-based firms) to classify and treat independent contractors as employees. How do you treat your gig workers?

Help Your Business Partners Prosper

Companies looking to effect social change have plenty of work to do in their supply chains. Can your company help its suppliers become more prosperous? Ben & Jerry's was a pioneer in using its business to drive more inclusive prosperity. In the late 1980s, the company hooked up with Greyston Bakery in Yonkers, NY to supply brownie wafers for its ice-cream sandwiches. The bakery provides "great desserts by great people doing great deeds." Combining an economic and social mission, it sells brownies to food purveyors and the public made by the "chronically unemployed"—ex-convicts, former drug abusers, and disadvantaged youth—whom it hires and trains in business and social skills. Since then, Greyston has created over 3,000 brownie-baking jobs, generating about $65 million in payroll and providing benefits to about 19,000 families through the Greyston Foundation.

Caterpillar's Supplier Diversity program focuses on increasing opportunities for small businesses owned by minorities, women, veterans, or the disabled. The program requires that all suppliers meet Caterpillar's requirements concerning quality, capacity, and cost. Caterpillar runs a 100-day transformation program to help suppliers adopt lean manufacturing processes and eliminate waste in their operations and Caterpillar employees serve as mentors to participants. A Supplier Development College offers both free and fee-based courses and "train the trainer" programs so participants can cascade knowledge to co-workers.

On a global scale, Coca-Cola's 5by20 initiative provides economic empowerment for nearly five million women entrepreneurs across the company's value chain—including retailers, suppliers, producers, and more. Women participating in 5by20 get business skills training, access to financial services and assets, and connections with peers and mentors. An early study of the program found that women increased sales by an average of 44 percent after receiving business skills training and that their average personal income increased by 23 percent over one year. Participants reported that, on average, they could better afford basic expenses for themselves and their families, such as expenses for children's education, medical visits, and clothing. And two-thirds reported they were able to put money into savings each month.

Would any of these approaches make your company's supply chain more prosperous and representative of society?

Invest in Your Community

How can your company support its local and regional business infrastructure? Here's two examples of companies investing in the future workforce and business ecosystem.

Improve Education. American businesses have for decades assisted K-12 schools with donations of money, books, technology and such, sponsorship of science fairs and competitions, employee volunteerism, and even "adopt a school" programs. Select high-tech firms go further with specialized training programs in communities that make use of corporate tools, know-how, and people.[21] IBM operates over thirty P-Tech (pathways to technology) schools that offer disadvantaged students the chance to receive a high school diploma and associate's degree within six years, as well as a shot at an IBM job. Students take traditional high school classes and get workplace training, intensive STEM education classes, college courses, and often real-world job experience as well—all at no charge. According to IBM's projections, there will be 16 million jobs by 2024 that require post-secondary degrees, though not necessarily a four-year college degree. To scale this venture, IBM's P-Tech founder Stan Litow forged partnerships with more than 600 businesses (like American Airlines and Volkswagen) to start over 220 P-TECH schools across the United States and around the world.

Support Small Business. Goldman Sachs' *10,000 Small Businesses* is a $500 million investment to help entrepreneurs create jobs and economic opportunity by providing them with greater access to education, financial capital and business support services. The *10,000 Small Businesses* program currently operates in 30 markets in the US through a network of more than 100 academic and community partners. Small business owners participate in 100 hours of education over the span of three months, either in a classroom or virtually, in a kind of crash course MBA. The subject matter: how to scale their own business. The emphasis is on peer-to-peer learning among the 30 or so entrepreneurs in a cohort, who also get one-to-one coaching and mentoring from Goldman employees. To date nationally, over 8,200 small business owners have graduated; some 67 percent of graduates see revenue growth and 47 percent report creating new jobs six months after completing the program.

The Global Dimension

Does your company source materials globally? Have plants and offices outside of your home nation? Is it a good neighbor in these locales? Recall how a few years ago some 1,127 textile workers—sewing clothes for Sears, J.C. Penney, Walmart, and the Gap—died in the collapse of a shoddy garment factory in Bangladesh. These companies joined in a coalition of businesses from 28 countries, international labor unions, and NGOs to work with the government of Bangladesh to reach an accord on fire and building safety in factories. As a result of the accord, 90 percent of the hazards reported at 1,000 factories in Bangladesh have been eliminated and the minimum wage for workers has increased from $38 to $95 a month.

What can businesses do to alleviate poverty? Banks, beginning with one launched by Nobel Peace Prize winner Mohammed Yunus, introduced micro-credit lending whereby the poor can pool their modest savings and get small loans. Repayment rates have been upwards of 97 percent. This model has spread into other businesses where, for example, Mexican cement-maker Cemex introduced its *Patrimonio Hoy* program that gives customers technical assistance and loans to design, build, and fund improvements in their housing.

Select companies today are building out Base-of-the-Pyramid (BoP) business models to provide more affordable goods and services, as well as employment opportunities, to the world's poor. We will look at these models in the chapter on products and services. But BoP investment is not only needed in developing nations. Many poor neighborhoods in the US are "food deserts" where locals cannot get access to fresh produce and affordable staples. Grocers Shaw's and Pathmark have built stores in inner cities that feature a dizzying variety of racially and ethnically targeted brands, at multiple price points, and locally originated store layouts and displays. Like other companies operating in BoP markets, Shaw's had to do its own sociological study of customers' needs. The Shaw's market team identified 42 different ethnic and religious affiliations within inner-city New Haven, Connecticut. To develop the right product mix, the management collaborated with community groups and organized meetings with the ethnic leadership to discuss product offerings. You can, for example, find fresh goat meat in some stores—meeting the needs of consumers from Caribbean countries.

Challenges on the Horizon

There you have it: your company *can* do more to promote equity and more inclusive prosperity. But consider two challenges that you may face in the seas of social change.

Meritocracy or Something Else? Thomas Piketty traces the rise of inequality to the shift in income away from labor and toward capital. But Daniel Markovits, in *The Meritocracy Trap*, argues that roughly 75 percent of the increase in the top 1 percent of earnings is caused by shifts in income within the workforce.[22] This is not just due to swollen CEO and top executive pay—it is because highly educated professionals earn so much more than everyday working people. These are bankers, attorneys, and consultants, but they are also found in elite universities (e.g., business school faculties), medical care (e.g., doctors but not nurses), and throughout the technology world.

Meritocracy has historically been a social ideal—the reformer's alternative to, say, a hereditary aristocracy. But questions are being raised as to whether meritocracy has gone amok. Today's high earners are more apt to have attended private or independent schools from kindergarten onwards and send their children to such schools, too. Top colleges are open to the best and brightest but screen students with standardized tests (for which the top earners' schools prepare them with better teaching and advanced courses) and favor the children of generous alumni in their admission decisions. Meanwhile, neighborhoods are ever more economically segregated and there are fewer everyday connections between peoples who are better and worse off.

Most people still hold to the belief that success—in business and life—is due to intelligence and hard work. But there is also the "paradox of meritocracy." It seems that when many people succeed they ascribe their success to their intellectual and moral superiority. A review of research in psychology and neuroscience finds that believing in meritocracy "makes people more selfish, less self-critical, and prone to acting in discriminatory ways."[23] The upshot: people who are successful tend to think that it is their "due" and that those who are less successful are deficient and less worthy of the fruits of economic life.

Naturally, this works against inclusive prosperity. It may have implications in your company relating not only to pay, but also to the size of offices, your company's eating facilities, and use of perks that are valued as status symbols. It also challenges you to create a more egalitarian work environment and to provide your "non-elite" employees with tuition support, development opportunities, and more chances to get ahead—subjects we will take up in the next chapter.

Is Democracy at Stake? Recent legislation in the United States lowered the statutory federal income tax to 21 percent (versus the previous 35 percent rate). A study found that profitable companies paid an effective federal income tax rate of 11.3 percent on their 2018 income (the first year the lower rate took effect) and that many big companies, including Amazon, Chevron, Halliburton, and IBM, did not pay federal income taxes at all.[24] Tax avoidance continues to date and it doesn't sit well with the American public, over two-thirds of whom say companies pay "too little" in taxes.

Mistrust of business is only one consequence of growing inequality and the sense that the system is rigged for the rich and powerful. In this moment of sweeping social change, the very legitimacy of capitalism as currently practiced is in question. The idea that business creates prosperity solely by increasing its profits is being challenged as both intellectually and morally bankrupt. Meanwhile, in many parts of the developing world, attention is turning toward the wealth-creating potential of state capitalism as found in China and the Persian Gulf versus the democratic capitalist model of the West.

As a business leader, you must be concerned that only one in three young adults in the US, UK, and Australia, as well as in Germany, France, and the Netherlands, now see it as "essential" to "live in a country that is democratically governed."[25] Recent elections of "strong men" autocrats in several democratic nations and the rise of extreme right- and left-wing populism are indicative of a potential social earthquake. There are, of course, many causes of disenchantment with democracy and with democratic capitalism, but this much is clear: the failures to produce inclusive growth and to redress inequities are paramount.

Can Your Business Step Up?

Many people are dubious that the private sector can reduce the wealth gap and improve the upward mobility of poor and low-income workers— domestically and abroad. It seems to them that capitalism is the culprit—that inequality is in its DNA. A much-repeated parable popularized by Orson Welles sums up this thinking:

> Scorpion met Frog on a riverbank and asked him for a ride to the other side.
> "How do I know you won't sting me?" asked Frog. "Because," replied Scorpion,
> "if I do, I will drown." Satisfied, Frog set out across the water with Scorpion
> on his back. Halfway across, Scorpion stung Frog. "Why did you do that?"
> gasped Frog as he started to sink. "Now we'll both die." "I can't help it," replied
> Scorpion. "It's my nature."[26]

Moving into this next wave of social change calls for forging a new kind of capitalism. Can your company step up and help create a more prosperous and inclusive economy in your host nation and wherever you do business? Hopefully, you found some ideas and inspiration here. After moving forward on purpose and prosperity, the next step in this direction concerns how you manage and lead your people.

07

Engage the "Whole" Person

Software and analytics company SAS Institute, based in Cary, North Carolina, with operations around the world, has been recognized as "a great place to work" in over 20 countries. It has a 35-hour workweek, recreation and fitness facilities at HQ with tennis and basketball courts, a weight room, and a heated pool, and a free on-site healthcare clinic, staffed by physicians, nutritionists, physical therapists, and psychologists. Deeply discounted childcare is available as well as no-cost "work–life" counseling which helps employees manage the stresses of everyday life. It also offers good pay, benefits, and an annual bonus. The business result: high-performing people and the lowest turnover rate in its industry (2–3 percent compared to an industry average of 22 percent).

How does SAS afford all of this? From monies the firm would otherwise have to spend on headhunters, training new staff, and restoring lost employee productivity. Tens of thousands of people apply for the few hundred openings available at SAS every year. Is this really nirvana? Marketing VP Jim Davis confesses:

> While we say we have a 35-hour workweek, I don't know anybody who really works 35 hours. The reality is if you trust people, and you ask them to do something—and you treat them like a human being as opposed to a commodity where you try to squeeze something out—they're going to work all sorts of hours. But they're going to enjoy those hours as opposed to "slaving in the office."[1]

The perks are an attraction, but the real motivator for SAS employees is the work—it's challenging, meaningful, and makes a real difference. This was the animating philosophy of company founder Jim Goodnight, who expressed it this way: "Treat employees like they make a difference, and they will." SAS software is used to detect bank fraud, improve child welfare, research cancer, and track climate change. Of course, not every employee at SAS is developing software, so the company makes a point of giving every worker a sense of purpose. For instance, members of the landscaping crew get an individual area of lawn or garden to attend to; they "own" that piece of acreage, the same way as software developers own every step of product development from conception to delivery and earn a portion of the profits from the sale of their tools (for as long as they stay with the company).

Fast Company recently cited SAS as a "best workplace for innovators." Naturally, you find its employees online at company hackathons and working with customers at SAS Vector Labs to incubate new products and services. They also present their ideas on solving societal problems at the company's annual Social Innovation Summit. In our research, we met with I-Sah Hsieh, whose job, as he told us, "is to find innovative ways to use SAS analytics for social good." He has worked to make SAS a key hub in the DATA4Good movement. This movement crowdsources information and the best thinking from scientists and experts to guide responses to social challenges and crises. In the case of Hurricane Florence, for instance, SAS volunteers and data scientists throughout the Southeast US analyzed social media data to direct supplies and workers to shelters and worked with hospitals to rapidly share patient data across the region. In another project, data scientists analyzed the movement of endangered animal species including rhinos, Bengal tigers, and polar bears to guide protective measures.

What Is the New World of Work?

The coronavirus pandemic taught companies that they cannot function without their "front line" workers. People whom the business world regarded as replaceable are now considered essential to success. Companies also learned about challenges faced by working parents, the effects of stress on people's productivity and mental health, and the import of resilience and adaptability in their workforce—from top to bottom. For some, this was a "wake-up call" and stimulated efforts to future-proof their workforce through better pay, flexible work schedules, continuous training and development, and treating people as full human beings.

Meanwhile, the pandemic awakened many working people to their situations and priorities. Some were reminded that they have a bad boss, do mindless work, feel disrespected and unappreciated, or have an uncaring employer. These issues may have already been present but their demotivating impact was magnified during the pandemic. Many people had the time and space to think more deeply about their work, lives, and careers. It seems some decided, based on working from home for months, that they wanted to continue to work from home—to gain more work–life balance and control over their work schedules. Others concluded that they wanted to work for someone else, launch their own business, or move into a new field. The result: "The great resignation of 2021" in the US and Europe, and four in ten in the global workforce considered resigning.[2]

This is not the only social change sweeping into business. We've noted that over three in four of the Millennial generation in the United States (born 1981–1996) want to work for an organization that "cares about how it impacts and contributes to society" and 83 percent of Gen Z (born 1997–2012) treat a company's social purpose as a core consideration when deciding where to work. Globally, across the full age spectrum, 70 percent of people say they want to work for an organization with a "powerful social conscience."[3] The upshot is that many seek "something more" from their jobs. They want to do something *meaningful* and want their work to make a difference and produce some *useful* for the world. And they want to work for a company that speaks out on social issues and takes seriously its purpose to make the world a better place. So consider this question about your company handprint: *Does your company develop and activate employees as "whole persons"?*

This chapter looks at the current state of play in employee engagement and what a company might do to deepen the engagement of people who want to be part of a company with an inspiring sense of purpose. Then we see how employees can express that purpose in good works inside the business, with consumers, and in society to effect social change. Let's start with a trip to a seeming nirvana, where a large and successful company leads its people as "whole persons."

Engaging Employees in an Era of Social Change

In the profit-maximizing era, many companies treated their employees as "costs" that could be easily dispensed with via downsizing, outsourcing, offshoring, or selling off a business. In its turn to stakeholder management, companies came to regard employees as "assets" to be invested in, but typically good pay, development opportunities, and personal attention from management were limited to professional staff and up-and-comers. Now there is an outcry to pay entry-level workers a living wage, to acknowledge and value frontline workers, and to redress inequities and foster a sense of belonging for all employees. What's going on?

Social change has brought business to a crossroads. Will it take the high road and future-proof its workforce? Or go back to business as usual? This much is clear: many more knowledge workers will operate in a hybrid environment (some days in the office and some at home) and will spend more time in virtual meetings, communicate mostly by text and chats, and struggle to stay connected to their company's culture and purpose. Companies that aspire to lead social change will have to address four big issues to retain and engage their people.

People Want Work and a Life. Over the past few decades, companies went from lean, to agile, to sprint to compete in the global marketplace. The results have been lower costs, higher productivity, and faster time to market: Who's to complain? For one, Roger Martin, whose *When More is Not Better: Overcoming America's obsession with economic efficiency*, shows how the arguably helpful pursuit of efficiency has turned into a damaging obsession.[4] Nowhere has the toll been more evident than on working people (see box below).

THE TOLL OF TOO MUCH WORK

For many the workplace has become a pressure cooker and this extends into the "off hours" for managers and knowledge workers who regularly receive and send work-related texts and emails during their evenings, and on holidays and vacations, and are presumed to be on call 24/7. Is it any wonder that so many US employees say they are "overworked" and that 77 percent, in a pre-pandemic survey, reported they experience "burnout" on their jobs? But this is not just a US problem. Three in five employees in the UK say they're working more hours than they would like, and in Asia, where employees have the longest working hours globally, a majority of workers report feeling unwell as a result of work-related stress.[5]

In his book *Dying for a Paycheck*, Jeffrey Pfeffer reports that stressful white-collar work is now far more hazardous than blue-collar work and that stress-related conditions account for 75 percent of visits to doctors' offices. As you may have heard, heart attack rates are highest on Monday mornings. On the other side of this, research finds that care and compassion shown by work colleagues can strengthen emotional connections at work and boost people's ability to function as productive employees.[6]

People Want to "Belong." Roughly 40 percent of Americans feel physically and emotionally isolated in the workplace, according to an EY Belonging Barometer Study, with even more saying they feel "ignored" at work.[7] This sense that "I don't belong here" is most common among Blacks, women, and LGBTQ employees in the United States. Globally, surveys find that nearly four in ten take an organization's "inclusiveness" into account when making career decisions and a significant number of women (44 percent), racial and ethnic minorities (45 percent), and LGBTQs (50 percent) have decided against pursuing and accepting a position from an employer they perceived would not provide an inclusive place to work.[8] Many say they have experienced "microaggressions" at work—such as receiving comments about their dress or speech, not receiving credit for their ideas, and hearing derogatory comments or jokes about "people like you."

People Want to be Fulfilled. The expectations of people have shifted as new generations have come into the workforce. Baby Boomers (born 1946–1964) were better educated than the generations that preceded them and many espoused an "anti-authority" outlook, having come of age amidst social protests and societal strictures. Employers engaged them with enriched jobs, fewer rules, and more say in work-related decisions. Gen Xers (born 1965–1980), by comparison, had strong material orientations yet also sought work–life balance. They were met with incentive systems, development programs, and the introduction of flexible work schedules and family-friendly benefits. Millennials, reared in an era of relative prosperity and schooled in social issues and service learning, came to work with "prosocial" motivations and a desire to contribute to social good. Their aspirations have been a powerful force moving firms forward on CSR and sustainability. Now a driving aspiration, especially among Millennials and entering Gen Zers, is to find and fulfill one's sense of purpose at work. Yet many are unfulfilled: only 28 percent of respondents in a PwC employee survey said they feel fully connected to their company's purpose.[9] How about your people?

People Want to Use Their Talents and Abilities. Here's a paradox for you: even as employees say they are overworked, large numbers feel underutilized! In a 2021 survey by a talent agency, over one in three US respondents reported that their company does not give them an opportunity to "shine" and one-half said they wish their employer had a better understanding of their skills. Another agency survey among US and UK workers found just 38 percent using their full knowledge and expertise at work, with 90 percent wanting to do so.[10] The usual fix here is for companies to better assess their employees' talents, and then, where feasible, to enrich their jobs and provide underutilized employees with the coaching, training, and development opportunities needed to prepare them for more skillful jobs. Good, but not good enough for Millennial and Gen Z workers. Many of them want time and space to develop personal projects that might help their company and also help to solve social and environmental problems. Employees in the Innovation Studio of AKQA in Melbourne, Australia developed open-source software that restricts the use of heavy-duty vehicles in protected areas of Brazil's rainforests. WeTransfer, a Dutch file-transfer company founded in 2009, gives its employees one full "Innovation Friday" each month to work on a project of their choosing, some of which are part of the company's suite of workflow tools. What might your people accomplish with an innovation Friday?

A Framework for Engaging the "Whole Person"

How do you engage your people? Most companies use Maslow's hierarchy of biological needs when they think about motivating and activating their employees. Step 1 in climbing the ladder has a company pay people a reasonable wage, including benefits, and afford them a measure of job security—all of which meets their material needs. Step 2 is to ensure that peers, direct supervisors, and the company treat people with dignity and respect—meeting their social needs. Step 3 is to make the work itself more stimulating—with some variety and challenge and personal responsibility—to meet people's need for self-esteem and growth. Voila! A more engaged workforce, or so this recipe tells us.

Now, if your company is falling down on any of these three steps, forget about having dedicated and productive employees. But suppose your firm is doing fine on steps 1, 2 and 3. Does that encompass everything your people hope for from their employment? Ironically, it was Maslow who, after defining his need hierarchy, recognized it did not fully reflect what moves people in their heart and soul. He spent his final years defining what he called "being values."[11] Atop his list of being values is "wholeness"—the integration of one's work and life roles and experiences into a unified sense of "self." Others are aliveness, justice, beauty, and goodness. We use these values, Maslow noted, to interpret and give meaning to what we do and accomplish. And, he added, they are integral to our personal identity and sense of purpose.

So let's throw a curveball into the standard employee engagement formula. Maybe engaging employees is not just a matter of meeting their biological needs but even more about enabling them to express their "whole self" and sense of purpose at work. This opens up a new frontier for activating and energizing employees whose aims are to contribute to social progress and to make the world a better place. Yes, you still have to meet their material, social, and growth needs but the opportunity is there to help them fulfill their life purpose and, in so doing, the social purpose of your company.

We have proposed a framework for employee engagement that emphasizes the importance of aligning personal and company values, of welcoming and including diverse employees, of respecting and supporting people in their work and life roles, and of helping them to find and fulfill their life purposes such that they can help their company fulfill its purposes.[12] It is not focused on meeting employees' needs. Rather, it's about enabling them to express and develop their identity in the workplace and beyond. Companies that move toward whole-person engagement not only affirm and enrich multiple dimensions of people's current identities, they also can help them to find "whom they want to become" (see Figure 7.1).

Let's examine each of these aspects of identity and what they mean for engaging employees (and you) at work.

Personal Identity. To say someone "needs" something emphasizes their individualistic and atomistic nature. Shifting attention to people's identity stresses their social and connected self. Developmental psychologists contend that the "self" cannot be separated from its relation to others and that an

FIGURE 7.1   Engaging the Whole Person

"interacting sense of self" is found in infants and informs development of the self over the life course.[13] This means that we construct and express "who I am" in relation to other people and the world around us.

Generation is a powerful socializing force. Members of a particular generation to some extent share similar experiences based in what is going on in the world around them and, at least in their formative years, are apt to adopt the language, dress, tastes, and sensibilities of their peers. Naturally, generational experiences differ across nations and circumstances, but mass media and global social networks influence what demographers call "intragenerational homogeneity." We know that generational identity runs deep: there are clear generational differences in fundamental attitudes and values and in how people think about and express themselves in their working lives.

We've seen how Millennials and Gen Z want to make a difference in the world. They want to find a "place" to fulfill those personal aspirations. This is what makes CSR such a potent motivator for workers under age 40 and why it is so important to many of them to work for a company that embodies their ideals. But people of all ages today also want to live healthier and more sustainable lives. Wal-Mart has motivated over 600,000 of its employees to develop Personal Sustainability Projects (PSPs) that encourage them to eat healthier foods, exercise more, and recycle. In some cases, employee family members develop their own PSPs. To date, 15,000 associates have stopped smoking. Interestingly, many eco-friendly or waste-reduction innovations prototyped by employees in their homes have been implemented in the Wal-Mart workplace. Would your employees value a PSP?

Social Identity. Identity theorists contend that we see the world and ourselves through the lens of our gender, race, ethnicity, and sexual orientation, among other facets of social identity.[14] Accordingly, leading firms host voluntary employee "affinity" groups (aka resource groups, networks) where people can connect to identity-based peers to share experiences, network, offer one another counsel and social support, and advance their shared interests in a company and beyond. The electronics retailer Best Buy exemplifies a multi-faceted approach to employee identity engagement.

Individual employees, for example, can be engaged through the company's "strength-based" HR model that encourages job involvement and development around their personal strengths and passions. On the work–life boundary, many employees are part of a results-only work environment (ROWE) that allows them to flexibly manage their work and personal time, so long as results are achieved. The company hosts a women's leadership forum (WOLF) that engages female managers, staff, and even customers in Wolf Packs that provide leadership tips and support. Best Buy also supports affinity groups revolving around race (Black Employees Network, Asian Employees Network, Latin Employees Network), age (Teenage Employees and SaGE—The wisdom of experience), sexual orientation (PRIDE), plus groups centering on faith, military service, and personal abilities/disabilities (INCLUDE).

Does engaging people's social identity pay off for companies? Gartner research shows that organizations that have identity-based networking groups are twice as likely to report they are effective at employee inclusion. More broadly, studies find that when workers feel like they "belong," they are more motivated, engaged, productive, and 3.5 times more likely to contribute fully and innovatively to reach their potential.[15] Do your employees feel a sense of belonging in your workplace?

Role Identity. People also incorporate and express identity via their roles at work and other domains of life. To foster a greater sense of belonging at work, for instance, companies refer to their people as associates (W.L. Gore), partners (Starbucks), members of a crew (Jet Blue) or cast (Disney), or brand them as, say, Owls (Hootsuite), Yelpers (Yelp) or Warbles (Warby Parker). This labeling lessens status differences and promotes camaraderie. It can also lift people's sights about the purpose of their work. "The term 'employee' carries a lot of baggage and can often imply an 'us and them' or feeling of division and objectification," explains Chris Mann, CEO of Guayaki, maker of Yerba Mate organic beverages:

> For us, we are all about Yerba Mate culture, service and sharing. In Argentina, the person who provides hospitality by serving and sharing yerba mate is called a Cebador. Recognizing that all of us at Guayaki are Cebadores aligns our culture, elevates our purpose and makes it clear that we are all here to provide service and to share.[16]

Carrying this a step further, boot maker Timberland connects employees' roles at work to their roles in their communities—as "Earthkeepers." It activates its retailers and consumers to serve alongside its employees in environmental projects in the spring on Earth Day, and in community service in the fall through its "Serv-a-palooza." The aims: develop young people's leadership skills and promote environmental and civic activism. A company executive says:

> Many companies pay thousands of dollars for the type of team-building skills we learn through giving ourselves, together. So not only is Timberland furthering positive change and community betterment, we are making an investment in our infrastructure. This is not philanthropy. I firmly believe that the minds we turn here at Timberland explode our productivity and effectiveness.

Employees are also engaged in good work in the business as Timberland greens its products by eco-innovations in sourcing, sewing, and construction and the use of an "ingredients" label that lets consumers know what's in their boots.

Life Purpose. How does one find a life purpose? It involves letting go of self-interest and discovering a calling larger than yourself. Psychologist Douglas LaBier, who has studied people with a strong sense of life purpose, says it this way: "[It] can be hard to imagine in our mercantile society, but giving your mental, emotional and creative energy from the heart comes naturally when you serve something larger than your self-interest. It beckons you; it calls forth your spirit."[17]

Building on this logic, the idea advanced here is that companies can benefit from engaging their employees with regard to their life *purposes*—their sense of self and place in the larger world that they live in. Psychologist Mihaly Csikszentmihalyi depicts humans as having an "evolving self" whose growth hinges on attaining fuller consciousness of their inner nature and of the world that surrounds them. In developmental terms, this posits that human potential expands as people gain a deeper sense of their personal aspirations and connect it to what is happening in their world. In so doing, Csikszentmihalyi contends, "One needs to step out of the cocoon of personal goals and confront larger issues in the public arena."[18]

Since 2012, German-based software maker SAP has sent over 1,250 employees on pro bono service assignments to consult with innovation hubs, incubators, and academic centers to build their capabilities and to brighten the prospects of over 450 social entrepreneurs and enterprises in 49 countries. Listen to one young SAP staffer, about to launch a social innovation lab for women entrepreneurs: "I want to help these women get new hope for a better future. And I want to use this time to get to know who I am and what my potential is...." Hear another older Millennial helping social innovators in Kenya:

> I am in my ninth year of working at SAP and have had a tremendous amount of support and coaching from leaders and mentors. I have increased confidence and learning that came with being placed in another country, drawing from my own knowledge and learning at the same time. The ability to make an impact on people's lives ensures it's an experience I will never forget, and I will make sure many SAP employees have a chance to gain the same experience.

We'll look further into how engaging employees in pro bono service is good for them, their companies, and the communities and people they serve. But first, it's time for another look in the mirror.

STRESS TEST: RATE YOUR COMPANY ON EMPLOYEE ENGAGEMENT

Think about employees and your company. Are people treated fairly? Does your firm truly support and value diversity? Are people really treated like your "most important asset"? Do you give your company a "thumbs up" for engaging employees in good work?

CHECKLIST 7.1

People: Does your company develop and activate employees as "whole persons"?

To what extent....   1 = Not at all   5 = To a great extent

	1	2	3	4	5
1. Can employees "be themselves" at work?	☐	☐	☐	☐	☐
2. Are *all* employees respected and treated fairly by your company (e.g., race, gender, ethnicity, sexual orientation)?	☐	☐	☐	☐	☐
3. Does your company help employees to balance their work and personal lives?	☐	☐	☐	☐	☐
4. Are employees encouraged to do volunteer work that benefits society?	☐	☐	☐	☐	☐
5. Does your company educate and involve employees in social and environmental improvement activities?	☐	☐	☐	☐	☐
6. Does the work employees do enable them to produce something useful for society?	☐	☐	☐	☐	☐

Again, add up the answers to these six questions: if you score 25 or more, your company strongly engages its employees as full human beings. If 12 to 24, not so much. If lower... why do people work for you?

How to Make Work More Engaging

Being overworked, not belonging, feeling unfulfilled, and not using their full talents and abilities not only disengage employees at work, they have spillover effects on people's health and well-being, and seep into personal relationships, marriages, and even child rearing. They also translate into lost productivity, shoddy workmanship, and lousy customer service. Many companies have employee assistance programs to help employees deal with their troubles, but good employers, and especially those that are great places to work, take proactive steps to be employee-centered and family friendly. How do they address the problems discussed here?

Put Boundaries Around Work. In our recent research visits to companies, we did not find any of them insisting that their people work fewer hours, take longer breaks, or ease up on their responsibilities. But several had new practices to help employees work smarter and without unnecessary distractions. These included designating one- to two-hour work periods when no meetings could be scheduled and calls and texts from managers and other employees were discouraged; instituting flextime so that employees could more or less manage their own comings and goings at work; and moving to remote work, such that employees could work at home one or more days a week or even full-time. The coronavirus pandemic gave a huge boost to remote work and, on balance, many prefer it rather than going back to the office every day. We also found two outliers taking additional steps (see box below).

LIFE IS SHORT. WORK HEALTHY.

You've probably heard how Silicon Valley companies feature ping-pong tables and arcade games at their offices, host yoga classes and cocktail parties, and have 24/7 cafeterias, snacking centers, and even nap rooms. This is so employees can "eat, sleep, and breath" their jobs. Software company Slack has a different ethic: work hard and go home. The company is trying to counter the "overwhelming zaniness" that its Silicon Valley neighbors embrace. The philosophy seems to work. By 6.30 pm, Slack's headquarters are mostly empty.

How about all those after-hours emails and texts—at night, over the weekend, and even when you're on vacation? France outlawed them in 2017 with its "disconnect law" that fines employers that make employees work outside of normal workday hours. In the United States, healthcare consulting firm Vynamic, whose corporate motto is "Life is Short. Work Healthy," has adopted a "zzzmail" policy. Employees are discouraged from emailing their coworkers between 10 pm and 6 am Monday through Friday, and all day on weekends and holidays. This policy has paid off. In its annual employer satisfaction surveys, Vynamic consistently scores 90 percent—almost double the national average of 48 percent.

Diversity and Inclusion + Equity and Justice. Most large companies today have made commitments to support diversity in their hiring and employment, dealings with suppliers and customers, and in their community relations. The best ones also commit to inclusion where people feel respected and valued for who they are and experience a sense of belonging. In these companies, diversity and inclusion is valued not only as an HR factor, but as a source of fresh ideas, as a means of mirroring and better serving the multicultural marketplace, and as a source of learning and effectiveness. Studies find that firms with a more diverse workforce generally perform better than their counterparts.[19]

Committing to equity and justice is a more complex consideration. Most agree that everyone should have equal opportunity to get a job, advance in a company, or do business with one, but not that there should be equality in outcomes—e.g., getting the same pay and rate of promotion, or operating on the same business terms. The idea that business should be "woke" and attend to and remedy historical injustices to Blacks (#blacklivesmatter) and women (#MeToo) adds to the complexity. What should a company do on these accounts? The Black Lives Matter protests in 2020 became a focal point of energy for African American affinity groups in companies. In addition to providing support to their members, the BOLDforce group of Black employees at Salesforce hosted "safe spaces" for several mixed-race conversations about racism, helped the company develop a more inclusive recruiting strategy, and worked with the supplier diversity team to source more goods and services from Black-owned businesses, including funding, guidance, and sponsorship for smaller suppliers. Listen to Tony Prophet, Salesforce Chief Equality and Recruiting Officer, on this count:

> Inequality, in all its forms—gender, LGBTQ, racial, or otherwise—is an issue that every company must address for its own benefit and to create a better world. We believe businesses need to focus on closing the equality gap with the same energy put into creating new products and markets.[20]

Will business deliver on this front? McDonald's is giving its executives bonuses for increasing the share of women and minorities in leadership roles; Nike is linking executive pay to achieving diversity goals; and Facebook committed to a 30 percent increase in the number of people of color in leadership positions in the next five years (others with big commitments are Google/Alphabet, HP, Levi Strauss, Microsoft, Mozilla, RBC, and Wells Fargo). As for gender equality in business leadership, we still have a long ways to go. In the United States, latest estimates are that women hold 5.8 percent of CEO positions in S&P 500 companies and 30 percent of board seats. Europe lags in terms of CEOs in big business, as 28 women headed companies in Europe's STOXX 600 index, which tracks companies across 17 European countries, but in France, Italy, Sweden, Finland, and Germany women account for more than 33 percent of board members.[21] What is the composition of your company's top management and board?

Make Work More Fulfilling. An interesting new idea is floating around about what can make work more fulfilling: design jobs such that people can help one another. Adam Grant, author of *Give and Take: Why helping others drives our success*, contends that "prosocial" motivation is a powerful driver of work engagement and a source of personal meaning and significance on the job.[22] His research studies find many different ways that employees can apply this motivation at work:

- Jobs that enable employees to see the positive impact they have on "beneficiaries" of their work (both inside and outside their companies) are more motivating than those that offer better pay or more "intrinsic" challenge.
- Salespeople who are "givers" and strive to benefit coworkers and customers are more productive than those who primarily look out for themselves.
- Employees who volunteer for community service through their employers are more satisfied and have higher commitment than those who do not volunteer.

In a felicitous turn of phrase, Grant says engagement is more about employees "giving" than "receiving."

Scholars who study mindfulness, caregiving, and compassion at work report that people who "give" take on the perspective of others and get a more complete picture of what is really going on in the world around them. This undermines self-centered tendencies of the ego and fosters empathy and concern for others. It also enables people to see their "reflected best self" in their positive impact on others.[23]

Empower Employees to Serve Society. Recent years have seen a marked increase in company volunteerism—employees giving time to mentor school children, care for the homeless, elderly, or disadvantaged, participate in disaster relief, build community playgrounds or Habitat for Humanity housing—along with more "skill-based" engagements where they use their technical and business know-how to address social concerns. At the leading edge, select companies offer employees a chance to do good through global pro bono service-learning assignments where corporate teams of volunteers work with nonprofit organizations and communities in need.

What do these pro bono programs look like? IBM's Corporate Service Corps (CSC) is modeled on the US Peace Corps, deploying over 500 people annually, and engaging teams of volunteers in three months of pre-work, one month in country, and two months in post-service where they harvest insights for themselves and their business. Ernst & Young's Fellows program is much smaller and focuses on improving small business in Latin America. But its volunteers spend three months in direct service—giving them more time to deliver tangible results. Pfizer's Global Health Fellows program "loans" individual employees to NGOs, primarily in Asia and Africa, to address local healthcare needs. In addition to its global program, SAP sponsors "local" pro bono programs where its employees staff Social Impact Labs in Berlin, Hamburg, and other German cities to assist social entrepreneurs that are set to scale.

PYXERA Global, a Washington DC-based NGO that places pro bono volunteers for over 30 companies around the world, has surveyed participants, their companies, and the people and communities they serve as to the impact of these programs. Among the findings:

- Nearly all participants acquired or improved their skills as a result of their assignments and gained a better understanding of the role of business in society. Other benefits cited by most were enhanced cultural awareness, improved communication and problem-solving skills, and greater adaptability.

- Nine in ten companies say they have designed their programs to achieve both business and social goals. Surveys of program managers find that companies that institute global pro bono programs benefit from staff with greater knowledge of countries important to business expansion and most see an increase in staff motivation, retention and performance. Companies also benefit from an enhanced reputation in the countries where programs are implemented—which improves their ability to win new business—and from being seen worldwide as a global corporate citizen.

- Nearly all of some 300 program clients surveyed are satisfied with their program and say that pro bono participants served as a "change agent" for their organization. Local organizations report operational benefits in areas of stakeholder management, leadership and governance, marketing and external relationships, and training and development.[24]

PYXERA values the services received by pro bono clients at $7.5 million in company outlays annually, with some 2,000 client organization staff helped by programs and over 57 million touched by the work of global service teams. To our eyes, pro bono service is a great way to engage employees and prepare them to lead in an era of rapid social change. By working collaboratively in a team of peers, and confronting and addressing clients' complex social challenges, pro bono participants take on new roles, experiment with new behaviors, and see markets and societies from a new vantage point. This readies them to be the agents of change that their companies—and the world—so desperately need. Would this form of employee engagement with CSR, whether globally or locally, benefit your business?

Engage Employees as Social Innovators

Intrapreneurship, the notion of operating like an entrepreneur within an established organization, was popularized in business three decades ago.[25] In our research we find leading companies developing and activating their employees as *social* intrapreneurs. Thus far we have highlighted social intrapreneurship in Ferrovial's innovation contests, Barclays' Social Innovation Facility, SAS's Vector Lab, and enterprise-wide in Danone's lab-to-land projects. What else is happening?

SAP runs a Design and Co-Innovation Center where employees can tinker with new ideas at their own pace and, when ready, move them into an internal incubator, the SAP.iO Venture Studio, where employee-led startups get technical assistance, go-to-market support, and venture funding. The studio helped to launch and fund Brilliant Hire, a bias-free, skill-based prescreening platform that helps digitize recruiting for companies looking to hire for and promote diversity. IBM features a suite of engagement vehicles for employees ranging from innovation jams to surface new ideas, hackathons to build them out, and an intrapreneurship support program to carry promising employee ideas through to development and the market. Lenovo's foldable PC was developed at the company's Beijing employee innovation incubator. And German industrial manufacturer Siemens has democratized the process via its Quickstarter program that enables Siemens' employees to allocate company money to support development of fellow workers' ideas.

Swedish tech company Ericsson has updated the suggestion box via its grass-roots Collaborative Idea Management Program that enables employees to propose and build on innovative ideas throughout the company. Over

300 Electronic IdeaBoxes set up by employees have to date cumulated over 16,000 ideas and comments from over 10,000 peers. These inputs are vetted, rated, and enhanced by technical experts in the business and bundled into innovations. We saw an Ericsson innovation in Kenya where a network of employees launched a Community Power Project that uses "off the grid" base stations, powered by wind and/or solar power, to share excess power among nearby communities. The base stations power mobile phone charging and in larger-scale deployment can electrify street lights, clinics, and schools for an entire community. Of course, bringing such innovations to market takes money. Ericsson added Innova boxes to provide internal venture funding for employees to gather data, develop prototypes, and fine-tune innovations through field tests.

Hopefully these examples stimulate you to think more about engaging your people as social intrapreneurs. David Grayson and colleagues liken social intrapreneurs to jazz musicians in that they must go through a period of "woodshedding" to develop social and technical skills, "listen" to what is happening in both the business and wider world, and then "improvise" continuously as their innovations take shape and unfold.[26] Imagine all that jazz being drummed up in your business.

Work for People Who Need Work

Several firms we studied have "hire local" or "welfare-to-work" programs that include customized training, apprenticeships, mentoring programs, work–family support, and subsidized transport to and from the job. The temporary employment company Manpower launched MyPath, an e-learning platform that assesses its user's skills, provides career path suggestions, and offers training through online courses. A partnership with Rockwell Automation in Milwaukee provides skills training to military veterans to help them secure advanced manufacturing jobs.

Meanwhile, an estimated 650,000 people are released from prison in the United States every year and 60 percent of them are unemployed a year after their release. We have seen how Ben & Jerry's partners with its supplier Greyston and supports its "open hiring" policies that open doors for ex-offenders. Baltimore-based Rowdy Orbit worked with software company GitHub Inc. to develop a curriculum for training workers returning from prison in quality assurance (QA) jobs. McDonald's and Walmart have specialized programs to hire and advance ex-offenders that include counseling and social support.

On the global stage, India's Nand Kishore Chaudhary (NKC) founded Jaipur Rugs in 1978 working with nine artisans on two looms weaving rugs. NKC started his business on the principle of dignity, employing "untouchables" and subverting centuries-old practices that had shunned the poor, women, and artists. Today, he employs a network of 40,000 artisans in more than 700 villages in India who, in their homes, weave rugs and pillowcases with exotic designs and colors that can be found in high-end stores throughout the world. The company supports its people with basic literacy and numeracy training, comparatively high wages (33 percent higher than the market rate for weavers), access to banking and payments via Vodaphone's M-Pesa mobile wallet, and new management development programs. As one newly promoted supervisor put it:

> I love being a weaver's friend (a Bunkar Sakhi) as it has transformed my
> existence as an individual and changed the course of my life. From someone
> who hesitated to consciously get out of her house, to visiting every loom in the
> village every day, I feel empowered. Nothing is impossible.

Challenges on the Horizon

There you have it: Your company *can* develop and activate employees as "whole persons." But new challenges are arising. Consider just a few of the big issues that you and your company will face.

Remote Work. Prior to the Covid-19 pandemic, only 3.4 percent of the US workforce worked remotely full-time and nearly one in four worked from home a day or more per week. During the pandemic that jumped to over 60 percent! In its aftermath, a substantial proportion of employees will continue, at least periodically, to work from home. Benefits of remote working include more freedom and flexibility, no commuting, and not having to "dress up" for work—at least from the waist down for those who zoom. Some 80 percent of remote workers say their jobs are less stressful than going into the office and 65 percent say they are more productive when working at home. On the downside, many report a heightened sense of social isolation and more challenges in maintaining work–life balance.[27] Some worry that working remotely makes them less "visible" to their boss and senior managers—"out of sight, out of mind"—and puts them at risk of missing out on new opportunities and chances for a promotion.

How does a good employer manage its remote workforce? Ensuring that people have the right tools (hardware and software), training, and technical support are requisites. Regular communication and periodic "check-ins" with a supervisor and both at-home and on-site work teammates are also important. It helps, too, when remote work teams set their own "rules of engagement" about when, how often, and how long to meet virtually. Adobe assembled a multi-level team of managers and employees to design its hybrid workplace. Checking in with the team, we learned that employees now have the option to work from home about 50 percent of the time and operate in a "digital first" environment with ready access to their company's cloud and AI services. An Adobe Life app includes news and information about company and location doings and enables personalized connections among employees and work teams.

Automation. Work today, and much more so tomorrow, will be affected by robotics, artificial intelligence, autonomous transport, chatbots, and the Internet of Things. While estimates of their impact vary, somewhere between 30 and 50 percent of jobs in Europe and the United States are at risk of elimination via automation by the mid-2030s. On the upside, experts project that from one-half up to nearly all of these jobs will be supplanted by new, higher-skilled jobs. On this count, Amazon intends to spend $700 million to train about 100,000 workers in the United States by 2025 to help them move into more highly skilled jobs.

Many blue-collar jobs will be handled by robots and AI applications will take over clerical and routine white-collar work. Human service jobs and those requiring judgment, creativity, or face-to-face interaction seem secure—at least for the foreseeable future. What are good companies doing as they enter this brave new world? Thomas Davenport and Julia Kirby make a case that employers augment, rather than automate, their jobs. That "means starting with what humans do today and figuring out how that work could be deepened rather than diminished by a greater use of machines."[28] Naturally, this means training and helping employees to continuously upgrade their skills and employability.

Surveillance. Sounds creepy, but over two-thirds of employers monitor employees' email and social media accounts at work and, with the pandemic, surveillance moved into remote employees' computers, tablets, and cell-phones. That means your company knows when you log in and off, what websites you visit, what numbers you are calling or texting, what's in your emails, who's on your calendar, and even where you are throughout the day. You should be aware of being surveilled not only as an employee, but also as a websurfer, consumer, and citizen. Your privacy and the security of your data are at stake. Companies that surveil their staff are advised to develop and publish a code of ethics on surveillance and data management—and follow it. What are your company's practices and policies in these regards?

Employee Voice and Activism. In June 2019, several hundred Wayfair employees staged a walkout in protest of the company's sale of furniture to an immigrant detention center at the US-Mexico border. A letter signed by 500 employees stated, "We believe that the current actions of the United States and their contractors at the southern border do not represent an ethical business partnership Wayfair should choose to be a part of." Workers in Hong Kong, Myanmar, the Philippines, Indonesia, Brazil, and Chile over the past three years have joined in protests against their governments and called on their employers to take a stand. We expect employee activism will increase in the years ahead with respect to the issues of the day and how your company is responding to them.

Are you prepared to engage your employees as "citizens"—of your nation, the world at large, and the planet? A 2021 Edelman survey of 7,000 employees in Brazil, China, Germany, India, Japan, the UK, and the US found that over seven in ten employees had "higher expectations" than before the pandemic about the "social impact" of their employer. And, amid the great resignation, some 76 percent feel more emboldened to "insist on change." What are their outlets? Nearly six in ten prefer to work "within the system," petitioning senior management or proposing changes to their manager or HR. But four in ten are ready to "take it public" by joining a social media campaign or protesting outside offices or factories.[29]

All of this has ignited a movement to bring employee "voice" formally into company policy making—directly in the boardroom or at least through board and management advisory committees. Whatever your and your company's position on this might be, it is clear that many employees, particularly the younger ones, are unafraid to speak out about their companies on social media. What will your employees post about your firm in the years ahead?

The Benefits of Engaging Employees as Whole Persons

When employees find that their company welcomes their "whole self", including personal desires to serve society and/or protect the planet, they feel welcome to bring their true self (who I am!) into the workplace. People whose aspirations and life purposes are fulfilled through their companies can serve as effective brand ambassadors for their firms through their word-of-mouth and social media commentary. They produce social capital—a web of positive relationships—that connects their companies to other stakeholders and the public at large.

It takes employees to bring a company's social purpose to life and, as we shall see in the following chapters, to produce the right products and services and to help your company make the world greener.

08

Design and Market Products and Services with Social Value

Foodies have an avid interest in the latest food fads. Bjorn Quenemoen and Jamie O'Shea's Bjorn Quorn are on their faves list. When Bjorn was a student at Bard College, he hosted popcorn parties using his farm family's traditional recipe, heavy on nutritional yeast. His freshman dormmate Jamie, an inventor, was experimenting with an inexpensive method of building big, curved mirrors which focus sunlight to create high temperatures. He knew Bjorn was gearing up to start a popcorn business and convinced him to heat his popcorn kettles using sunlight. The two partnered to produce Bjorn Quorn— non-GMO popcorn, sourced from family farms, solar popped, and seasoned with all-natural flavors and nutrients high in vitamin B.

Their popcorn was a hit and migrated from Hudson Valley stores and craft breweries to Eataly markets to online retailer Etsy. Protein-rich and solar-popped popcorn hits the mark not only on conventional customer criteria but also with those looking for social and environmental benefits. A visit to Bjorn's office at Kelder's Farm in Kerhonkson, NY, found him busy completing a complex supplier application for Whole Foods, which prominently supports small, local vendors. The application included the usual questions on food safety, supplier insurance, retail labels and the like, plus queries on non-GMO certification, compliance with responsible farming practices (soil health, pest management, water conservation, waste reduction, air, energy, and climate impacts, etc.), social accountability (farm worker welfare), sustainable packaging, and traceability (sources of ingredients, where and when packed and shipped, and so on). Welcome to the modern food world, Bjorn and Jamie.

Meanwhile, two billion people worldwide (37 million in the United States) are moderately-to-severely "food insecure," with limited or uncertain access to enough food, and the growth of 150 million children has been stunted by malnutrition.[1] On a research visit to Ghana we came across Shobhita Soor, founder of Legendary Foods, who is tackling this problem by turning insect larvae from the palm weevil into the most affordable source of protein in West Africa. Protein-rich foods like chicken and beef are expensive and can't be stored at room temperature. Edible insects are comparatively inexpensive, have a long shelf life, and are chock full of protein, good fats, zinc, B vitamins, iron, magnesium, and calcium. African consumers grill them, use them in soups and sauces, and grind them to add to bread and cookies. Insects provide over 60 percent of the protein consumed in rural Ghana. Could they be fare for foodies in the West? Go online or to a natural foods grocer and you'll find edible insects in protein bars, pasta, spicy chips and burgers, and in powder formats for baking throughout Australia, Europe, and the United States.

What Do You Have on Offer?

Marketing has moved beyond the 4Ps (product, price, place, promotion) into a world of value-based consumption. Just as we saw with employees, consumers today also expect "something more" from companies they buy from. Nearly two-thirds of global consumers prefer to purchase products and services from companies with a purpose that reflects their own beliefs and values. Over three-quarters say supporting companies that address social and environmental issues helps them feel they are doing their part. On the downside, one-third of all consumers say they have stopped buying their preferred products because they lost trust in the brand.[2]

Philip Kotler, the father of modern marketing and author of the 4Ps, contends that the new purpose of marketing is to create a better world. He offers practitioners 4Ws to consider: do your products or services create 1) economic *wealth*, 2) environmental *wellness*, 3) social *well-being*, and/or 4) human *wisdom*?[3] Many people are shopping for a better world and want products and services that are not only good for themselves personally but also good for the world we live in. And here there is a big gap between what companies promise and what they deliver. A 2021 Meaningful Brands study of over 2,000 brands used by 395,000 consumers in 30 markets, found consumer expectations are at an all-time high; 73 percent say that brands "must act now for the good of society and the planet." Yet trust in brands is at an all-time low; just 36 percent of consumers feel satisfied with companies' "concrete actions to make the world a better place" and only 34 percent say brands are "transparent about their commitments and promises." Cynicism abounds, with 71 percent saying they are tired of "empty promises."[4]

So, take a look at your handprint: *Does your company deliver products or services that are both good for people and good for the world?*

This chapter first looks at what is happening in the realm of products and services and the implications for companies that aspire to lead social change. Then it examines what a company and its leaders can do to deliver products and services that produce social value for the business, customers, and society.

Products, Services, and Social Change

Product development and marketing have changed significantly over the past several decades. In the profit-maximizing era, commodity purveyors mostly competed on price but top consumer companies differentiated themselves by their brand value propositions. First, their products had to give customers functional benefits (does it achieve my practical objectives?) and factors like cost, quality, reliability, and ease of use were at the base of a brand's value proposition. As a "value add," market leaders also provided emotional benefits (do I like it and what does it say about me?) to customers. Here aesthetics come into play and how consumers feel when they consume or use your product becomes a brand differentiator. Typically, people pay a premium for emotional benefits. As luxury car maker BMW marketed it, "A BMW is not just a car, not cold and impersonal, but a precision instrument that comes to life when you drive it—one that makes driving a joy." But they don't always pay more: Southwest Airlines aims to "Connect people to what's important in their lives through friendly, reliable, and low-cost air travel." Fly Southwest and your bags fly free.

With a shift to sustainability and stakeholder management, two new criteria entered into the customer equation: 1) the social and environmental impact of products and services, and 2) the "trustworthiness" of the company that provided them. We've seen how progressive niche companies were acquired by big companies who thereupon began to make and market their own "good for you" brands (e.g., all-natural, organic, sustainably sourced, and Fair Trade certified). Cost more? Yes, but an analysis of 83 research papers found that 60 percent of people are willing to pay extra for a socially responsible product—at an average premium of 17.3 percent.[5] What's next? Brands that feature a social value proposition (see box).

WHAT IS YOUR BRAND'S SOCIAL VALUE PROPOSITION?

Just as companies are seeking a higher purpose, so also are they crafting "social value propositions" for their products and services. Consider these criteria:

1 Does your brand address a real social, economic, or environmental problem?

2 Is your brand's social value proposition authentic and connected to how you do business?

3 Are your products or services priced fairly and are you transparent about their sourcing, making, and impact?

Companies that lead social change answer these questions affirmatively and many find ways to enlist their customers in changemaking.

Consumers Want to Live Better Lives. Globescan recently surveyed 25,000 people across 25 countries to explore their current concerns, expectations, and opportunities to support a healthier and more sustainable lifestyle. While 54 percent say that living in a way that is good for themselves, others, and the environment is a "large" or "major" priority for them, only 37 percent say they "mostly" live this way now.[6] What could close this gap? Respondents report that they could eat healthier, exercise more, pay closer attention to their own and their family's well-being, spend more time in nature, and consume more socially and environmentally conscious products and services. For business, this translates globally into an estimated $1.2 trillion opportunity for "good" brands.

The "tech for good" movement is stepping smartly into this space. Nearly six in ten smartphone users have downloaded a mobile health app onto their phones. There are over 300,000 apps to stimulate or monitor your running, jogging, weightlifting, cardio workouts, or yoga routines. And some 30 million people use Fitbit—wearable technology that can track the distance you walk, run, swim or cycle, as well as the number of calories you burn and take in. There are also countless apps on nutrition and diet, weight loss, stress management, personal grooming, spirituality, and mindfulness. And while more games are downloaded than any other kind of app, not far behind are those geared to education.

Consumers Want to Buy Brands That Are Purposeful—and No More "Empty Promises." You may have read (or seen on YouTube) Pietra Rivoli's disturbing account of *The Travels of a T-Shirt in the Global Economy*.[7] It is a tale about the exploitation of poor farmers and sewers and their lands, all of which is typically invisible to consumers. Well, not now if you shop for T-shirts (and most anything else) at Marks & Spencer (M&S). The UK-based retailer provides "raw material to store" traceability on every single clothing and home product it sells. With its traceability program, labeled "String," when you buy a T-shirt from M&S, you can trace the full "string" of actions backward to find out where the cotton was grown, the yarn was spun, the fabric was produced and dyed, and the shirt was sewn and finished. While M&S was the first retailer to commit to full traceability for non-food products, Wal-Mart, Levi Strauss & Co., and select others have been fast followers.

Nowadays consumers can see ratings of over 150,000 products on the GoodGuide app as to whether they are safe for use, healthy, green, and made by a socially responsible company. Websites like *Just Capital*, *Good On You*, and *Done Good* report on where a company stands on issues like labor conditions, material sourcing, emissions, and waste. *Open Secrets* reports on which political campaigns and charities a company contributes money to. How does your company score on these sites?

Consumers Want Products with "Collective Benefits"—Good for Them and for the World. There certainly is more good stuff on offer for consumers today, but whose stuff is also good for the world? Natura, a Brazilian cosmetic company, puts its purpose into a social value proposition for its customers and society. The company's mantra "bem estar bem" (Well-being/ Being well) is its guide for developing products that preserve biodiversity, traditional knowledge, and culture in Amazonia. For instance, its Ekos product line contains fruits, oil, and berries that are sustainably sourced from Amazonia rainforests—which promotes conservation and keeps land from being deforested. In addition, all Ekos products are biodegradable and come in bottles and packaging made from recycled material. In recent years, Natura acquired two global B Corps, the Body Shop and Australia's Aesop, as well as Avon, to become a global powerhouse.

On cultural preservation, Natura established agreements with 2,500 small suppliers to guard against "biopiracy"—the unethical commercialization of the region's genetic and cultural heritage. The company also promotes education and entrepreneurship in Amazonia. Former CEO Alessandro Carlucci stresses the value of developing business leaders in this way: "When you have local leadership in the communities, they develop, they grow." He reports, "We also invest in the production chain to allow them to have some business there too." Natura is building a multi-million-dollar soap factory in

Amazonia that has space for suppliers to establish manufacturing capacity as well. Carlucci adds that bringing its suppliers together is "a way for them to learn to be sustainable as a company."[8]

Consumers Want to Be Engaged and Activated by Brands. While brand loyalty and reward programs still feature, many consumers are digitally engaged by brands today. They get "push" messages from marketers that send them to brand apps or websites where they can watch appealing adverts with brand-driven storylines and get their questions answered by chatbots. Celebrities and social media influencers (paid and unpaid) post pictures, videos, and commentary about brands on TikTok, Twitter, and in blogs. At the leading edge, customers tell their own stories about brands and see their content featured in messaging and marketing campaigns—like at Ashley Parker. We're also in an age where brands are subject to digital protests. Digital campaigns against racist trademarking led to brand makeovers for Aunt Jemima, Uncle Ben's, Cream of Wheat, Mrs. Butterworth's, and Eskimo Pie.

How about marketing for good? Cause marketing took a big step forward in the early 2000s when U2 musician Bono and activist Bobby Shriver partnered with companies such as Apple, Coca-Cola, Converse, Gap, Hallmark, and Starbucks in the Product (RED) campaign to raise more than $600 million for the Global Fund to Fight AIDS, Tuberculosis, and Malaria. Surveys report that 91 percent of global consumers are likely to switch brands to one that supports a good cause, given similar price and quality.[9] Cause-related marketing ads on YouTube have grown four-fold in recent years. Still, this is tricky. Look at what happened to PepsiCo with its "woke ad" featuring Kardashian supermodel Kendall Jenner. The ad, set to music by Skip Marley, followed an ethnically diverse group of young people, fashionably dressed, joining a protest. Jenner sheds her dress, removes her blonde wig, and challenges police brutality with a can of Pepsi. Social media erupted about the company trying to "cash in" on the Black Lives Matter protest movement. The ad was pulled within 24 hours and Pepsi issued a public apology.

STRESS TEST: RATE YOUR COMPANY'S PRODUCTS AND SERVICES

Think about your own company: Does it offer products that conform to what your customers expect from a socially conscious producer or service provider? Do they add benefits to your customer's health, well-being, or welfare or in any way educate or uplift them? And, how about transparency and customer engagement?

CHECKLIST 8.1

Products: Are your company's products and services good for the world?

To what extent....   1 = Not at all   5 = To a great extent

	1	2	3	4	5
1. Are your company's products or services "good" for customers—adding direct or indirect benefits to their health, education, or well-being?	☐	☐	☐	☐	☐
2. Does your company have "environmentally friendly" products or services?	☐	☐	☐	☐	☐
3. Is your company open and transparent about what's inside its products and, when necessary, about unsafe or defective goods and services?	☐	☐	☐	☐	☐
4. Does your company work with its suppliers to ensure that they do business fairly—in terms of wages, working conditions, employee health, etc.?	☐	☐	☐	☐	☐
5. Does your company engage its customers in social campaigns and in adding social value to your products or services?	☐	☐	☐	☐	☐
6. Is the world a better place because of your company's products and services?	☐	☐	☐	☐	☐

By now, you know the drill: 25 or above—good; 12–24—needs work; below that—fix things or risk the public's disapproval! What does it take for companies to provide products and services that are good for people and society? More socially conscious product design, marketing, and supply chain management practices.

New Requirements: Product Stewardship + Social Impact

The past two decades have seen companies embrace product stewardship to reduce their footprint on the environment and get rid of the "bad" ingredients in their goods. Product Stewardship is defined as "the act of minimizing the health, safety, environmental, and social impacts of a product and its packaging throughout all lifecycle stages, while also maximizing economic benefits."[10] We've seen throughout this book how responsible companies deliver healthier and more environmentally friendly products and services. What more can a company do to satisfy its customers?

FIGURE 8.1   Product Stewardship + Social Impact

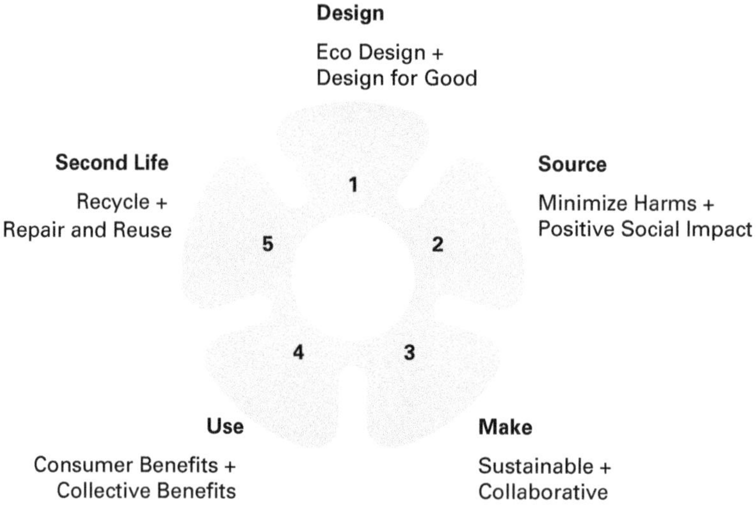

Design

Eco Design +
Design for Good

Second Life

Recycle +
Repair and Reuse

1

5   2

Source

Minimize Harms +
Positive Social Impact

4   3

Use

Consumer Benefits +
Collective Benefits

Make

Sustainable +
Collaborative

How about incorporating positive social impact alongside stewardship through the full product lifecycle (see Figure 8.1)? Let's play this out:

- **Design.** In their move to sustainability, companies turned to *eco-design* that emphasizes less consumption of raw materials and resources, protects flora and fauna, reduces waste and emissions, and makes recycling easier. The *design for good* movement has further ambitions: to improve people's lives and help create positive change.

- **Source.** Well-run businesses *minimize social and environmental harms* in sourcing raw materials and in-process goods in their supply chains. Leading ones are taking steps to have a *positive social impact* on their suppliers and their lands.

- **Make.** Environmental protection and the safety, health, and well-being of employees are top of mind in companies committed to *sustainable production* of goods and services. Companies leaning into the future collaborate with customers to enhance their products and help them lead better lives.

- **Use.** Healthy and environmentally friendly products and services have *customer benefits*. The next challenge for business is to create *collective benefits* with products and services that also improve society and heal the planet.

- **Second Life.** Top companies make their goods *recyclable* and give materials a second life. What's next: *repair* and *reuse.*

Design Products or Services with Social Impact

There is a revolution underway in business (and society) with the use of design thinking and human-centered design practices to develop socially beneficial products and services, built environments, and living communities. Variously termed social design, social impact design, design for social good, and design for social change, this movement has three inter-related features: 1) designs based on social criteria; 2) a user-driven and participatory design process; and 3) development of innovations that help to solve societal problems.

Criteria for "Good" Design. Dieter Rams is a German industrial designer who was responsible for the design of Braun's consumer products for many years (and an inspiration for Apple). He developed 10 principles of good design: innovative, aesthetic, unobtrusive, honest, makes a product useful, makes it understandable, long-lasting, thorough down to the last detail, environmentally friendly, and "involves as little design as possible."[11] Do these criteria apply to your company's goods and services?

Ram's emphasis on environmentally friendly design is manifest today in an explosion of green architecture, furniture, and fixtures, in transport and power, apparel and appliances, and in most every category of product or service today, including the option to not have your towels washed every day you stay at a hotel. But what makes a product or service "socially" useful—both to users and to society?

This was a central concern of Unilever in its efforts to eliminate the "bad" stuff from its brands and add in more "good" stuff. Each food and personal care brand was put through a "brand imprint" and then improved to yield *less environmental impact* (water use, waste, greenhouse gas emissions), produce *more personal vitality* (benefits to health and well-being), and create *social value* (effecting social change). Progress on this journey continues apace. As of 2021, Unilever provides more than 125 billion servings of foods or beverages that are fortified with at least one of the five key micronutrients—vitamin A, D, iodine, iron, and zinc—and is aiming to reach 200 billion servings in the next few years. Meanwhile, its Dove campaign emphasized "real beauty" (not just "inner beauty") and took on the advertising industry with campaigns against "super-skinny" fashion models and photo-shop editing of "imperfections" in beauty ads. Unilever then partnered with the world's largest stock photo agency Getty Images, and with Girlgaze, a group of female-identifying and non-binary photographers, to build a publicly accessible library of "unedited" pictures of real beauty. Its #ShowUs photos feature in Unilever ads, with taglines like "beauty doesn't rest at 67" and "all skin is beautiful," and Unilever hacked the industry by agreeing to cover the fees of any #ShowUs models who appear in other companies' ads!

The Social Design Process. "Design is the best way to get from A to B when you don't yet know what B is," or so says our Babson colleague Cheryl Heller. She founded the Design for Social Innovation program at the School of Visual Arts in NYC, is now Director of Design Integration at the Design School of Arizona State, and teaches a course on "Design for Good." In *The Intergalactic Design Guide*, she explains the social design process in this way:

> instead of a small team of expert designers being responsible for the creative output or product, social design is done by cross-disciplinary teams, including both people inside the company, and in external stakeholder communities. The goal, in addition to breakthrough products and services, is breakthrough interactions between people that lead to ongoing innovation.[12]

Naturally, different design processes feature in different kinds of innovations. For instance, in their large-scale eco-innovations, big companies invest in basic research and engineering to develop technologies to open new markets and make the planet greener. Similarly, in developing new food recipes and product ingredients, Pepsi, Unilever, and others draw on chemistry, biology, and other life sciences to produce functional foods and beverages —or what some call "nutraceuticals," as they offer nutritional and medical benefits. An early mover in this area, Unilever developed a low-cost iodized salt called Annapurna and introduced it into India. It has since made this available in sachet sizes as small as 100 grams and at prices equivalent to six US cents, to place it within the price reach of poor families. PepsiCo introduced an iron-fortified cracker in India that addresses iron deficiency and has cookies on offer in Mexico that are fortified with Vitamin A. But no big food company is doing as much to blend food and medicine as Nestlé. Nestlé's Health Science unit has worked with partners to make drinks for people with meta-bolic disorders and a medical food sold for the dietary management of Alzheimer's disease.

Other kinds of social innovations involve co-creation with users who might operate as both producers and consumers.[13] For instance, Ericsson, the Swedish maker of telecom equipment, partnered with the World Meteorological Organization and the Uganda Department of Meteorology to co-create a mobile weather alert application that enhances the safety of fishermen in Lake Victoria through detailed, customized weather forecasts. In turn, it jointly developed with DataProm, Vivo, and Telefónica a fleet management system in Curitiba, Brazil to connect buses wirelessly that has increased public confidence in travel safety and reduced fuel costs and travel time.

Innovations That Solve Social Problems. We've seen how B2C companies develop products and services that improve diets, help children learn, enable people to monitor their health, and support socially conscious living. In the B2B space, IBM's Watson computer has moved from competing on (and winning) the game show *Jeopardy!* to treating cancers through cognitive computing. When we visited IBM's new innovation "garage" in Times Square, New York City, we saw technologists, medical librarians, and doctors from Memorial Sloan Kettering Cancer Center using AI to analyze patient records, medical studies, and clinical trial results to help physicians make treatment decisions. Their project connects patients' genomic data with "evidence-based" treatment options and can also match patients with the best available clinical trials. In the future, Watson will act as a physician's assistant by examining a clinical case from different angles and then—using reference materials and its collaborative learning experiences—enable a physician to support or refute etiological hypotheses.

Add Social Value to Your Supply Chain

With their shift from doing less harm to doing more good, leading companies are having a positive social impact throughout their value chains. Take three examples:

Support Rural Lives. By 2050 we'll need to feed two billion more people than today. How can we do that responsibly? To ensure a sustainable and secure supply of foodstuffs, and to support the productivity and well-being of small farmers, many companies are innovating in their supply chains and securing certifications of sustainable sourcing and adhering to ISO standards. Some of the innovators studied include global farm-to-food giants like

Nestlé, Unilever, and Danone, and regional businesses like Charoen Pokphand in Thailand, Jollibee Foods in the Philippines, and Haigh's Chocolates from Australia.

Royal FrieslandCampina, a Dutch dairy cooperative with markets worldwide, receives milk supplies from over 19,000 member dairy farms in the Netherlands, Belgium, and Germany and thousands of smallholder farms in Asia, Africa, and Eastern Europe. Due to the sheer number of smallholder farmers supplying fresh milk to FrieslandCampina in Asia, the company needed an efficient and effective way to support them. Its innovation was the Dairy Development Program. The first phase of local DDP implementation involves building a local network of farmers or, where one exists, aligning with a farmer cooperative. The second phase involves establishing a development program to address their greatest needs, including training, expert consultancy, knowledge partnerships, or specific tools or infrastructure to improve milk hygiene, young stock breeding, or feed and water use. Through a Farmer2Farmer exchange program, Dutch dairy farmers also share the dairy knowledge and expertise that has been developed in the Netherlands with smallholder suppliers.

Help Build a Local Living Economy. Listen to Judy Wicks, founder of the natural food restaurant White Dog Café, and promoter of a "local living economy," passionately describe her calling:

> I love nature and animals and the abuse of animals in the corporate farm system
> is just unbelievable. It's barbaric the way that pigs and cows and chickens
> are raised in the corporate system; to me it's a spiritual issue. I believe in my
> interconnectedness environmentally, spiritually, and economically with other
> people and with other forms of life. So I feel it's my moral duty, you know, to
> work on these issues.

Under Judy's leadership, White Dog purchased sustainably grown produce from local family farmers, and only humanely and naturally raised meat, poultry and eggs, sustainably harvested fish, and fair trade coffee, tea, chocolate, vanilla, and cinnamon. The cafe also ticked every box on social responsibility and sustainability: paying a living wage, mentoring inner-city high school students, plus recycling and composting, solar-heated hot water, eco-friendly soaps and office supplies, and buying 100 percent of its electricity from renewable sources.

Is this a one-off? We first met Judy over a decade ago as she was making muffins. She has since sold her business to local owners who have maintained her traditions and now Judy speaks, blogs, and is an activist in the

Business Alliance for Local Living Economies (BALLE), comprising some 80 community networks throughout North America and representing over 22,000 socially responsible businesses.

Practice Fair Trade. We've mentioned fair trade a few times, but what is it all about? The Fair Trade movement took off when world coffee prices slumped in the late 1980s, roasters saw their incomes shrink, and coffee farmers and workers were further impoverished.[14] A Dutch development agency proposed a system of certification for roasters and retailers who would adopt fair trade principles, including a guaranteed minimum price for producers, an additional 10 percent for investments in social and environmental projects, and 60 percent advance payment so they wouldn't have to sell their beans immediately after harvest—when prices are low. All of this evolved into fair trade certification for bananas, honey, coffee, oranges, cocoa beans, cocoa, cotton, dried and fresh fruits and vegetables, juices, nuts, quinoa, rice, spices, sugar, tea, and even wine. The FAIRTRADE label appears on over 35,000 products sold around the world and encompasses over 1.65 million producers across 75 countries. The market for fair trade goods grew to nearly $12 billion worldwide in 2019, and producers earn roughly $200 million annually in premiums for their fair trade production. So, what are you doing, or could you do, to add social value through your supply chain?

Collaborate with Customers

Savvy marketers prepare customer "journey maps" and digitally engage consumers at their every touchpoint with a product or service, from initial urges and search to purchase decisions, use, and discard—enhancing the full experience. How about using digital technology to help your customers consume more responsibly? Many companies today use a QR (quick response) code on their packages so consumers can get information about ingredients, processing, packaging, and transport, up to its delivery to the store (or your home). Ben's Original (Mars Group) partnered with app maker Blippar to showcase its supply chain using augmented reality (AR). Customers can scan a box of rice to learn how the rice makes its journey from farm to fork through interactive maps and infographics. Dutch natural food company Eosta enables its consumers to engage in a virtual conversation with the grower of their organic produce or flowers. Is your company doing anything good with QR codes or AR experiences?

In this era of social change, companies crowdsource product ideas, operate open innovation platforms, and gain constant feedback from early users of new goods and services. Threadless, a fashion e-commerce company, pushes collaboration further by letting users design, choose, and buy the product of their choice. Consumers post a design on the company's website, other users vote on it, and the creations that receive the most support from the community are produced. How about co-production? Look at how LEGO pioneered brand co-creation with its legions of brand fans (see box). And why just involve your own customers? Several businesses, including Google, M&S, and Unilever, support and join in the work of Collectively, a network that enables young people to share stories about creating positive personal and social change.

FROM BRAND FANS TO CO-CREATORS: LEGO

At its founding in 1932, LEGO took its name from a combination of the Danish words "leg" and "godt," meaning "play well." It doesn't just sell toys—it strives for "the development of children's creativity through play and learning." To fulfill its brand promise, it designs colorful blocks and figures that can be assembled to build a house, castle, airport, or whatever might be imagined. Time for an update: it used to do the designing—now it crowdsources many of its concepts, designs from brand fans, and invites super-users into its innovation center to co-create new products with its multidisciplinary design team.

LEGO's move to open innovation all started in 1998 when it introduced Mindstorms, a line of programmable robots built with LEGO blocks, and the software program was hacked! Rather than going after the culprits, LEGO saw the benefits of their ideas and gave all Mindstorms users a "license to hack." Meanwhile, powered by the internet, a disparate group of AFOLs (Adult Fans of Lego) began to connect online, developed their own Facebook pages and websites, and got together to show their LEGO creations at annual BrickFests. CEO Jørgen Vig Knudstorp attended an early BrickFest in 2005 and was stunned by fans' enthusiasm and creativity.[15] How could he bring this into the company?

LEGO Group first leapt into online open innovation in Japan with a design contest, and users came up with the company's iconic DeLorean *Back to the Future* car and 30th-anniversary *Ghostbusters* building set. In 2014, open innovation was institutionalized with LEGO Ideas. Here's how it works: 1) submit your proposal for a new LEGO set, complete with a model, photos, and a description; 2) gather support from the brand community—once you get 10,000 supporters, your set qualifies for a review by the LEGO Review Board; and 3) if successful, your idea becomes a real LEGO set that any fan can purchase around the world. You even get a royalty on sales, and recognition as the set's creator!

LEGO continues to expand its open innovation work—for the benefit of the company and to teach people (adults and kids) design skills. Recently, it partnered with Tencent in China to develop "creative and safe digital play experiences for Chinese children." On this games platform, children develop skills in 3D design, coding, construction, and building, and create "virtual" landscapes and stories in a video game format. With this gaming product, LEGO hopes to harness the creativity of its young users to inspire the next generation of product ideas.

Good for You, Good for All of Us

To give you some inspiration on products that create social change, we studied up on how the buy-one-give-one model of Tom's shoes and Warby Parker eyeglasses has been picked up by the social business Hey Girls to raise awareness around menstrual periods and increase accessibility to hygiene products. Hey Girls created an organic, environmentally sound sanitary product that, when a box is purchased, another one is donated to a girl in need. We also met with Mattel, which offers gender-neutral dolls. Gen Z does not subscribe to traditional gender norms and, according to the Pew Research Center, almost 60 percent of young people believe forms and online profiles should include options besides man or woman.[16] What else is going on?

Plant-Based Protein. In the United States, an estimated 4 to 5 percent of the population are vegetarians, and in Europe this jumps to 10 percent. The percentage of people in the West who identify as vegans or flexitarians (mostly vegetarian) has grown dramatically in the past 10 years and the market for plant-based protein has a projected annual compounded growth rate of 14 percent from 2021 to 2026. Who had the foresight to trailblaze this market? Companies like Impossible Foods and Beyond Meat (US) and Vbites (UK and Europe) were early movers into the plant-based "meat" market, and the plant-based "milk" market is already crowded. "Raising the Good in Food" is the social value proposition of Canada's Maple Leaf

Foods, who point to the benefits of their plant-based meats for animal welfare, climate, food security, and nutrition. Research finds that consumers go for these social benefits, more so than the taste, when they buy plant-based meats. Consumer tests find that several plant-based burgers taste like the "real thing," though a few had the consistency and texture of "cat food."[17]

As for good food delivery, we all saw fresh food and meal home delivery scale during the coronavirus pandemic, and food e-tailing continue its surge. Florida-based Natural Machines is taking this a step further. The company has created a 3D printer that has consumers load in a few fresh ingredients, choose a recipe from the touchscreen menu, hit print, and the machine does the rest. Other early movers like NovaMeat and Redefine Meat offer 3D printed beef steaks made from plant-based compounds that taste like the fat, muscle, and blood found in animal meat.

Slow Fashion. Fast fashion is inexpensive, trendy clothing whose makers translate designs from the catwalk or celebrity culture and turn them into garments in a matter of weeks. It used to be that fashion revolved around "seasons"—now new styles are introduced into stores weekly. At an outfit like Fashion Nova, that means 600 to 900 new styles per week! Who buys fast fashion? Mostly young women, aged 18 to 25 years old, many of whom, according to one study "feel pressured to wear a different outfit every time they go out."[18] What's the problem? These garments are often made by underpaid and exploited workers overseas and produce an outsized environmental footprint. But trends are changing.

One sign is the growth in secondhand store shopping for apparel, shoes, and accessories. More than one in three Gen Zers bought secondhand clothing in 2019. Another is the switchover by fashion retailers. In 2019, fast-fashion Forever 21 went bankrupt and H&M and Zara began to turn to "slow fashion." H&M has a Conscious Collection, in which garments must contain at least 50 percent sustainable materials, such as organic cotton and recycled polyester, and Zara pledges that it will only use sustainable, organic, or recycled material in all of its clothing by 2025. They had better hurry this up because thousands of entrepreneurs are moving into this space and fashion incubators are multiplying all over the world.

Fair Financial Services. According to the Reputation Institute, an outfit that annually surveys consumers worldwide, financial services are rated lower than every industry, besides energy companies, on transparency.[19] Antoni Ballabriga, the Global Head of Responsible Business at BBVA, has tried to differentiate his bank in these regards. Serving nearly 10 million low-income customers in Spain and throughout Latin America, the bank offers low-interest payday advances ("Adelanto de sueldo"), mobile banking, and through its Microfinance Foundation provides financial support to vulnerable populations, including a program providing financial literacy and funds to women entrepreneurs. Where BBVA really separates itself from the pack is in its commitment to "radical transparency." Customers get full information—on costs and benefits—of every bank product in clear language without the usual small print disclaimers or hidden fees.

Affordability. IKEA sells couches, armchairs, and tables for about half of what its competitors do. "We could be misinterpreted as a low-price company doing cheap stuff," says its top designer Marcus Engman, "But we're all about affordability."[20] What are the key ingredients in IKEA's design recipe? The company starts with users' needs and visits people in their homes to identify their needs and pick an appropriate price point. Then it engages in "democratic design" whereby a mix of product specialists, marketers, and engineers use a 3D printer to develop prototypes in an open development swap where everyone exchanges ideas. Finally, the company uses the most affordable materials and flat packs its goods for customers to assemble on their own. IKEA also has a Buy Back program where consumers call sell back unwanted furniture and home goods that may otherwise end up in landfills—and receive store credit toward future purchases.

How about affordable products that are healthy and environmentally friendly? There are now upwards of 35,000 "dollar" stores throughout the United States that cater to households earning less than $40,000 per year. What these stores don't stock is much in the way of good stuff. Dollar Tree, for instance, earns a grade of D+ on the use of toxic chemicals in its offerings. The retailer Target is turning this to its advantage. It has introduced a private-label Target Smartly brand for price-conscience shoppers that includes home and personal care items, like hand soaps, paper plates, razors and more, priced at $2 or less. These affordable products get a grade A on toxic chemicals and its Smartly lotions and potions are not tested on animals.[21] In addition, Target stores are now signed with bright green Target Clean icons letting consumers know that 4,000 products in their beauty and home and personal care aisles (and online) are free of phthalates, propyl-parabens, formaldehyde, butyl-parabens, sodium laureth sulfate and other unpronounceable toxins.

A Second Life. On a global level, we produce 2.12 billion tons of waste every year. About 13 percent of that is recycled. At current rates, the ocean will have in it more plastics than fish (by tonnage) in 2050. In 2018, several big companies (including Mars, M&S, PepsiCo, Coca-Cola, Unilever, and Walmart) pledged that they would have 100 percent reusable, recyclable, or compostable packaging by 2025. What's next? A Reuse Revolution is gaining speed, with moves toward reusable cups, containers, and, as we shall shortly see, fashion.

The Global Dimension

The United Nation's first Millennium Development Goal target—to cut the 1990 poverty rate in half by 2015—was reached in 2010, five years ahead of schedule (though poverty rates jumped during the pandemic). The next challenge for global business is to meet the aspirations of the world's growing middle class (doubling to 3.2 billion in 2020 from 1.8 billion in 2010)—what do they want?

Socially Conscious Consumers are Everywhere. When we first began tracking what the world wants from corporations, over 10 years ago, we were not surprised to find that Scandinavians and the Dutch put more weight than Americans on social responsibility, environmental practices, and corporate ethics. But we were stunned that South Koreans, Brazilians, Chileans, and Indians weighed them more significantly than Americans, too.

Now this is translating into socially conscious consumerism. This sentiment is stronger in Asia-Pacific, Latin America and Middle East/Africa than in North America and Europe. But what is crucial in purchase decisions worldwide is whether or not a brand can be trusted to "do what is right."[22] One implication of this is that top multinational companies have adopted "global" standards on product safety, packaging, labeling, and truth in advertising, rather than simply complying with local requirements which, outside of the US and Europe, are often lax or less demanding.

The Base of the Pyramid. When C.K. Prahalad and Stuart Hart popularized back in 2002 the idea that there is a "fortune" to be made by companies who serve the BoP, they could only point to a few exemplars such as Unilever's Project Shakti, which turned poor women into entrepreneurs and had them travel to nearby villages in India to sell hygienic soap and toothpaste and dispense health advice to rural customers. Today there are many more. [23] SC Johnson, the world's leading maker of insect control products, such as Raid and Baygon, is another exemplar. Their challenge was, first, to gain a local supply of a key ingredient, pyrethrum. Along with partners USAID and the Borlaug Institute of Texas A&M, SC Johnson worked hand in hand with Rwandan farmers and their communities to sustainably farm and harvest the plant. Next there was the challenge of learning how to market insect control products, in a culturally compatible format, to protect people from malaria and related diseases. The SC Johnson innovation team slept under mosquito bed nets on nights when the temperature was 100 degrees Fahrenheit with 95 percent humidity, and learned firsthand that the nets are hot and heavy and get dirty. The lessons learned were that rural consumers want insect protection products that work well but also are affordably priced and multifunctional.

Accordingly, SC Johnson developed a "bundle" of insect control products, ranging from repellents to home cleaning sprays, in refillable formats. They marketed them through WOW clubs, of seven or more homemakers, who also participated in group coaching sessions around home and family-care best practices. Says Mark Martin, Vice President of International Markets for SC Johnson, on this point: "We do not believe in taking a 'one-size-fits-all' approach to entering BoP communities. It is important for us to have a keen understanding of each market's needs as well as the time it takes to successfully enter these markets."[24]

Challenges on the Horizon

There you have it: your company *can* develop and deliver products and services that are good for people and for the world. But again there are developments ahead that will test your good intentions and call for resilience and adaptability.

Reuse and Repair. Can you imagine urging your customers to buy less? Patagonia shocked the retail world in 2011 with a "demarketing" ad on Black Friday telling people, "Don't Buy This Jacket." Through its Common Threads and Worn Wear initiatives, the company encourages people to buy used clothing and teaches them how to repair clothing with its repair kits. As founder Yvon Chouinard said it, "We want customers who need our clothing, not just desire it." He goes on "Reusing something instead of immediately discarding it… can be an act of love which expresses our own dignity."[25] Others are following along. Levi's promotes durability with its "Buy Better, Wear Longer" jeans that are meant to be worn "for generations, not seasons," and Sweden's Nudie Jeans Repair Shop buys back your old jeans, reconditions them, and sells them secondhand in its Re-use program. H&M is piloting an in-store repair program and Timberland will either refurbish used boots for sale on its re-commerce platform or upcycle/recycle them into future products.

The reuse-and-repair movement goes beyond clothes and shoes. In a strike against planned obsolescence and constant upgrades, the social enterprise Fairphone makes and sells repairable and upgradeable phones. Consumer "right to repair" rules are being advanced that apply to electronic goods like televisions, smartphones, tablets, and laptops as well as tractors, autos, and machinery of all types. These would require manufacturers to make their parts and source code available to independent repair shops and do-it-yourself consumers.

The Sharing Economy. Recent years have seen disruptions in the businesses of music, movies, and television programming with rental services, and in transport, lodging, and the exchange of goods and services via myriad peer-to-peer (P2P) markets. P2P consumers can locate and hire freelance professional and personal service providers; borrowers can get funds; and gig workers can find office space and support in the "sharing economy." The pioneer in the P2P market, eBay, reaches 183 million buyers annually and offers them over 1.6 billion listings of new and used goods. China's Alibaba has more sales than eBay and Amazon combined. How do people pay for all this? Forget cash or checks. Sped up by the pandemic, P2P mobile payments are expected to grow to $4 trillion by 2024.

What could all this sharing mean for your business? On the plus side, it opens up new ways to raise capital, expand payment arrangements, outsource specialized work, reduce the costs of business travel, and stay connected to consumers on a resale platform. In the B2B space, you can rent production capacity from other businesses, easily acquire and sell used machinery, join with other companies to increase your buying power, monetize underused assets (e.g., meeting rooms, parking places, warehouse space, trucks), and work with co-located firms to set up a carpooling service, borrow and lend employees, and collectively manage waste. On the downside, your margins may shrink and markets collapse. Adapt or die.

Brand Activism, Slacktivism, and Blowback. We've highlighted the growing import of companies speaking out on social issues and using their brands to "take a stand." Why is this important with regard to your products and services? Some 87 percent of US consumers said they purchased a product because a company "stood up and advocated for" an issue they cared about, and US and UK consumer activists agree that it is "more important now than ever to show support for companies that 'do the right thing' by buying from them." But note this: 76 percent will refuse to purchase a company's products or services upon learning it supported an issue contrary to their beliefs.[26]

As an example, fitness companies SoulCycle and Equinox were targeted when it was reported that one of their investors, Stephen Ross, hosted a fundraiser for Donald Trump's 2020 re-election campaign. The Brits staged a tea protest when Rishi Sunak, Boris Johnson's chancellor, posted a picture of himself on Twitter with a large bag of Yorkshire Tea and social media erupted over his support of Brexit. Tempest in a teapot? Yorkshire Tea and P&G Tips next got caught up in the culture war over racism (remember their colonial history).

So there are risks and rewards with brand activism for companies. On the consumer side, critics also complain about "slacktivism" (which combines the words slacker and activism) whereby people give your company a thumbs-up or down for taking a stand but doing little else. Likes on Facebook, pictures on Instagram, and retweets on Twitter are seen as a "lazy" response to social issues or, as Malcolm Gladwell put it, "the revolution will not be tweeted." So, too, signing an online petition for or against a company is largely ineffective. The message for companies is to translate your activism into "real life" campaigns. And lest we dismiss the slacktivists (aka clicktivists), studies suggest that for many, a social media click is but a first step toward gaining a better understanding of the issues, connecting with a like-minded peer group, and ultimately taking action.[27]

Are You Ready For Brand Democracy?

Brands have evolved from being owned and controlled by individual companies to being influenced by consumers and other stakeholders to being part of a larger ecosystem of actors and interests around the globe—some friendly to you and others not so much. This includes potential boycotters who may turn against you based on your purpose, products, and advocacy and "BUYcotters" who will support you and buy your goods and services because of who you are and what you deliver to them and to society. In this emerging era of "brand democracy," some two-thirds of the world's public subscribe to these three tenets:

1 I believe brands can be a powerful force for change.

2 I expect them to represent me and solve societal problems.

3 My wallet is my vote.[28]

Next up: the planet.

09

Help the Planet to Flourish

IKEA announced its People + Planet Positive platform in 2012, with the purpose to "balance economic growth and positive social impact with environmental protection and renewal." Its green journey began in the mid-1980s, when it discovered that its particleboard furniture products had formaldehyde emissions exceeding legal standards. It also faced calls for boycotts from environmental groups over the use of tropical rainforest wood in its furniture. With this "wake up" call, IKEA (like Interface) brought in Sweden's Natural Step to help it clean up its environmental problems and formulate and drive an agenda to reduce its footprint. The results are notable: nearly 60 percent of IKEA's current offerings feature renewable materials and 12 percent contain recycled materials. All of the non-recycled wood used in its products is Forest Stewardship Council certified, meaning that its harvesting did not contribute to deforestation. All laudable, but P+P Positive shifted its focus to the company handprint: helping customers to live better and restoring and regenerating the planet.

Go into an IKEA store today and you'll find it's powered by rooftop solar panels or purchased renewable energy. Every store has LED lighting, many use rainwater harvesting, and newer ones have a geothermal system for heating and cooling. Every supplier and service provider is vetted through the company's IWAY supplier code of conduct that sets mandatory standards on their environmental, social, and working conditions, and IKEA recently announced that its direct suppliers in Poland, China, and India will operate with 100 percent renewable energy, followed by a global stepwise rollout. There's more: IKEA's parent company Ingka Group now owns more than 136,000 acres of forest in the United States that have been "set aside" for nature restoration and carbon sequestration. The company has also committed to making half of its cooked meals and 80 percent of its packaged foods plant-based by 2025. Next IKEA is taking its 4Rs (reuse, repair, repurpose, and recycle) into customers' homes and communities.

On the consumer side, you may have seen IKEA's "trash" advertisements. One shows trash piling up in a landfill with people's thrown-away furniture (with the purchase price of each item shown). Another depicts a giant meteor made of trash—discarded appliances, toys, and single-use plastics—hurtling toward Earth. These two ads heralded IKEA's campaign against "unsustainable consumption" in a "throwaway society." In the spirit of caring for human habitats, IKEA has partnered with the construction firm Skanska to build affordable and sustainable homes throughout Scandinavia and now the UK. The modular timber-frame homes are manufactured in a factory (with less than 1 percent waste) and feature an open living plan with natural light, living spaces, tiled washrooms, and, as you can imagine, IKEA kitchens. The company says it recycles over 99 percent of leftover construction materials and that its carbon footprint is less than half that of normal building projects. What's the impact on the community? A local UK councilor reports that it gives "lower-income, hard-working individuals a genuine chance to buy their own home without having to move out of the town."

The Anthropocene Age: A Sixth Extinction?

Elizabeth Kolbert's *The Sixth Extinction: An unnatural history* puts us in the Anthropocene Age, in which human activity is the dominant influence on climate and the environment. Unlike the previous five extinctions, she argues, it is our passion for expansion and exploration—a "madness gene"—that threatens a new one. She writes:

> As the effects of global warming become more and more difficult to ignore, will we react by finally fashioning a global response? Or will we retreat into ever narrower and more destructive forms of self-interest? It may seem impossible to imagine that a technologically advanced society could choose, in essence, to destroy itself, but that is what we are now in the process of doing.[1]

Greta Thunberg, born 2003, is stimulating a global response. A Swedish environmental activist, at age 15 she picketed Sweden's parliament calling for a "strike" against climate change by school-age children. After her address to the 2018 United Nations Climate Change Conference, student strikes took place every week somewhere in the world and a year later there were multi-city protests involving over a million students each. To avoid flying, Thunberg sailed to North America to attend the 2019 UN Climate Action Summit. Listen to her first words at the summit: "This is all wrong. I shouldn't be up here. I should be back in school, on the other side of the ocean. Yet you all come to us young people for hope. How dare you! You have stolen my dreams and my childhood with your empty words."[2]

At one of Ray Anderson's first talks about Interface's journey, he was given a poem by an attendee, Glenn Thomas, called "Tomorrow's Child." It speaks of meeting a child, "though yet unborn," and learning that "the things I do might someday, somehow, threaten you." Ray would read this poem at meetings in the company and in public presentations. At one, we heard him say, "We are, each and every one, a part of the web of life. The continuum of humanity, sure, but in a larger sense, the web of life itself. And we have a choice to make during our brief, brief visit to this beautiful blue and green living planet: to hurt it or to help it." So look at your handprint: *Does your company help to protect, restore, and regenerate the planet?*

This chapter highlights the current status of Mother Earth and the challenges faced by companies that want to lead green social change. It then looks at new ideas on how business can take account of its planetary impact and move beyond sustainability to help create a world where nature flourishes. These ideas could help your company make a better future for "tomorrow's child."

Planet and Social Change

Industry was slow to respond to the green movement in its early years. Most firms complied with environmental protection regulations but little more. 3M was one of the first big businesses to step up and go beyond regulatory requirements. In the mid-1970s, it launched its Pollution Prevention Pays (PPP) program to reduce harmful chemicals in its processes and products, including developing water-based solvents to reduce air emissions from the manufacture and use of its tapes and sandpaper. 3M's Life Cycle Management (LCM) process was developed in the late 1990s to assess how products, from raw materials to consumer use to disposal, were impacting the environment, and has since become a corporate standard. Post-it® Notes are now made from 100 percent de-inked, recycled fiber with 20 percent post-consumer waste.

The new millennium was a "tipping point" for the green wave in business. Paul Hawken and Amory and L. Hunter Lovins, drawing on early lessons at Interface, wrote *Natural Capitalism: Creating the next industrial revolution* and presented a "road map" for moving forward[3] (see box).

NATURAL CAPITALISM

The move toward Natural Capitalism called for four radical transformations in industry and eco-entrepreneurs and leading companies are answering the call:

1 **Dramatically increase the productivity of natural resources, through energy efficiency and the use of wind and solar power.** Progress has been substantial on reducing energy use in appliances, home heating and cooling, industrial production, and fuel use by vehicles. Wind and solar power generated a tenth of the world's electricity in 2020.

2 **Shift to biologically inspired production through cradle-to-cradle (C2C) and closed-loop production systems.** Recycling of paper, paper board, and glass has increased substantially over the past 20 years. Hermann Miller was among the first companies to receive C2C certification for its line of recyclable office chairs.

3 **Move to new business models involving leasing or sharing.** Dow pioneered the leasing of chemical solvents with its SAFECHEM solutions. Its customers rent a container of solvents and then Dow takes back the container and used solvents for recycling. Zero emissions. As for the sharing economy, early entrants like Couchsurfing and Zipcar were supplanted by Airbnb in 2008 and Uber in 2009.

4 **Reinvest in natural capital through reforestation, wetlands reclamation, and promotion of biodiversity.** Rather than build a $40 million wastewater treatment plant, Dow spent $1 million to restore a wetland that naturally filters wastewater, with significantly lower construction and operational costs.

Looking for other signs of green social change? Toyota's hybrid Prius sold 5,000 cars when it entered the United States in 2000—the only hybrid then in the market. In 2019, over 400,000 hybrids were sold in the US (from all makers) and Tesla sold over 200,000 all-electric vehicles. Bike-sharing services have increased exponentially and electric scooter and bicycle sales reached 40 million in 2020. And, to reduce energy use, Microsoft sank one of its data centers into the ocean off the coast of Orkney, Scotland to keep it cooler than on land.

Assessing industry's progress on the green front, Andrew Hoffman characterizes much of the work to date as Sustainable Business 1.0: *Industry Integration*. It has been inwardly focused and has seen companies "clean up" their emissions and reduce waste. Today, Hoffman contends, we are moving to Sustainable Business 2.0: *Market Transformation*. It is focused outward on customers, supply chains, and markets—to provide greener goods and to incentivize investors to save the planet.[4]

But here's the bad news: we have already passed three of the "planetary boundaries" that represent "thresholds above which humanity cannot safely operate": climate change, biodiversity loss, and biogeochemical flows (nitrogen and phosphorus cycles). And we are nearing the boundaries for ocean acidification, freshwater use, and deforestation.[5] Who is responsible for this calamity? Businesses, governments, and all of us—as investors, consumers, employees, and citizens. Can this be turned around?

Sustainability Is Not Sufficient: The Planet Needs to Be Repaired, Restored, and Regenerated. Paul Hawken's book *The Ecology of Commerce* inspired Ray Anderson to begin his ascent up Mt. Sustainability. His new volume, *Drawdown: The most comprehensive plan ever proposed to reverse global warming*, gives businesses, cities, and people 100 different technologies and practices to "draw down" greenhouse gas levels in the atmosphere. When they tackle climate change, companies mostly talk about "mitigating" their environmental impact and slowing their rate of emissions. A few make bold promises to reach net-zero emissions—in, say, 10, 20, or more years. Hawken takes exception to this approach, "If we're going in the wrong direction, why would we want to slow down in the wrong direction? Why wouldn't we stop and turn it around?"[6]

Have you seen buildings that combat air pollution? The façade of apartment block 570 Broome in New York City is covered in Pureti's titanium dioxide nanoparticle treatment that reacts to ultraviolet rays from the sun and converts air pollution and grime into non-toxic minerals and water vapor. Its impact is equivalent to taking 625 cars off the road. On a broader scale, shingle manufacturers are embedding 3M's titanium dioxide-coated roofing granules into roofing products that covert the nitrogen oxides in smog into harmless water-soluble ions, in effect cleaning the air!

Nature-Based Solutions Can Help to Heal the Planet. Interface carpets pioneered this frontier in industry by using biomimicry to develop environmentally friendly Cool Carpets. Now it is running its own "factory as a forest." The company takes account of the full ecology around its LaGrange, GA plant and measures and sets targets on carbon sequestered, water stored and purified, sediment retained, pollination supported, pollution detoxified, biodiversity supported, and soil fertility enhanced by the system. Next in the product space: Proof Positive (carbon-negative) carpet tiles that store more carbon in the tile and its backing than is emitted during the production process.

The Nature-based Solutions Initiative at the University of Oxford catalogs restoration and regeneration efforts on farmlands, coastlines, and urban areas. Projects studied include tree planting, peatland restoration, and regenerative livestock grazing in forested areas in the Scottish Highlands, and the reconversion of portions of farming fields into grasslands to combat soil erosion and flooding in the South Downs of England. The Wild West End in London has brought together a coalition of partners including the real-estate developer Crown Estate and design firm Arup to connect London's green spaces through infrastructure including green roofs, living walls, planters, street trees, and flower boxes. The aim is to attract birds, bees, and bats back to the UK capital. Nearby, the Portman Estate in the Marylebone area has seen hundreds of Georgian buildings retrofitted for energy efficiency to create homes and offices that fit modern-day sensibilities but preserve historic architecture.

The Future Is a Green and Blue Economy. FTSE Russell estimates revenues for companies operating in the green economy at $4.3 trillion globally in 2021.[7] This sector is expected to grow fast, outperform the rest of the economy, and create upwards of 25 million jobs by 2030. The value of goods and services provided by the blue economy, the planet's oceans, is estimated at $2.5 trillion globally.[8] This sector is expected to grow fast, too, but much investment will be directed at cleaning up marine plastic pollution, repairing deltas, mangroves, salt marshes, and coral reefs, and protecting wild and farmed fisheries. Expect a boom in the use of micro and macro algae for carbon sequestration and renewable energy.

Blue entrepreneurs are leading social change here. You may have heard the story of Florida surfers Andrew Cooper and Alex Schulze, who embarked on a post-college surfing trip to Bali and found the beaches buried in plastic garbage. Their shock led them to found 4Ocean, a for-profit business that pulls plastic and glass waste from oceans around the world and repurposes it by making bracelets out of those recycled materials. 4Ocean sells each bracelet for $20 with the promise that the money from each purchase will fund one pound of trash removal. To date the company has pulled eight million tons of plastic from the sea. You can also find recycled ocean plastic in sunglasses (Norton Point), denim jeans (G-Star Raw), and sneakers (Adidas). GreenWave is pioneering regenerative ocean farming using a mix of seaweeds and shellfish with zero inputs—no freshwater, fertilizers, or feed. Their aquatic farms sequester carbon, provide storm surge protection, and rebuild marine ecosystems. Anyone with 20 ocean acres, a boat, and $20–50K can start their own farm.

People Want to Live a Greener Life and Want Companies to Help Them Do So. We've shown you that green consumers want to buy products from companies that protect the environment and will boycott those who harm it. It seems that the pandemic has sped up an "eco-awakening," with over half of all global consumers saying they are more health- and environmentally conscious in its aftermath.[9] In 2021, 73 percent of people globally said they want to reduce their impact on the environment and nature by a "large amount"—up from 63 percent just one year prior. How can they reduce their impact? Here's what people say they can do: 1) reduce energy and save water in my household; 2) recycle materials and resell/donate used products; 3) repair broken products; and 4) generate or buy renewable energy (if possible). Large majorities also say they would like to minimize their negative impact on the environment when traveling and choose environmentally friendly hotels and accommodations.[10] Can companies help them live greener lives?

A 2000 survey found that consumers based their perceptions of a green brand on the color of its packaging and logo and "healthy" or "natural" messaging. Today nearly half want products in biodegradable or recyclable packaging, with traceable and transparent origins, and with certification of their social and environmental bona fides.[11] Expectations continue to rise, as consumers also want companies to help them live healthier and greener lives. Two thrusts are underway: educating consumers about eco-living, and making it easy for them to practice it. A quick example of making it easy: reverse vending machines that accept used (empty) beverage containers and return money to the user in places that have mandatory recycling laws or container deposit laws.

STRESS TEST: RATE YOUR COMPANY'S GREEN AGENDA

Think about your own company: Is it a "plunderer of the earth" or a protector? Does it have sustainability targets? Does it take steps to "green" its offices and operations? Do employees have a chance to participate in environmental initiatives—in the organization? In communities? Does your company provide eco-friendly products or services?

CHECKLIST 9.1

Planet: Do we protect and restore the natural environment with our business?

To what extent....   1 = Not at all   5 = To a great extent

	1	2	3	4	5
1. Does your company have environmental goals for reducing waste and emissions?	☐	☐	☐	☐	☐
2. Does your company have environmental programs to recycle, reduce energy use, and protect water quality?	☐	☐	☐	☐	☐
3. Do employees have a chance to improve the natural environment on their jobs or through green teams/ projects?	☐	☐	☐	☐	☐
4. Does top management take good environmental performance seriously?	☐	☐	☐	☐	☐
5. Does your company measure and report on its environmental performance?	☐	☐	☐	☐	☐
6. Does your company make an effort to improve the natural environment in communities where it does business?	☐	☐	☐	☐	☐

OK: 25 or above—good; 12–24—needs work; below that—fix things, fast What does it take to move forward on greening? Getting employees and customers involved, producing eco-friendly products and services, and joining up with social entrepreneurs, other businesses, and government to care for the planet.

Three New Ways to Think About the Planet and Humanity

As nations and companies strive to reduce greenhouse gas emissions, policy makers, business, and the public also focus on the full roster of environmental impacts: ocean acidification, biodiversity loss, chemical and air pollution, freshwater loss, desertification and land conversion, and so on. Many big companies measure, monitor, and report on their impacts in these areas, too. How about your firm? Attention is turning to the relationship between the state of the environment and people's economic and social well-being. Here matters like access to food, water, housing, and energy come to the fore as well as inequities as to who has more or less access—and at what price. This extends into the political domain as well—who has influence over national policy and regulation and what will it take to effect change? Consider three new ways to think about all of this—and to take action.

Doughnut Economics. In 2012, Kate Raworth set the stage for Rio +20 UN summit on Sustainable Development when she presented a visual framework—shaped like a doughnut—which brings planetary boundaries together with social boundaries and highlights a safe space between the two in which humanity can thrive. Outside the doughnut, humans overshoot an "ecological ceiling" and the earth's carrying capacities for human life. Inside the doughnuts are shortfalls that threaten the social foundations of our collective existence. Her popular book, *Doughnut Economics: Seven ways to think like a 21st-century economist*, details seven strategies to achieve a "regenerative and distributive economy."[12]

Who's putting doughnut economics into practice? Professors and school-teachers are using it in the classroom; urban planners in Amsterdam, Stockholm, and KwaZulu Natal are designing "Doughnut Districts" in their cities; and community groups worldwide have hosted Doughnut Hackathons and invented Doughnut board and digital games. Pioneering businesses and B Corps are assessing their social and environmental performance against the Doughnut's dimensions. Want to know more? Check out the Doughnut Economics Action Lab where there are resources, case studies, and opportunities to work with communities and other businesses on putting your business into the doughnut.[13]

Net Positive. Jeffrey Hollander, founder of Seventh Generation, speaks of movement toward "net positive" in this way:

> As individuals and organizations, we need a new vision of the future—a vision
> driven by what we want rather than what we want to avoid, what we aspire to

rather than what we seek to prevent, what is good for "we" rather than "me." We should base decisions on what will be best for tomorrow, not just today [...] In the net positive framework, "good" means regenerative: providing restorative and positive impacts on people, planet, and society.[14]

The Net Positive movement was launched in 2013 by London's Forum for the Future, The Climate Group, and WWF who enlisted several companies for "beta" tests. We've seen IKEA's agenda; what are other companies doing?

- Berlin-based Dycle makes a 100 percent biodegradable diaper that is collected after use at community meeting points and composted to create terra preta, a fertile black soil found in rainforests that supercharges the growth of trees and plants.

- European home improvement company Kingfisher has new "Connect to Nature" and "Healthy Home" products that enable a 50 percent reduction in customers' energy use and a 50 percent improvement in their water efficiency.

- Computer company Dell is using plastics from used electronics in over 250 of its new products and recycles gold from old motherboards into new ones. It has set an ambitious 10x20 Goal to create 10 times the amount of "good" through technology compared to the footprint it creates.

- Fetzer Vineyards installed a new wastewater treatment system that uses worms and microbes to naturally clean its wastewater for use in irrigating its vineyards. The winery harvests the system's worm castings for use as an on-site fertilizer.

Flourishing. John Erhenfeld set the bar even higher in his call for business and society to move from sustainability to "flourishing"—"the possibility that humans and other life will flourish on earth forever."[15] Flourishing, as currently expressed, is more of a mindset than methodology. It involves "whole brain" thinking, living with rather than against nature, and being committed to designing a greener future. One company we visited exemplifies all three. California's Tablas Creek Vineyard became the first Regenerative Organic Certified™ (ROC) vineyard in the US in 2020. Relying on nature-based models, it uses its herd of 250 sheep for soil fertility and perennial gardens for pest management. It also does not till the ground between vine rows, thus maintaining the soil's microbial life, reducing the need for irrigation, and providing for carbon sequestration. On the social side, ROC certification requires companies to pay workers a living wage, provide safe working conditions, and give them a say in work-related decisions. As for other pioneers, energy company Anesco is collaborating with Europe's largest nature conservation group to enhance biodiversity at solar farms. Tiger Beer is working with Gravity Labs, an Indian startup, to capture vehicle emissions and transform them into ink. The ink has been used to create artworks in cities that call attention to the problems of urban pollution.

Doughnut economics, net positive, and the move to flourishing all shift our thinking beyond sustainability to something more. Figure 9.1 presents the array of frameworks and tools that companies use to care for the planet. Which ones does your company use? Let's now see how regenerative and restorative practices can be put to work in your business.

How to Green Your Business

No doubt your company is doing something to reduce its environmental impact and mitigate the effects of climate change. In previous decades, many businesses have taken steps to lower their CO_2 emissions and apply the 3Rs (reduce, reuse, recycle) to cut back on waste. Progress is undeniable but the general consensus is that it is "not enough" and companies will have to "pick up the pace" to meet the Intergovernmental Panel on Climate Change target of cutting emissions in half by 2030 (from a 2010 baseline) to avoid the worst consequences.[16] What's on the agenda?

Green Your Buildings. Over a decade ago, a group of 40 eBay employees in San Jose formed a green team to promote sustainable business practices in the company. This scaled to over 3,000 employees in more than 20 countries in three years. Green teams were a driving force in the construction of eBay's

FIGURE 9.1 Frameworks to Care for the Planet

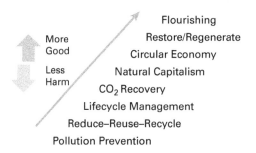

corporate headquarters, "Mint," the first building built to LEED Gold Standards in San Jose, CA, which also features the city's largest solar panel installation. Soon 100,000 customers and sellers joined employees in green teams and traded knowhow on sustainable packaging, waste reduction, and carbon-neutral shipping. With its focus on selling pre-owned products (about 16 percent of eBay's revenues), the company now promotes itself as the sustainable alternative to Amazon.

Green Your Products. Many startups go green from the get-go. Michael Baker, founder and CEO of SOLE, in Great Falls, Montana, suffered a back injury that caused the full-bearded Canadian adventure-seeker to recognize a market need: affordable and eco-friendly orthotics. He launched SOLE to make heat-moldable, over-the-counter orthotics that are produced from recycled wine corks. To ensure its supply chain, the company founded ReCORK, a wine cork recycling program that, to date, has recycled 100 million wine corks, working with wine retailers and public collection partners. Want more? Austin-based startup GrubTubs repurposes food waste from restaurants and grocery stores to create a nutrient-rich, affordable animal feed for local farms. Looptworks reuses and repurposes other companies' waste. It turns the worn-out seat leather from Southwest Airlines planes into soccer balls and turns Alaska Airlines' used seats into handbags and purses.

Green Your Supply Chain. Nestlé is working with over 500,000 farmers and 150,000 suppliers to enable them to implement "regenerative" agriculture practices that improve soil health and maintain and restore diverse ecosystems. In return, Nestlé rewards farmers by purchasing their goods at a premium, buying bigger quantities, and co-investing in needed capital expenditures. Cereal maker General Mills vows that it will have regenerative agriculture in place on a million acres of North American farmland that supply oats and other grains to its factories. The company worked with the Nature Conservancy, the Soil Health Institute, and the Soil Health Partnership to develop a road map for farmers. It has its farmers reduce tilling, increase crop diversity, keep the soil covered year-round, plant cover crops in winter to maintain living roots in the ground, and reintegrate livestock into the landscape. Among the projected benefits are greater soil fertility, more carbon sequestration, strengthened water-holding capacity (and drought resistance), better water quality, reduced runoff, less need for pesticides and herbicides, better biodiversity above and below the soil, and, according to experts, a slightly reduced yield, but higher profit per acre.[17]

How to Green Your Employees (and Yourself)

People score low on environmental literacy and those in the United States are among the least literate in the world. A study by the Yale Project on Climate gave 50 percent of the US population a grade of F on their knowledge about climate change and another 40 percent scored a D or C.[18] Fewer than six in ten knew about the greenhouse effect; just 45 percent understood that carbon dioxide traps heat from the earth's surface; and only 25 percent had ever heard of coral bleaching or ocean acidification. The study also found that only half of the public understand that global warming is caused mostly by human activities. However, this may not reflect misunderstanding but instead religious and political beliefs: as of 2020, the US has the largest percentage of "climate deniers" in the world.

Businesses have stepped into the education gap. According to survey research by the National Environmental Education Foundation, 73 percent of US respondents said that their company is educating employees across the organization about corporate sustainability goals.[19] As an example, Stonyfield Yogurt keys its education around "Mission in Action" projects where employees participate in one or more teams to improve the company's environmental performance and get "just in time" training on, say, the company's carbon footprint, water use, waste, or specific impacts that pertain to their mission. New hires spend a day or more working on a dairy farm to learn the business and organic agriculture. This kind of hands-on exposure to environmental impacts is a great way to sensitize employees to the issues.

Hands-On Engagement. Green teams are common nowadays in businesses of all types and throughout education from kindergarten through college. In many businesses, the teams not only green their business, they also have community-oriented environmental improvement projects. Does your company have a green team? If not, start one. There are plenty of how-to guides and videos. Here are some keys to the success of green teams in companies: 1) enlist people with a passion for nature; 2) educate them about the environmental impact of your business; 3) provide the teams with high-level organizational support and an executive champion; and 4) develop measurable targets and get feedback on results.

Timberland has green teams throughout its business and enlists its most ardent and able "Earthkeepers" as Global Stewards to run service-learning programs for staff. Recent projects had the stewards mobilize hundreds of employees to create an urban green space in Philadelphia's Rail Park and a community garden in the Bronx; run an incubator to train organic farmers; and join in a company-wide effort to plant 50 million trees from 2019 to 2023, including "The Great Green Wall"—an 8,000 km line of trees across the entire width of Africa to fight climate change, drought, famine, conflict, and migration. The Global Stewards meet annually to define their personal purposes and goals, share best practices and key learnings, and welcome and socialize new members.

Dow Corning sponsors employee service on a global scale. A team of 10 from Dow Corning Citizen Service Corps went to Bangalore, India to develop renewable energy products for rural housing. Describing the assignment, Ronda Grosse, from the United States, blogged:

> We interviewed urban planners, developers, architects, engineers, citizen sector organizations and university scholars in order to gain insight into affordable housing needs in India. And we spent time talking with families living in slums and other low-income communities, allowing us to gain deeper insights into their daily lives and challenges.

When confronting technical challenges, the Dow team emailed, blogged, and tweeted ideas with scientists and engineers back home, bringing the expertise of not just 10 but hundreds of fellow employees to their mission.

Eco-Innovation Contests and Awards. Intel uses an annual contest and Environmental Excellence Awards to recognize employees or employee groups that have created an eco-innovation. In 2018, a team of employees developed a 24/7 micro-climate monitoring system that covers 20 times more locations per zone than traditional air quality monitors, and offers significant improvements in cost, size, coverage, and power consumption. The solution was deployed at Intel sites in Arizona and India. In 2019, another team developed a more eco-friendly way to ship silicon wafers. Replacing front-opening shipping boxes with new smaller, horizontal shippers provides better protection for wafers while reducing freight and materials costs and environmental impact from fuel and materials consumption. The team also replaced previously used packaging foam with a recyclable material.

Awards are also given to employees who innovate for society. Two Intel employees in 2019 operated a nonprofit called Outside2Inside (O2I), which recovers thousands of pounds of "wonky produce" that would otherwise be discarded. O2I donates the produce to low-income families and schools, thereby reducing food waste through awareness and food recovery while also lowering waste to landfill and water and carbon emissions associated with food production and disposal.

Strategies to Heal the Planet

Companies that we have studied have three strategies to help heal the planet: 1) conserve and restore nature, 2) repair and rebuild, and 3) invest in a greener future. Consider these examples:

Conserve and Restore. McKinsey & Co. make a compelling case for nature conservation. We can reduce atmospheric CO_2 by up to 2.2 gigatons annually by avoiding deforestation and promoting natural forest regrowth. We also reduce the risks of zoonotic diseases (like the coronavirus) by curbing human encroachment on nature. To reduce the erosion of natural capital, scientists and policy makers have called for the permanent conservation of at least 30 percent of the planet's surface by 2030, nearly doubling nature conservation on land and in national waters. Yes, this will be costly but it could create over half a million new jobs in conservation management and be a boon to eco-tourism and sustainable fishing.[20]

Historically, companies involved in forestry and fishing, mining and drilling, construction, and agriculture have had horrific environmental records—as Ray Anderson names them: "plunderers of the earth." Well, some of these firms have turned to restoration. Forestry company Weyerhaeuser says that 100 percent of its timberland has been certified by the Sustainable Forestry Initiative. This certification covers protection of biodiversity, species at risk, and wildlife habitat; protection of water quality; and sustainable harvesting and prompt regeneration. The company reports that it harvests only 2 percent of its forests each year and plants over 150 million trees annually. The National Mining Association reports that, since 1978, more than 2.8 million acres of mined lands in the United States have been restored for wildlife and wetlands, recreation areas, economic development parks, farms, golf courses, and the like. The Pittsburgh Botanical Garden sits atop over 400 acres of land despoiled by coal mining. Four streams on the site were seriously polluted with acid mine discharge; a private–public partnership removed the mine, reclaimed the site, reduced pH levels in the water, and now 111 different species of birds flock to the Garden as a result of remediation and restoration.

Repair and Rebuild. When Bill Ford took over as head of Ford Motor Co. in 1988, "I was told to stop associating with any known or suspected environmentalist." Instead, he led a $2 billion renovation of the River Rouge plant that turned it from a hellhole into one of the most eco-friendly production facilities in the world (capped by a 10.4-acre "living" green roof); Ford also created a renewable energy park, and oversaw the launch of hybrid cars and, most recently, an all-electric Mustang. Henry Ford II tore up a section of Detroit riverfront in the 1970s to build seven interconnected skyscrapers, the Renaissance Center, later abandoned by Ford and taken over by General Motors. His nephew Bill is instead making a net positive investment in the city, restoring Detroit's Central Train Station and several factories in the Corktown area of town. Over 2,500 Ford employees will work there in a couple of years.

Invest in a Greener Future. Today nearly 1,500 self-driving cars, trucks, and other vehicles are in testing at more than 80 companies across the United States. This portends a future of less car ownership, more ride sharing, fewer accidents, and congestion-free driving because autonomous cars could be programmed to interact with other cars to make routes more efficient. Self-driving cars could also drive close together in "packs" to reduce air resistance and potentially reduce vehicle energy consumption by as much as 25 percent. Tesla's Powerwall 2, a battery that stores excess solar energy and makes it available on demand, is being installed in 50,000 homes in South Australia, which would create the biggest virtual power plant in the world. From 2010–2020, more than two million residential solar panels were installed in the United States. How soon before we share our solar power with one another? Other advances include bio-based plastics, products designed via biomimicry, foods made from mycoproteins and insects, software and apps that manage energy use, waste gasification technology, and on and on. Are any of these technologies and applications in use in your company?

Eco-Innovation

Researchers at MIT make a distinction between sustainability-oriented versus sustainability-driven innovations where progressively more attention is given to an innovation's ecological benefits.[21] What does a sustainability-driven innovation look like? Sanergy is an MIT spinoff established to solve sanitation problems in the developing world. Knowing that nearly eight million people in Kenyan slums lack access to proper sanitation, the Sanergy team used $25,000 from the MIT Public Service Center to develop a circular solution to human waste management.

Sanergy builds low-cost toilet units and sells them to local entrepreneurs who become franchise partners. The franchisees maintain the unit and in exchange earn an income by charging for use of the toilet. Sanergy collects the waste at the end of every day and transports it to a centralized facility, where it's converted to energy and organic fertilizer. From there, Sanergy sells the fertilizer to local Kenyan farms at a far more reasonable price than the petrochemical-based alternatives available. As of 2020, the company provide "fresh lite" services to over 120,000 per day at a cost of $13 per person per year, with the government bearing $6 per person per year of that cost. This is five times cheaper than building sewers.

Carbontech. Technology is in place today that pulls CO_2 out of the air and uses it in the making of asphalt, cement, concrete, plastic, biofuels, and, as Interface is doing, floor tiles. The Carbon180 report projects a global market opportunity of over $5 trillion for companies that replace existing materials with those derived from captured carbon—in fuels ($3.82 trillion), building materials ($1.37 trillion), and plastics ($0.41 trillion).[22] RP Siegel, an engineer who writes for the GreenBiz Group, reports that San Francisco-based startup, Mango Materials, is making bioplastic from methane gas. The company's production plant is co-located with a methane producer so that the feedstock is directly pumped in instead of being vented into the atmosphere. Meanwhile, UBQ is making thermoplastics — polymers that soften when heated and harden when cooled — from municipal solid waste.[23]

Cleantech. The Cleantech Group monitors industry developments in cleantech and publishes an annual list of the top 100 companies to watch and invest in. The Innovation Group of J Walter Thompson tracks trends in the "new" sustainability through consumer surveys and analyses of regenerative eco-innovations.[24] Is cleantech relevant to your business?

CLEANTECH

- **3D printing** is used in food, fashion, and a vast range of materials, often using recycled plastics or organic waste. The Million Waves Project has turned ocean plastic waste into 3D-printed prostheses; Spanish brand Nagami features 3D-printed chairs; the Netherlands has a 3D-printed steel bridge; and Texan startup Icon 3D-printed a single-story home from cement in less than 24 hours for only $10,000. The home produces almost zero waste and is energy efficient to run.

- **Smart technologies**—ranging from AI and apps to sensors and satellites—are used to monitor and manage energy use, plan transportation and logistics, reduce waste, and help to decarbonize emissions. Energy customers can use apps to monitor their energy consumption and providers can assist them with data-based guidance. In service of reforestation, BioCarbon Engineering uses drones to plant trees. Sensors aboard a fixed-wing drone observe ground topography, biodiversity, and obstructions to create an optimized planting pattern. A planting drone that can cover a hectare in 18 minutes deploys 300 biodegradable seedpods, and then monitors growth.

- **Fintech** is used by the Scandinavian bank Ålandsbanken to track the environmental impact of each of your credit card transactions. China's online payment giant Alipay teamed up with Ant Financial Services Group to enable users to track their eco-friendly activities, such as paying bills online, to earn virtual "green energy" points and grow virtual trees. Once users earn enough points, Ant Financial plants a real tree.

- **Bio-based ingredients and processes** are big in foods—for animals and humans—as we saw in the prior chapter. Zoa bioleather, created by Modern Meadow, replaces leather with collagen produced by a gene-edited yeast. Checkerspot designs and manufactures high-performance materials and launched skis made from a high-density composite derived from microalgae polyol.

Partnerships for the Planet

Sustainability professionals in business, government, NGOs, and academe believe that the best way to address planetary problems is through partnerships between businesses, NGOs, governments, and universities.[25] Today there are hundreds of global multi-business and multi-sector initiatives regarding climate change (alliances for carbon trading, energy conservation, and green IT) and natural resource stocks (partnerships around sustainable fish, water, agriculture, and food), plus thousands at regional, state, and local levels. Why so?

First, the challenges are complex and defy single-company solutions. Companies that join in these partnerships learn together the many dimensions of the problems they face and which practices do and do not address them effectively. Second, the problems typically extend beyond the corporate fenceline and potential solutions require expertise, resources, and buy-in from different sectors. Third, some solutions call for the development of standards of conduct, around, say, environmental impacts, resource preservation, and the like. No company alone can certify its practices and products—who would believe it?—so an independent, industry-wide or government certification is needed. Finally, sometimes solutions call for large-scale investment that can impact a company's bottom line. Having multiple businesses join in levels the competitive playing field and ensures there are no "free riders."

Take the Marine Stewardship Council (MSC), an association of fisheries and food companies formed to deal with preservation of seafood stocks following the collapse of fishing in the North Atlantic. From 2010 to 2020, the percentage of the world's marine wild fish caught with MSC certification increased from 6 percent to nearly 20 percent. Go to a store and see the blue MSC label at the fish counter. As a result of this partnership, and other efforts, researchers now report that over half of the world's fish stock is recovered—or increasing—in oceans that used to be overfished.[26]

The story is less sanguine when it comes to deforestation for palm oil production. The Roundtable on Responsible Palm Oil certifies some 19 percent of the palm oil harvested worldwide. Studies show that certification has reduced deforestation by 33 percent in Indonesia, a major producer, but nevertheless its overall forest cover continues to decline and orangutan habitats and biodiversity are threatened.[27] Close the plantations? Over five million small farmers harvest palm oil in Indonesia and their livelihoods depend on it. So companies like Unilever and Pepsi now trace the sources of their supply to 1,500 or so palm oil mills that are committed to natural habitat conservation and no deforestation.

Could your company benefit from joining in green partnerships in your community, region, nation, or even the world? We'll look at how some of these partnerships effect systemic social change in the next chapter. Before turning to it, consider some planetary challenges up ahead.

Challenges on the Horizon

There you have it: your company *can* help to restore and regenerate the planet. But there are some issues that need thoughtful attention as you develop a way forward.

The Degrowth Movement. Amidst widespread criticism of global capitalism and the threats of climate change, a "degrowth" movement has taken shape. Research and Degrowth, an academic association dedicated to research and awareness-raising about the topic, defines degrowth as a "downscaling of production and consumption that increases human wellbeing and enhances ecological conditions and equity on the planet."[28] The idea has spread from the margins to mainstream economic and political discourse. Proponents make a case for degrowth because GDP is a poor predictor of "National Happiness," the earth cannot sustain current rates of global growth, and the inequities that result from unchecked growth portend ever more political polarization and popular unrest. What alternatives do they propose?

In *Prosperity Without Growth: Foundations for the economy of tomorrow*, Tim Jackson, a professor of sustainable development at the University of Surrey, in England, frames the situation this way: "Questioning growth is deemed to be the act of lunatics, idealists and revolutionaries. But question it we must."[29] He recommends a shift toward less resource-intensive service, rather than product-based business, and operating within a more localized economy (à la Judy Wicks!). Others point to the practical examples of industrial cooperatives like Israeli kibbutzim, Spain's Mondragon, and Italian Solidarity Economy Networks, or B-Corps that prioritize their mission and values over profit growth and market share. As for the political implications, degrowth options include a more highly regulated type of capitalism, planned socialism, or an economy where companies along with consumers, investors, employees and executives are committed only to sustainable long-term growth. Where do you stand on these three options?

White Skies. Elizabeth Kolbert's latest book, *Under a White Sky: The nature of the future*, is a cautionary tale.[30] It's about how humans mold nature to their purposes and then face unexpected and undesirable consequences. It begins with an account of how the diversion of a river in Chicago created a hospitable routing for invasive silver carp to enter the Great Lakes and threaten to destroy the indigenous fish population. Solution: set up fish gates in the river and electrocute the carp! Then we tour the Mississippi Delta where the mighty river has been dammed and diverted and polluted by oil and gas drilling to the point that coastal communities are routinely flooded with toxic waters and New Orleans is sinking into the sea. The book finishes with a look at how solar geoengineering is being applied to save drought-stricken lands and bleached coral seas from global warming. This has geoengineers inject particles into the atmosphere to reflect sunlight back into space, cooling the planet. Major drawback: the resulting haze turns the color of the sky from blue to white.

In a 2015 TED talk, Microsoft co-founder turned healthcare expert Bill Gates warned that a virus-like 1918 Spanish flu would spread "very quickly" around the world. He went on to say, "We've actually invested very little in a system to stop an epidemic," adding, "We're not ready for the next epidemic." He has now added urgency to our survival in *How to Avoid a Climate Disaster*. It is an optimistic, can-do sort of book, full of ideas on the "solutions we have and breakthroughs we need."[31] Many opine that the development of Covid vaccines demonstrated (once again!) our human ingenuity and capacities to devise a technological "fix" for the challenges posed by nature. Kolbert's message about the white sky reminds us of the second-order consequences of relying exclusively on technology to solve our problems.

A Whole of Society Approach

How we handle climate change will be determined by interests and forces beyond the scope of any business and all of them. Andy Hoffman makes a compelling case for a whole of society approach that has government activating citizens and businesses enlisting their employees and consumers in the challenge of our times. He writes:

> If it's only corporations, it's going to be driven by money, and it will not focus on the core of the issue. If it's only technologists, it's only going to be driven by technology, and the result will be equally inadequate. But if it's a full Re-enlightenment, then religious values, community, education, technologies and corporations all have a role to play.[32]

This is a call for systemic social change—the subject we address in our final chapter.

10

Collaborate For Systemic Social Change

We first met Denmark's Lisa Kingo in 2000 when she was an EVP at Novo Nordisk where she led several company units and its overall sustainability effort. Thereafter she became a guiding force in the development of the Sustainable Development Goals (SDGs) and in 2015 was named Executive Director of the UN's Global Compact (UNGC), an association of over 13,000 companies across 160 countries that have committed to universal principles on human rights, labor, environment, and anti-corruption. The UNGC's mission: change the way the world does business and, with Lisa's doings, focus companies' energies on achieving the SDGs.

Joining the UNGC involves more than making a commitment to principles and leaving it at that. The Compact requires member companies to report on their social and environmental performance annually and publishes the findings on its website. It delists those who don't report—no measurement, no membership—and has over the years dropped 600 companies from its ranks. We've been engaged with the UNGC since it was established in 1999 by then-UN Secretary-General Kofi Annan, who launched it this way: "I propose that you, the business leaders, and we, the United Nations, initiate a global compact of shared values and principles which will give a human face to the global market." From 2002 onward we worked alongside Spain's Manuel Escudero to help establish Principles for Responsible Management Education and enlist business schools globally to tilt their curricula and research toward responsible business management. Another initiative with our Global Network on Corporate Citizenship was to create a forum where leading UNGC companies could together assess their experiences and lessons learned in moving toward a more responsible business model.

The launch of the SDGs was supposed to be a "game changer" for business. Some background: the UN set the original Millennium Development Goals (MDGs) in 2000 using a top-down approach with the idea that UN member national governments would spearhead progress toward them. By contrast, the SDGs were created through a large participatory process as 10 million people worldwide expressed their views on global goals, and business and civil society organizations had several seats at the convening table. An initial list of about 300 proposed goals was negotiated, prioritized, and aggregated over three years and by 2015 winnowed to 17 goals. Goal #17 set a new agenda for taking action on the SDGs via local, regional, and global partnerships.

But when Lisa became head of the UNGC, she sounded an alarm on the SDGs: "Despite real progress being made by the business community, there is clear recognition that action is not measuring up to the size of the challenge."[1] Accordingly, she set up a "Making Global Goals Local Business" campaign to motivate and make it easier for UNGC members to take up the goals. Leveraging Goal 17, she and her team facilitated the creation of more than 4,000 multi-party SDG partnerships in Global Compact Local Networks. Next, taking a page from social innovators, her team launched accelerator labs where companies could incubate initiatives focused on gender equality, climate change, and integrating the overall SDGs into their businesses. Then came a lab for young SDG innovators and a partnership with the B Lab to develop the SDG Action Manager, an interactive software program that enables B Corps and small businesses to link their practices to the SDGs, measure and report on progress, and network with similarly motivated companies. Finally, there was outreach to the investment community to fund work on the SDGs, recruitment of leading CFOs in a task force to align company financing with the SDGs, and the launch of an annual award for SDG pioneers.

Takeaway: Lisa successfully transformed the UNGC from a membership body into a partnership for collective action.

Go Big or Go Home

Chapters 5 through 9 detailed five big problems facing business in the swirl of social change, highlighted new ways of thinking about solutions to these problems, and showed you concrete actions that entrepreneurs, small and midsize companies, and progressive large firms are taking to address them.

Here's the worry: 10 years from now it will be apparent that these efforts, even those well-conceived and ably executed, will be seen as good, but not good enough. Why so? A one-company by one-company approach is not sufficient. Complex problems call for complex solutions and organizations from different industries and sectors bring unique and essential assets to the work of social change. Recognition of this is leading to collective advocacy and action and to collaboration within and across the sectors to solve societal and ecological problems.

Big companies we've studied such as IKEA, Nike, Natura, PepsiCo, SAS, SAP, and Unilever have joined in many of these efforts—sometimes as an ally but often as a roll-up-your-sleeves partner. Smaller ones partner too, whether with the B Corps community, in one or more social issue partnerships, or in grassroots groups such as the Business Alliance for Local Living Economies. In the logic of the handprint, several or all of the five Ps (purpose, prosperity, people, products, and planet) are in play with systemic social change, and you are now reaching out to other hands (e.g., the company handshake!). So how about your business: *Is your company a member of any alliances, coalitions, and/or partnerships that aim to solve social problems and advance social change?*

This final chapter looks at the rationale for and impact of partnerships geared to promoting systemic social change. It then examines what leading companies are doing by 1) joining up with NGOs and social entrepreneurs to produce solutions to complex social problems; 2) starting or joining multi-company or multi-sector efforts to effect system-wide social changes; and 3) shaping public policy and public opinion to make a better future.

The Role of Business Amidst Social Change

It is clear to business that its role in society has to change. Widening unease has provoked a series of incremental remedies that, while good in their intentions and outcomes, are not good enough to create the type of systemic changes needed to address today's social and environmental challenges, let alone those of tomorrow. The issues we've raised about purpose, prosperity, people, products, and the planet are not unfamiliar to businesspeople today and they are surely on the agenda of CEOs and boardrooms across the globe. What isn't so clear is what a company and business overall should do about tackling all of them.

The intractable issues of our time cannot find real solutions without a new alignment of the social contract. Business, operating amidst weakened public institutions and supporting civil society organizations with its philanthropy, can no longer stay in its own lane, tend solely to its own interests, write some checks, and rely on other sectors and interests to care for society writ large and the planet. Moments like business is now facing are not unknown or without precedent. Joseph Schumpeter wrote of the "gale of creative destruction" to describe the "process of industrial mutation that continuously revolutionizes the economic structure from within, incessantly destroying the old one, incessantly creating a new one."[2]

We've seen throughout this volume new theories and models for repurposing business, getting to a fair and inclusive economy, treating people as full human beings, putting societal impact into products and services, and restoring the health of the planet. To accomplish all of this at scale, a new kind of capitalism must take hold in which businesses, NGOs, and governments worldwide work together to address global health, climate change, and equitable growth. What about you and your company? Are you ready to step up your efforts and work with other organizations to tackle the grand challenges we face? Here are some "shifts" required to effect systemic social change.

Business and Its Leaders Need a New "Mindset" to Lead Social Change. Derrick Feldmann and Michael Alberg-Seberich make a persuasive case for this in *The Corporate Social Mind*, which contends that a business leader needs to "keep society on your mind" to "lead social change from the inside out."[3] One indicator of this new mindset is that socially conscious start-ups and future-forward businesses take a holistic view that considers not only their relationships with specific stakeholders but to society as a whole. A second sign is that these companies tune in to emerging social issues early and are unafraid of advocating for social change and "doing the right thing." A third is that many of their leaders embrace the tenets of positive leadership and conscious capitalism. They care about the world we live in and say so in internal discussions and public forums. And they focus their companies' assets and attention on doing business for the common good.

Social change-leading companies take an "all in" approach that has them activate their people, customers, and other stakeholders to co-create a better future. Scholars tell us that their socially conscious leaders set problems into their systemic context and use the "whole brain" to look for creative solutions.[4] New goals and measures, like social value creation and social impact assessments, figure into their companies' strategies and performance scorecards. Some even have a CPO (Chief Purpose Officer). But the real test of authenticity is when social value creation is led from the boardroom, not the marketing department.

The Next Big Shift: From Shared Value to Collective Action. Our colleague Jane Nelson, Director of the Corporate Responsibility Initiative at Harvard's Kennedy School, has been a longtime advocate of multi-stakeholder and -sector approaches to problem solving and has worked with the UNGC, World Economic Forum, World Business Council for Sustainable Development, and countless governments, NGOs, and companies to set them up and monitor their impact. She reports that multisector efforts are moving beyond creating standards, making pledges, and setting goals. Collective action, she contends, is the "only way" we can effectively address climate change, corruption, and equitable development in the world.[5]

Multi-party alliances and partnerships enable organizations to perform tasks and achieve goals that are too costly or complicated for a single organization to do on its own. In the commercial arena, companies regularly work with other businesses in their supply chains and distribution systems, in shared R&D and product development, in co-marketing and social media promotions, in delivering customer solutions, and some join forces in mergers and acquisitions. One of us edited a volume of case studies of multi-party collaboration in the social and environmental arena that highlighted several "collaborative advantages" to organizations that work together. Specifically, partnerships can enable them to:

- forge relationships that transcend the perspective of a single organization and address multiple stakeholders' interests;
- combine resources and diverse expertise to tackle complex problems;
- spread the costs and risks of investment and innovation;
- increase trust and reduce transaction costs between differing interests;
- help common interests to enlarge and conflicting parties to cooperate;
- open new market opportunities; and
- scale solutions to effect systemic social change.[6]

Self-interest, competition, and profit seeking by firms can, under the right conditions, contribute to innovation and wealth creation. But collective interests, cooperation, and social value creation are needed when it comes to the successful operation of multi-organization partnerships focused on meeting society's needs.

Systemic Social Change is Hard. Effecting systemic social change involves "a systemic transformation, over time, in patterns of thoughts, behavior, social relationships, institutions and social structure… it is complex, uncertain and dynamic."[7] The approach and practices that companies use to build and transform themselves (as described in Chapter 4) apply to systemic social change with three amendments: 1) multiple organizations are working together to build and/or transform; 2) complexities are compounded because systemic problems have interlocking causes and require multi-faceted solutions; and 3) power differences, resource limitations, mistrust, and many other barriers to change are magnified in multi-party efforts which can lead to pseudo-cooperation, false starts, lagging energy and, ultimately, to defeat. What's involved in creating systemic change (see box)?

There are myriad theories and models of how to effect systemic social change. Sally Uren, Chief Executive of the UK's Forum for the Future, has devised one aimed at collaborative ventures. Key components include: 1) *engagement* and *collaboration* to bring relevant actors together; 2) *capacity building* so that they have the knowledge and resources to look beyond the quick fix; 3) *catalytic action* "which means you design some change and then that change in and of its own right sparks further change in the system"; and 4) continuous *adaptation, reinforcement*, and *learning*.[8] Certainly Lisa Kingo's systemic change efforts to activate the SDGs in business features each of them and more.

WHAT'S INVOLVED IN CREATING SYSTEMIC SOCIAL CHANGE?

Our research has identified some key characteristics of successful systemic social change efforts that differentiate them from traditional philanthropic, CSR, and sustainability projects of companies:

1 **360° Engagement.** To effect systemic social change, companies work with a full range of relevant interests to understand a social problem and develop a shared perspective on its causes and action implications. This often

requires outreach from a firm beyond its traditional stakeholder network and means engaging people and interests that may have different viewpoints on the problem at hand and how to best address it.

2 **Activism and Advocacy.** Systemic social change immerses business in the maelstrom of politics and the issues of the day—in the immediate circle of relevant actors and interests and the distal realm of local, national, even global divisions. It takes patience and persistence to build a coalition, find the "right" partners, and gain entry to an arena where your company's motives may be suspect and your involvement challenged.

3 **Collective Action.** Systemic social change is best effected through alliances, coalitions, and/or partnerships—a go-it-alone strategy isn't up to the challenge. Different parties need to be enlisted and coalesce around shared interests, develop deep working relationships, and operate as equal partners. Among businesses, this sometimes includes "coopetition" where competitors agree to cooperate in hopes of mutually beneficial results.

4 **Structure, Process, Deliverables.** Collaboration needs careful development and continuous reinforcement. A collaborative structure sets up roles and relationships; a management process establishes ground rules and methods for working together; and agreed-upon deliverables focus energy and attention on getting things done. Think project management, change management, and relationship management as interconnected streams of work.

5 **Disruption.** Partners that create systemic social change don't settle for "easy answers" or cosmetic changes. They disrupt the status quo and look for fresh, even "radical," solutions to overcome inertia and accelerate progress. Go for a "moonshot" yet stay grounded in the art of the possible.

6 **Social Innovation.** Systemic change requires infusing something "new" into the system. This can be an idea, technology, process, product, organization, or symbol that alters the existing patterns or replaces them. We've described many individual company social and eco-innovations that benefit business, society, and the planet. Systemic social change is all about collective impact and involves interactive value creation with users.

7 **Openness, Transparency, and Accountability.** Critics confound any effort to effect serious social change. Contempt, secrecy, and overpromising and underdelivering can lead to a feeding frenzy on social media. Instead, tell your story openly and fully, listen and respond to criticism, and document your progress (including missteps) factually, plainly, and honestly.

> **8 Scale.** Experiments, prototypes, demonstration projects, and small wins can
> be steps to systemic change, but the aim is to devise something new that
> can be scaled via replication, adaptation, and widespread use. Often this
> means adopters have to repeat the whole process outlined above but can
> learn from prior efforts, leverage successful ideas and tools, and move ahead
> with confidence that systemic social change is possible.

We Need to "Learn" to Create Social Change. Charles Darwin summed his views on evolution in this way: "In the long history of humankind (and animal kind, too) those who learned to collaborate and improvise most effectively have prevailed."[9] Peter Senge stimulated a revolution in business with his writings on mental models and systems thinking and his idea that organizational learning is key to success. He amplified all of this in *The Necessary Revolution: How individuals and organizations are working together to create a sustainable world*, where he points out that the world is full of smart people but the only way we can solve our massive problems is if we shed our particularistic assumptions and preferred solutions, combine our smarts, and learn together.[10]

Researchers who have studied and convened multi-party systemic change efforts emphasize that knowledge exchange and collective learning among parties are integral to successful system transformation.[11] What kinds of knowledge need to be shared and created in partnerships? For one, the parties need deep knowledge about the problem at hand and on-the-ground issues and conditions. Subject matter experts and non-business partners often have that knowledge ("know-what") and can work with the partners to conduct necessary indigenous research. Second, the parties need to develop "hands on" knowledge of potential levers for change and how this might affect the overall system. Partners typically develop this capability ("know-how") experientially through experimentation and demonstration projects before moving on to system-wide changes. Third, there is a need to engage those who will be implicated in or affected by change. These might be farmers in a food waste project, educators in a youth skill development effort, or CEOs in a multi-business coalition on climate change. It is important to connect to users and influencers ("know-who") and build necessary social ties to them in a partnership. Finally, there are matters of creating and sustaining energy, countering resistance, and building momentum. Partnerships built on social purpose and social value creation ("know-why") provide an added boost of motivation to all parties.

STRESS TEST: RATE YOUR COMPANY ON PARTNERING FOR SOCIAL CHANGE

Creating systemic social change calls for partnering with other organizations in common cause. How about your organization? Has it founded or joined in multi-party alliances or partnerships to effect social change? Spoken out on the issues of the day? Tackled large-scale challenges through its philanthropy, business models, and/or advocacy? Rate your organization on its efforts to effect positive social change.

CHECKLIST 10.1

Partnerships: Does your company speak out and partner with other organizations to create social change?

To what extent....   1 = Not at all   5 = To a great extent

	1	2	3	4	5
1. Does your company certify any of its products or services—Fair Trade? Sustainable Sourcing? Rainforest Alliance? Others?	☐	☐	☐	☐	☐
2. Is your company a part of any partnerships to address social or environmental issues—Local? Regional? National? Global?	☐	☐	☐	☐	☐
3. Is your company a part of any associations of good companies—Businesses for Social Responsibility? Shared Value Initiative? Conscious Capitalism? UNGC? B Corps community? Others?	☐	☐	☐	☐	☐
4. Does your company "take a stand" on social issues?	☐	☐	☐	☐	☐
5. Does your company work with NGOs or other businesses to advocate for positive social change?	☐	☐	☐	☐	☐
6. Does your company work with elected officials or civic leaders to promote positive social change?	☐	☐	☐	☐	☐

Again, add up the answers to these six questions: if you score 25 or more, your organization is taking a lead on systemic social change. If 12 to 24, this may be an arena to expand your influence. If lower... now is the time for collective action.

What Kind of Partnership Could Work for Your Company?

Companies engage in different kinds of multi-stakeholder partnerships—with NGOs, other businesses, and in multi-sector partnerships. Five years ago, John Elkington and Sustainability made a call for collaborations to shift from a narrow focus and transactional relationships to a more systemic and transformational agenda. It looks to us as if this shift is starting to take place (see Figure 10.1). Consider three types of partnerships involving business and other interests that are making this shift.

Business/NGO Partnerships. Companies today rely on respected NGOs to certify that their supply chains pass sustainable screens and that their products qualify as organic, "cruelty free," or Fair Trade. NGOs and companies also exercise collective influence via associations such as the Forest Stewardship Council and the Ethical Trading Initiative. And in philanthropic and CSR activities, companies often partner with charities and NGOs to deliver services to society. Why so? Few firms have the appropriate mix of staff, resources, and know-how to operate in this space on their own and in any case may lack the legitimacy with local communities to do so. A study by Austin and colleagues finds NGOs to be far more knowledgeable about social needs and more effective at planning social action than businesses. There is also evidence that partnering with NGOs gives a business more credibility when entering into social terrain and a stronger "license to operate" in society. Picking the right partners is key.[12]

FIGURE 10.1   Partnership Types and Scope

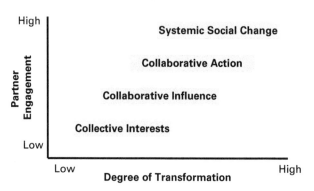

SOURCE Adapted from *Sustainability* (2016) Catalyzing the next generation of multi-stakeholder collaboration for sustainability, LinkedIn, https://www.linkedin.com/pulse/catalyzing-next-generation-multi-stakeholder-denise-delaney/

Many companies working with NGOs have had a significant positive impact on social problems in their organizations, supply chains, communities, and global operating arenas.[13] But when it comes to tackling larger-scale systemic social change, and addressing society's "wicked problems," a more extensive and inclusive approach is needed. Take, as an example, the Global Fashion Agenda (GFA), formed in 2016 around the Copenhagen Fashion Summit, which joined together NGO activists with companies like H&M, Nike, Target, and others to "transform the way we produce and consume fashion." The parties collaborated in areas of supply chain traceability, use of water, energy, and chemicals, closed-loop manufacture, better wages, and creating respectful and secure work environments. In 2021, the GFA joined forces with eight other fashion NGOs and their company partners to form the Fashion Conveners, which encompasses a larger swathe of the fashion industry and has worldwide reach.[14] The aim is to leverage collective knowledge, reduce duplication of effort, and drive systemic change.

Multi-business Partnerships. As for partnering between multiple businesses, we have cited initiatives on climate change, natural resources, human rights, and access to medicines, energy, and education. Many of them reconcile collective interests in an industry (e.g., the Extractive Industries Transparency Initiative) and some exercise collective influence (e.g., Business Roundtable's call for stakeholder capitalism). But here, too, we see multi-business groups pivoting toward creating systemic social change. Starbucks, for instance, hosted and invited its competitors to a "Cup Summit" to find ways to reduce waste and promote recycling of coffee cups. Initiatives have been launched among these companies with the Foodservice Packaging Association to increase the recyclability of cups and with waste management firms to increase volume and thereby make recycling more economically viable.[15]

On a broader scale, 250 CEOs from US companies large and small have banded together in a group called CEO Action for Racial Equity. Still at an early stage, the group has formulated action-oriented policies for promoting racial equity within companies and entered the public arena with proposals on food security, equitable policing, closing the digital divide, increasing access to telehealth and early childhood education, and on the decriminalization of poverty where the inability to pay fines, fees, or bail in the justice system disproportionately affects Black Americans. CEO Action has started the ball rolling toward systemic change with collaborations between business, government, and community leaders in five US cities.

Multisector Partnerships. "Any business that wants to profoundly alter its operating environment, any government that seeks to undertake fundamental reform, and any people who want to improve the world must partner with others from outside their sector," writes Steve Waddell, a specialist in global action networks.[16] Deirdre White, CEO of PYXERA Global, the NGO that works with over 30 companies operating global pro bono employee service programs, also operates a global engagement forum that brings together activists in business, government, education, and civil society to tackle "solvable" problems—from reducing post-harvest loss to reclaiming ocean plastics. Two leading lights at consulting firm Deloitte, William Eggers and Paul MacMillan, have pulled together rich examples of multiparty collaboration in effecting systemic change in *The Solution Revolution: How business, government, and social enterprises are teaming up to solve society's toughest problems*. These systemic changemakers and other pioneers have produced action guides that can help your company navigate the multisector terrain.[17]

One promising new form of multisector collaboration involves action tanks. A pioneer is France's Action Tank and Social Business (Action Tank Entreprise et Pauvreté), begun in 2010 under the leadership of Martin Hirsch, a former High Commissioner in the French government, and Emmanuel Faber, then CEO of Danone. It brought together companies, public actors, and academics in action projects to reduce poverty and exclusion in France. The action tank operates like an innovation lab where multiple parties combine their knowledge and work together to design solutions to social problems, test them out in different venues, and scale the most successful and cost-effective ones. Various configurations of organizations and people have innovatively addressed problems in the areas of employment, housing, nutrition, mobility, access to banking services, and caring for the elderly. The academics working on these projects provide technical advice, conduct project assessments, and prepare case studies to disseminate the findings and lessons learned. Students at HEC Paris are actively involved in many of the projects. This collaborative approach to systemic change is spreading. Similar action tanks are operating in India, Brazil, and throughout Africa, and at Babson College Cheryl Kiser has action tanks running on food systems, the future of mobility, and achieving social impact with the Internet of Things where entrepreneurs, leaders in business, government, and civil society, and faculty and students design and produce social innovations. What social issues could your company tackle via an action tank?

Scaling Social Impact

Now is not the time for small thinking or cautious action. Take climate change. Decades ago business didn't have to assume any responsibility for its emissions and pollution beyond complying with environmental regulations. Now more than 1,000 businesses are working with the Science Based Targets Initiative (SBTi) to achieve a net-zero carbon future by 2050. The We Mean Business Coalition has 2,000-plus companies taking joint initiatives to halve their emissions by 2030 with working groups on decarbonization in industry, transport, energy, and built environments. Companies in the World Wildlife Fund's Climate Business Network share their knowledge and practices to become "climate positive." There is also a climate hub for SMEs and WWF has a buyer's alliance that enables small firms to purchase renewable energy at reduced rates.[18] Plus there are thousands of other climate coalitions variously convened by the United Nations, national, state, and local governments, industry associations, chambers of commerce, and universities, foundations, and think tanks.

A March 2021 assessment of these efforts finds that net-zero commitments cover 61 percent of global greenhouse gas emissions, 68 percent of global GDP, and 56 percent of the world's population. This includes pledges by the national governments of the US, China, UK, and the EU, one-fifth of the world's largest companies, including oil producers Shell and BP, and legislative mandates for net zero in seven nations and four cities. The assessment concludes, "Net zero has come a long way in a very short time." Still, this collective movement is at an early stage, progress so far is modest, and the Intergovernmental Panel on Climate Change, a scientific body convened by the United Nations, warns that we are "locked into 30 years of worsening climate impacts no matter what the world does." But climate experts contend that with aggressive, rapid, and widespread emissions cuts, beginning now, we could limit global warming beyond 2050.[19]

Besides climate, there are business and multisector coalitions targeting inclusive growth, living wages, racial, gender, and LBGTQ equity, human rights in supply chains, work–life integration, healthy food, fashion, and living, and most every one of the SDGs, as well as corporate responsibility and sustainability. As more companies join in these collective efforts, positive social change will reach a "tipping point" and much of the public's skepticism and naysaying about business as a force for good could abate.

The Future of Business: A Voice and Force for Social Change

Many of the executives we met in our studies are visible and vocal advocates of using business to make a better world and select ones have pushed for necessary changes in policy and practice among their peers, elected officials, and the public at large. Ben and Jerry, for example, often collaborate with the activist group Moveon.org and the two were arrested while at the Democracy Awakening protest in Washington, D.C. in 2016. In July 2021, they announced their support for the boycott of sales of Ben & Jerry's products in Israeli settlements in the occupied Palestinian territories. On a different path, some years ago Virgin's founder Richard Branson brought together former UN Head Kofi Annan, Jimmy Carter, Nelson Mandela, Archbishop Desmond Tutu, human rights activist Mary Robinson, Muhammad Yunus, and others in a group called "The Elders." Their original focus was peacemaking but their agenda expanded into advocacy for universal healthcare, equality for women and girls, and issues pertaining to refugees and migration. The Elders led the global #WalkTogether movement in 2018 that spawned myriad grassroots initiatives.[20]

Throughout this volume we've reported how current-day business leaders like Larry Fink of Black Rock, John Mackey of Whole Foods, and Howard Schultz of Starbucks speak out and take action in the public arena to promote stakeholder capitalism and equitable employment. But moving into the public sphere is not just for big company bosses. Graciela Tiscareño-Sato is a Latina military veteran and CEO of the Gracefully Global Group, a Silicon Valley educational publisher whose content "motivates multicultural audiences to act." She focuses on the rights of US immigrants and their children. She reports, "My opinion is aligned with our corporate mission and my values as a person, mom, veteran, and entrepreneur."[21] Paola Dyboski-Bryant is the founder of Dr Zigs, a Welsh company that makes soap bubble kits, and advocates for social justice by filling the air with huge soap bubbles at political rallies, protests, and celebratory events like International Women's Day. She helped to push through the British government's "Kickstart" program that incentivizes businesses to hire unemployed youth and pays their salaries and National Insurance for six months. Latest doings: a "Bubbles Not Bombs" campaign that has her company send bubble wands to kids in regions torn by war and conflict. As the press reports it, she is "changing the world one bubble at a time."[22]

CEO Activism. In years past, most CEOs kept a low public profile and their companies entered the public arena through lobbying, political contributions, and image-burnishing sponsorships and philanthropy. Today, CEOs speaking out on social and political issues is the "new normal". Whether it's climate change, inclusive growth, economic, racial, or gender equity, business leaders are giving speeches, writing op-eds, and joining their peers in the Alliance of CEO Climate Leaders and the CEO Water Mandate, associations like Equality is Our Business and Paradigm for Parity, and many more. In the United States, they've entered into the political fray advocating for legal protections for LBGTQs, police reform, gun control, and voting rights, earning a rebuke from Senate Minority Leader Mitch McConnell to "stay out of politics" (except for political contributions). What's going on?

A 2020 global survey found activists and PR professionals agreeing that CEOs today are change agents and will be even more so in the future. The two groups ranked community leaders, celebrities, and citizens as most effective at making social change, followed by CEOs, who were rated as more influential than politicians, philanthropists, NGO leaders, journalists, religious leaders, and social media influencers. Salesforce CEO Marc Benioff explains his motivations to speak out in this way: "Today CEOs need to stand up not just for their shareholders, but their employees, their customers, their partners, the community, the environment, schools, everybody." Yet he notes that Salesforce board member Colin Powell, the former US secretary of state and four-star general warned him, "The farther you go up the tree, the more your backside is going to be exposed, and you'd better be careful."[23]

Aaron K. Chatterji and Michael W. Toffel report that beyond "raising awareness," activist CEOs also exert economic power by relocating business activities and funding activist groups. For instance, US states with "bathroom bills" that would require trans and gender non-binary persons to use facilities based on their sex assigned at birth, saw Salesforce halt all employee business travel to their states, PayPal cancel a planned business expansion in one of them, and high-tech companies pour money into political action groups calling for these bills' legislative defeat or reversal (if already enacted). The upshot, as some wags put it, is that most of the bathroom bills were "flushed away." Chatterji and Toffell's research finds that CEO activism affects the political contributions of their employees and can influence public opinion on controversial issues. They also discovered that CEOs who have taken a clear stand on such issues didn't cause a drop in company sales by alienating those who disagreed with them; on the contrary, consumers were more likely to buy their company's products.[24]

A Woke CEO? Still, moving into the public arena isn't for the faint-hearted. Recall how JPMorgan Chase CEO Jamie Dimon "took a knee" with his staff after the killing of George Floyd. He won plaudits for this within the bank but was pilloried for "performativity" in some of the media and in Vivek Ramaswamy's *Woke, Inc.*—a broader critique of "America's social justice scam."[25] Undaunted by the catcalls, JPMorgan Chase introduced The Path Forward in October 2020, committing $30 billion over the next five years to address the racial wealth divide, reduce systemic racism against Black and Latin people, and support its diverse employees.

Some of these pledged investments are philanthropic, some involve employees working with economically distressed inner cities in the JPMorgan Chase Service Corp, but most are commercial and find the bank in the US promising to: 1) open over 115 branches in underserved and low-income communities and offer customers low-cost, no overdraft checking accounts; 2) enable Black and Latin families to buy or refinance their homes at favorable rates; 3) increase lending and support to small and mid-market minority-owned businesses; 4) expand its base of Black and Latin suppliers; 5) issue a $1 billion social bond to increase affordable housing in poor areas of cities and towns; 6) partner with NGOs and civic groups on minority employment; 7) work with minority-owned banks to provide them with better access to capital and institutional investors; and 8) hire 300 Black and Latin financial advisors by 2025 (an area where its performance to date has been abysmal) and make diversity training mandatory for all employees. This adds some substance to woke capitalism—a lot more so than CEO virtue signaling by taking a knee.

Then Dimon lifted his voice into national politics in his 2021 letter to shareholders (see box). Now Dimon is not partisan and has said, "My heart is Democratic, but my brain is kind of Republican," and in the letter he took shots at both parties. What's notable about his recent moves is that, according to one insider, he has transformed from being a "whiner" who used to complain about his bank being besieged by regulators and social campaigners, into a "would-be statesman."[26] If Dimon can make such a shift, how about you?

A CEO GETS "POLITICAL"

JP Morgan Chase CEO Jamie Dimon got "political" in his 66-page 2021 letter to shareholders where he:

- cited the need for government regulation to ensure a fair and efficient system;

- supported tax increases to pay for infrastructure, saying that the wealthy should "keep in mind that if tax monies improve our society and our economy, (they) will be, in effect, among the main beneficiaries."

- said the US should learn from German and Swiss apprenticeship programs, healthcare in Singapore, infrastructure in Hong Kong, and inclusion from Ireland, where a homosexual Indian immigrant was recently elected prime minister; and

- laid out 15 policies leaders should focus on, including improved wages for low-skilled work, training for jobs, making it easier for those with a criminal record to get a job, better fiscal and tax policy, reforming social safety net programs, reviewing regulatory red tape, modernizing infrastructure, intelligent industrial policy, and proper immigration policies.

Dimon also took on US politicians by noting, "Politics is increasingly divisive, and government is increasingly dysfunctional, leading to a number of policies that simply don't work," adding, "The fault line is inequality. And its cause is staring us in the face: our own failure to move beyond our differences and self-interest and act for the greater good."[27]

The Power of the Whole. David Cooperrider facilitated the first summit meeting of the UN Global Compact in 2000 using a positive approach to collective dialogue called "appreciative inquiry." The intent was to identify common interests and build on the strengths each business could bring to solving global problems. Since then he has worked with companies and communities to harness "the power of whole" to create systemic change. The National Grid Group, for instance, brought together townsfolk in communities and hosted industry-wide gatherings in regions of the US and UK to generate ideas and action plans to expand the use of renewable energy. Fairmont Minerals brought the "whole system in the room" (employees plus hundreds of customers, global supply chain partners, NGOs, and community leaders) in Cleveland, Ohio to create "a green city on a blue lake." Walmart used the "convening power of our brand" to connect the dairy industry and create a platform where dairy farmers should share ideas, best practices, and problems encountered in their moves toward regenerative agriculture. This is business activism translated into community organizing and leadership at a local, regional, national, and even global level.[28]

Business as Statecraft and Diplomacy

The possibilities of partnerships and of companies making a positive impact on society extend well beyond the 5Ps we've addressed in this book. The UNGC has a Business for Peace platform with 150 companies and business associations from 37 countries that promote collaborative action to advance peace. Our ground-level research has taken us to the Rawabi Tech Hub, where Palestinian software engineers work with high-tech Israeli companies. Tech2Peace is an NGO that works with the partners to build the skills of the engineers and promote cross-cultural understanding. One of the Palestinians reports, "At first it was awkward, but by the third day we were discussing deep thoughts and our political opinions." Another says, "I believe that technology can break walls between any two sides of the conflict because it's borderless."[29] We also studied Jollibee in the Philippines where Muslims and Christians work together in plants and farm fields on both produce and peacemaking.

IKEA is a part of the Tent Partners for Refugees program involving over 140 major companies committed to integrating refugees in their host communities. The company used its core competencies to design a modular shelter for Syrian refugees in Jordan in 2011 with recycled plastic panels and solar-powered illumination. As refugees flooded into Europe, the company committed to supporting 2,500 of them with language skills and job training and is hiring many of them as positions open. It now employs refugee women at its Jordan production center to make hand-woven rugs and textiles. In 2019, the company sold these products in five nations and will scale to 30 by 2022, increasing the number of Jordanian weavers from 250 to 400.

Now these may sound like do-good activities, far afield from running a business, but they are part of the job for any business leader—and employee—who is connected to society and seeks to create social change. On this point, we increasingly hear CEOs speak to their work as "statesmanship." As our colleague David Grayson is quick to point out, this does not mean that business leaders aspire to "rule the world," nor that they use their platform to run for public office. Rather it shows that they actively engage in the issues of their times, speak out, take a stand, and join forces with other influencers in society.[30]

This calls for more "private sector diplomacy" where business uses its hard economic power and soft brand-and-people power to solve problems and promote positive social change. As Richard Haass, Head of the Council on Foreign Relations, elaborates it, corporate diplomacy cannot be handled out of a "small office" or led by "some vice president for government relations (who) calls a congressional staffer when he's got an issue." Instead, he says it is now "intrinsic" to the workings of business and that "every person in the company—certainly the upper echelon of leadership—needs to take this into account".[31]

Nike has assigned over 100 managers with governance responsibilities inside and outside the company and involved thousands of its employees in multistakeholder initiatives. These include collaborations with footwear, apparel, and fabric companies to inspect and ensure the safety and health of workers in their supply chains; partnerships with other businesses and NGOs in the Textile Exchange, Sustainable Apparel Coalition, and organic certification schemes; and involvement with the UN in its human rights agenda. Broadly speaking, while each of these ventures involves different issues and interests, what companies and the employees engaged in them have in common is that they are practicing corporate diplomacy. Are you ready to be a business statesman? To activate your company in private sector diplomacy?

Step Into the Public Arena

To effectively lead systemic social change takes you and your company into the public sphere and requires more than just a social mindset—you also need a social skillset. As Alain Gauthier, an advisor to many global partnerships, tells us, "Exercising leadership in cross-sector or multi-stakeholder contexts requires a higher level of both inner and interpersonal skills to deal effectively with the diversity of worldviews, values, assumptions, languages and experiences."[32] Scholars report that successful business diplomats have key competencies that include international business acumen, knowledge of relevant governing bodies and codes, political skills in dealing with diverse interests and the media, comfort with role versatility, and a high tolerance for ambiguity. They also say that while various MBA courses touch on these areas, MBA education overall is not well suited to the development of corporate diplomats.[33]

So how do managers and employees acquire these skills? We've noted how Tex Gunning at Unilever led his people on "learning journeys" to awaken them to the social and environmental issues in their world.

Companies that operate global pro bono programs also immerse their people in complex socio-political environments where there are no easy answers to solving systemic problems. Global service provides a "boot camp" in which company volunteers are schooled on how to get things done with limited resources, how to work in complex, multi-stakeholder environments and, of course, how to operate in another culture. They also learn a lot about themselves. On a more everyday basis, businesspeople can step into the public sphere and learn to work across sectors when they join nonprofit boards, participate in community associations and groups promoting social change, and join in the multi-party partnerships described here.

Make Your Move to the Edge of the Future

So here we are: your company *can* work with others to create systemic social change. We hope we've made the case that business in general, and your company in specific, will be on the right side of history in stepping up to help solve the problems wracking our world. The move from sustainability to social change, and from managing risk to creating social value, is not just an emerging *trend*. As David Cooperrider likes to say, it's really a *trajectory* that has been building for decades and gathered real momentum in the shadow of the pandemic and social unrest of today.

Business leaders and companies that move toward the edge of the future and take a lead on creating social change will find themselves among fervent supporters, some unlikely allies, and plenty of critics from the left and right. But we believe that as your company handprint enlarges and you join hands with others on this journey, your employees will be with you, your customers will support you, and your investors will ultimately thank you. Be smart, take stock along the way, learn from your wins and defeats, and take pride and sustenance from knowing that you and your company have done your part to make a better world.

Remember the wisdom of Margaret Mead: "Never doubt that a small group of thoughtful, committed citizens can change the world; indeed, it's the only thing that ever has."

NOTES

Introduction

1   Deloitte (2021) 2021 climate check: Business' views on environmental sustainability, www2.deloitte.com/global/en/pages/risk/articles/2021-climate-check-business-views-on-environmental-sustainability.html (archived at https://perma.cc/7GM6-YBAX)

2   Ulukaya quoted in Martinez, M (2018) More businesses commit to helping refugees thrive with new jobs, trainings, investment, The UN Refugee Agency, www.unhcr.org/en-us/news/latest/2018/9/5babbecf4/businesses-commit-helping-refugees-thrive-new-jobs-trainings-investment.html (archived at https://perma.cc/XL65-BE74)

3   Friedman, M (1970) The social responsibility of business is to increase its profits, *New York Times*, www.nytimes.com/1970/09/13/archives/a-friedman-doctrine-the-social-responsibility-of-business-is-to.html (archived at https://perma.cc/ERL4-T3MS)

4   Business Roundtable (nd) Statement on the purpose of a corporation, https://opportunity.businessroundtable.org/ourcommitment/ (archived at https://perma.cc/H3TL-YE82); World Economic Forum (2020) The Davos Manifesto, www.weforum.org/the-davos-manifesto (archived at https://perma.cc/ZR7N-6M2Z)

5   Survey results from: UNGC – Accenture (2019) The decade to deliver: A call to business action, www.accenture.com/lu-en/insights/strategy/ungcceostudy (archived at https://perma.cc/A9TB-59JQ); Globescan (2020) Report: Stakeholders rate corporate purpose in time of crisis, https://globescan.com/report-stakeholders-rate-corporate-purpose-2020/ (archived at https://perma.cc/GCC9-FWEB); Just Capital (2021) Two years later: Do Americans believe companies are living up to the Business Roundtable's redefined purpose of a corporation? https://justcapital.com/reports/do-americans-believe-companies-are-living-up-to-business-roundtables-purpose-of-a-corporation-2021/ (archived at https://perma.cc/H3LY-3ZKR)

6   Survey results from Edelman (2019) Edelman Trust Barometer 2019, www.edelman.com/trust/2019-trust-barometer (archived at https://perma.cc/8CBB-RU5F); Edelman (2020) Edelman Trust Barometer 2020, www.edelman.com/trust/2020-trust-barometer (archived at https://perma.cc/4N8D-Z49Y)

7   Edelman (2020) Trust Barometer.

8   For a primer on B Corps, see Marquis, C (2020) *Better Business: How the B Corp movement is remaking capitalism*, Yale University Press.

9   The British Academy (2019) *Principles For Purposeful Business*, www. thebritishacademy.ac.uk/publications/future-of-the-corporation-principles-for-purposeful-business/ (archived at https://perma.cc/9AX7-JQQT); see also Mayer, C (2018) *Prosperity: Better business makes the greater good*, Oxford University Press.

10   Porter Novelli (2020) *Executive Purpose Study*, www.porternovelli.com/wp-content/uploads/2020/09/PN_Executive_Reasearch_Report_9.8.2020.pdf (archived at https://perma.cc/K3PL-UKLY); Zeno Group (2020) Unveiling the 2020 Zeno Strength of Purpose study, www.zenogroup.com/insights/2020-zeno-strength-purpose (archived at https://perma.cc/8N9K-VN8F)

11   Credit Suisse (2021) Global wealth report 2021, www.credit-suisse.com/about-us/en/reports-research/global-wealth-report.html (archived at https://perma.cc/3KLU-6CDQ)

12   CEO survey results from UNGC – Accenture (2019) *The Decade to Deliver*, www.accenture.com/_acnmedia/pdf-109/accenture-ungc-ceo-study.pdf (archived at https://perma.cc/657M-X5HJ)

13   Gallup (2021) *State of the Global Workplace: 2021 report*, https://commsweek.ragan.com/wp-content/uploads/2021/07/state-of-the-global-workplace-2021-download.pdf (archived at https://perma.cc/GVG3-ZW56)

14   Cone (2016) 2016 Cone Communications millennial employee engagement study, www.conecomm.com/research-blog/2016-millennial-employee-engagement-study (archived at https://perma.cc/DYB6-ZPEW); Gen Z attitudes from Porter Novelli/Cone (2109) 2019 Porter Novelli/Cone Gen Z purpose study, www.conecomm.com/research-blog/cone-gen-z-purpose-study (archived at https://perma.cc/J5W9-L7G2)

15   Edelman (2020) Trust Barometer special report: Brand trust in 2020, www.edelman.com/research/brand-trust-2020 (archived at https://perma.cc/X6QC-ZFSX)

16   Edmond, C (2020) Global risk report 2020: These are the top risks facing the world in 2020, World Economic Forum, www.weforum.org/agenda/2020/01/top-global-risks-report-climate-change-cyberattacks-economic-political/ (archived at https://perma.cc/99US-LX7W)

17   Cone (2016) Millennial engagement.

18   See Mirvis, PH and Googins, B (2017) The new business of business: Innovating for a better world, Conference Board.

19   See Schwab, K (2017) *The Fourth Industrial Revolution*, Currency.

Chapter 1

1 Googins, BK, Mirvis, PH, and Rochlin, SA (2007) *Beyond Good Company: Next generation corporate citizenship*, Macmillan.

2 Elkington, J (1997) *Cannibals With Forks: The triple bottom line of 21st century business*, Capstone.

3 Brolick, quoted in Campbell, A (2014) Food at Wendy's will get clean label makeover, *Liberty Voice*, https://guardianlv.com/2014/03/food-at-wendys-will-get-clean-label-makeover/ (archived at https://perma.cc/K8DD-TG3D)

4 Cone (2017) 2017 Cone Communications CSR study, www.conecomm.com/research-blog/2017-csr-study (archived at https://perma.cc/KY6G-2MTA)

5 Esty, DC and Winston, A (2009) *Green to Gold: How smart companies use environmental strategy to innovate, create value, and build competitive advantage*, John Wiley & Sons.

6 Elkington, J (2018) 25 years ago I coined the phrase 'Triple Bottom Line.' Here's why it's time to rethink it, *Harvard Business Review*, https://hbr.org/2018/06/25-years-ago-i-coined-the-phrase-triple-bottom-line-heres-why-im-giving-up-on-it (archived at https://perma.cc/YLW4-FK2Q)

7 Porter, ME and Kramer, MR (2006) The link between competitive advantage and corporate social responsibility, *Harvard Business Review*, **84** (12), pp. 78–92; Porter, M and Kramer, MR (2011) Creating shared value, *Harvard Business Review*, **89** (1/2), pp. 62–77.

8 Hollender, J (2006) *What Matters Most: How a small group of pioneers is teaching social responsibility to big business, and why big business is listening*, Basic Books (AZ).

9 Just Capital (2019) A roadmap for stakeholder capitalism: 2019 survey results, https://justcapital.com/reports/roadmap-for-stakeholder-capitalism/ (archived at https://perma.cc/S4MV-PTPH)

10 Giridharadas, A (2019) *Winners Take All: The elite charade of changing the world*, Vintage; Chakrabortty, A (2019), Winners Take All by Anand Giridharadas review—superb hate-reading. www.theguardian.com/books/2019/feb/14/winners-take-all-by-anand-giridharadas-review (archived at https://perma.cc/DQ3Q-DEHR)

11 Quote from George, WW, Palepu, KG, Knoop, C and Preble, M (2013) Unilever's Paul Polman: Developing global leaders. Case 9-413-097, Harvard Business School.

12 Edelman (2019) 2019 *Edelman Trust Barometer: Expectations for CEOs*, https://edl.mn/2ZKenfN (archived at https://perma.cc/YZ6H-E9A6)

13 Edelman (2020)—see Note 6, page 210; Accenture (2018) From me to we: The rise of the purpose-led brand, www.accenture.com/us-en/insights/strategy/brand-purpose (archived at https://perma.cc/G8AZ-XHH9)

14 Browne, J, Nuttall, R, and Stadlen, T (2015) *Connect: How companies succeed by engaging radically with society*, Public Affairs.

15 Googins, B and Mirvis, PH (2011) Share value or shared values? US Chamber Foundation, www.uschamberfoundation.org/blog/post/share-value-or-shared-values/31243 (archived at https://perma.cc/R5DC-6KR5)

16 Porter Novelli (2020) *Executive Purpose Study*, www.porternovelli.com/wp-content/uploads/2020/09/PN_Executive_Reasearch_Report_9.8.2020.pdf (archived at https://perma.cc/K3PL-UKLY); Zeno Group (2020) Unveiling the 2020 Zeno Strength of Purpose study, www.zenogroup.com/insights/2020-zeno-strength-purpose (archived at https://perma.cc/8N9K-VN8F)

Chapter 2

1 Dees, JG (2001) *The Meaning of Social Entrepreneurship*, Duke University, Durham.

2 Samuelson, J (2021) *The Six New Rules of Business: Creating real value in a changing world*, Berrett Koehler.

3 Schumpeter, J (1909) On the concept of social value, *The Quarterly Journal of Economics*, **23** (2), pp. 213–32.

4 Vogel, D (2006) *The Market for Virtue: The potential and limits of corporate social responsibility*, Brookings Institution Press.

5 Edmans, A (2020) *Grow the Pie: How great companies deliver both purpose and profit*, Cambridge University Press.

6 Mackey, J and Sisodia, R (2014) *Conscious Capitalism: Liberating the heroic spirit of business*, Harvard Business Review Press.

7 Statistics from Economic Policy Institute (2021) The productivity–pay gap, www.epi.org/productivity-pay-gap/ (archived at https://perma.cc/C45B-73S9); Ortiz-Ospina, E and Roser, M (2019) Economic inequality by gender, *Ourworldindata.org*, https://ourworldindata.org/economic-inequality-by-gender (archived at https://perma.cc/KGL6-A6TR)

8 Mirvis, P (2012) Employee engagement and CSR: Transactional, relational, and developmental approaches, *California Management Review*, **54** (4), pp. 93–117; also see Mirvis, P and Googins, B (2018) Engaging employees as social innovators, *California Management Review*, **60** (4), pp. 25–50.

9 Aaron (2018) Consumers want brands to help them make a difference, *Queue*, www.wearequeue.com/blog/marketing-2/consumers-brands-help-make-a-difference/ (archived at https://perma.cc/QWT9-2CZ6)

10 Elkington, J (2020) *Green Swans: The coming boom in regenerative capitalism*, Greenleaf Book Group.

11 Bonini, S, Koller, TM, and Mirvis, PH (2009) Valuing social responsibility, *McKinsey on Finance*, **32**, pp. 11–18.

12 Fauci, A (2020) White House Coronavirus Task Force Briefing, April 7, https://mobile.twitter.com/nowthisnews/status/1248385955297251331 (archived at https://perma.cc/7VA8-B4CC)

13 Edelman (2020) Edelman Trust Barometer special report: Brand trust and the coronavirus pandemic, www.edelman.com/research/covid-19-brand-trust-report (archived at https://perma.cc/X2DR-E2TJ)

14 Masercola, N (2021) Corporate climate pledges proliferate, *Just Capital*, https://justcapital.com/news/corporate-climate-pledges-proliferate/ (archived at https://perma.cc/UJD4-4MAU)

15 Quote from Sacks, B and Samaha, A (2020) Starbucks won't let employees wear gear that supports Black Lives Matter because it is political or could incite violence, *BuzzFeed*, www.buzzfeednews.com/article/briannasacks/starbucks-is-now-very-pro-black-lives-matter-but-it-wont (archived at https://perma.cc/QH5C-KNKE)

Chapter 3

1 Globescan (2013) Large numbers remain unable or unwilling to name a socially responsible company,   https://globescan.com/large-numbers-remain-unable-or-unwilling-to-name-a-socially-responsible-company/ (archived at https://perma.cc/VKG2-RVN4)

2 Books by or about the founders of these companies: Cohen, B, Greenfield, J, and Maran, M (1998) *Ben and Jerry's Double Dip: How to run a values led business and make money too*, Simon and Schuster; Edmondson, B (2014) *Ice Cream Social: The struggle for the soul of Ben & Jerry's*, Berrett-Koehler Publisher; Anderson, RC and White, R (2009) *Confessions of a Radical Industrialist: Profits, people, purpose—doing business by respecting the earth*, St. Martin's Press; Knight, P (2016) *Shoe Dog: A memoir by the creator of Nike*, Simon and Schuster; Polman, P and Winston, A (2021) *Net Positive: How courageous companies thrive by giving more than they take*, Boston: Harvard Business School Press.

3 For background, see Mirvis, PH (1991) Ben & Jerry's: Team development intervention (A and B), in A Glassman and T Cummings (Eds.) *Cases in Organization Development*, Irwin.

4 For the inside scoop, see Lager, F (1994) *Ben & Jerry's: The inside scoop: How two real guys built a business with a social conscience and a sense of humor*, Crown Business.

5 For background, see Bayle-Cordier, J, Mirvis, P and Moingeon, B (2015) Projecting different identities: A longitudinal study of the whipsaw effects of changing leadership discourse about the triple bottom line, *The Journal of Applied Behavioral Science*, **51** (3), pp. 336–74.

6 Anderson, RC (1998) *Mid-Course Correction: Toward a sustainable enterprise, the Interface model*, Chelsea Green Publishing.

7 Hawken, P (1993) *The Ecology of Commerce: A declaration of sustainability*, HarperCollins.

8 For background see Amodeo, M (2018) *Beyond Sizzle: The next evolution of branding*, Maven House Press.

9 Harman, W (1988) *Global Mind Change: The promise of the 21st century*, Knowledge Systems.

10 Ballinger, J (1992) From Nike, the new free-trade heel, *Harper's*, August, pp. 46–47.

11 Larimer, T (1998) Sneaker gulag: Are Asian workers really exploited? *Time International*, p. 30.

12 For background see Mirvis, P (2011) Unilever's drive for sustainability and CSR—changing the game, in *Organizing for Sustainability*, Emerald Group Publishing Limited.

13 Bravard, C, Pontillo, J, and Hoffman, A (2021) *For Whom We Play the Game: Advice to the next generation of business leaders from Paul Polman*, Ross School of Business, University of Michigan.

14 Quotes from Farrell, S (2019) 'Damaged ideology': Business must reinvent capitalism – ex-Unilever boss, *The Guardian*, www.theguardian.com/business/2019/oct/29/damaged-ideology-business-must-reinvent-capitalism-ex-unilever-boss (archived at https://perma.cc/4W5Q-96Y4)

Chapter 4

1 Schlesinger, LA and Kiefer, CF (2012) *Just Start: Take action, embrace uncertainty, create the future*, Harvard Business Review Press.

2 Quote from Conlin, E (1990) The peace pops puzzle, *Inc.*, www.inc.com/magazine/19900301/5058.html (archived at https://perma.cc/Z72W-GM4R)

3 Background on this from Hall, C (2018) Everything you need to know about Lush's crazy controversial #spycops campaign, *Elle*, www.elle.com/beauty/a21098901/spycop-lush-cosmetics-explainer/ (archived at https://perma.cc/EJ4E-RT2N)

4 Kiser, C, Leipziger, D, and Shubert, JJ (2017) *Creating Social Value: A guide for leaders and change makers*, Routledge.

5 Wicked problems defined by Rittel, HWJ and Webber, MM (1973) Dilemmas in a general theory of planning, *Policy Sciences*, 4 (2), pp. 155–69.

6 BHAGs in Collins, JP and Porras, JI (1994) *Built to Last,* Harper Collins.

7 More on Unilever learning journeys in Mirvis, PH and Gunning, L (2006) Creating a community of leaders, *Organizational Dynamics*, 35 (1), pp. 69–82.

8   Heifetz, RA, Heifetz, R, Grashow, A, and Linsky, M (2009) *The Practice of Adaptive Leadership: Tools and tactics for changing your organization and the world*, Harvard Business Press.

9   Lorenz, E (2000) The butterfly effect, *World Scientific Series on Nonlinear Science Series A, 39*, pp. 91–94.

10 Nooyi, IK and Govindarajan, V (2020) Becoming a better corporate citizen. *Harvard Business Review*, **98** (2), pp. 94–103.

11 Vogel, L (2012) Nike's gameplan for growth that's good for all, *Management Exchange*, www.managementexchange.com/story/nike%E2%80%99s-gameplan-growth-that%E2%80%99s-good-all (archived at https://perma.cc/W326-QCAK)

12 See a review and analysis of different types of coalitions in Grayson, D and Nelson, J (2013) *Corporate Responsibility Coalitions: The past, present, and future of alliances for sustainable capitalism*, Stanford University Press.

13 Kanter, RM (2020) *Think Outside the Building: How advanced leaders can change the world one smart innovation at a time*, PublicAffairs; Mirvis, P and Googins, B (2018) Corporate social innovation: Top-down, bottom-up, inside-out and outside-in, in *Business Strategies for Sustainability*, Routledge, pp. 179–96; Sull, DN (2003) *Revival of the Fittest: Why good companies go bad and how great managers remake them*, Harvard Business School Press.

14 More on Danone's social innovation lab at Vilanova, M and Dettoni, P (2011) Sustainable innovation strategies: Exploring the cases of Danone and interface, ESADE, Institute for Social Innovation.

15 Quote from Greenland, R (2010) Social innovation, Danone style, *The Social Business*, www.thesocialbusiness.co.uk/blog/2010/07/social-innovation-danone-style (archived at https://perma.cc/VE9M-BZ2H)

Chapter 5

1   Quote from WARC (2017) Ashley Stewart's brand driven comeback, www.warc.com/newsandopinion/news/ashley-stewarts-brand-driven-comeback/39788 (archived at https://perma.cc/22YG-J8WH)

2   Quote from Abeyta, L (2021) How kindness took this brand from bankruptcy to success, *Inc.*, www.futurethink.com/blog/kindness-took-brand-bankruptcy-success (archived at https://perma.cc/Y8W3-34FT)

3   Quotes from Davis, D (2017) Plus-size retailer Ashley Stewart promotes empowerment to social followers, *Digital Commerce 360*, www.digitalcommerce360.com/2017/05/26/plus-size-retailer-ashley-stewart-promotes-empowerment-social-followers/ (archived at https://perma.cc/5RJP-7MJC)

4 Handy, C (2002) What's a business for? *Harvard Business Review*, **80** (12), pp. 49–55.

5 Kanter, RM (2010*) Supercorp: How vanguard companies create innovation, profits, growth, and social good*, Crown.

6 Sinek, S (2009) *Start With Why: How great leaders inspire everyone to take action*, Penguin.

7 Nimwegen, GV, Bollen, L, Hassink, H, and Thijssens, T (2008) A stakeholder perspective on mission statements: An international empirical study, *International Journal of Organizational Analysis*, **16** (1–2), pp. 61–82.

8 United Way Social Purpose Institute (2021) What's the difference between CSR and social purpose? https://socialpurpose.ca/social-purpose/ (archived at https://perma.cc/2ZQC-6HZM)

9 Survey results from Globescan (2020) GlobeScan Radar: The latest trends that will shape 2020 and beyond, https://globescan.com/radar-latest-trends-that-will-shape-2020-beyond/ (archived at https://perma.cc/6RB6-GFY7)

10 On the purpose gap, McKinsey (2020) Purpose: Shifting from why to how, *McKinsey Quarterly*, www.mckinsey.com/business-functions/organization/our-insights/purpose-shifting-from-why-to-how (archived at https://perma.cc/HXG2-RBAE); Rosenburg, W (2020) The purpose gap, *PWC*, https://pwc.blogs.com/corporatereporting/2020/10/the-purpose-gap-october-2020.html (archived at https://perma.cc/6XKR-NK5Q)

11 Survey results from Weber Shandwick (2019) Employee activism in the age of purpose: Employees (up)rising, www.webershandwick.com/news/employee-activism-age-of-purpose/ (archived at https://perma.cc/39DK-HYYM)

12 On how companies are dropping the ball on corporate purpose, see PwC (2016) Putting purpose to work: A study of purpose in the workplace, www.pwc.com/us/en/purpose-workplace-study.html (archived at https://perma.cc/U9QD-VUPR); Robison, J (2019) The future of your workplace depends on your purpose, *Gallup*, www.gallup.com/workplace/257744/future-workplace-depends-purpose.aspx (archived at https://perma.cc/XDJ9-9L2G).

13 Zeno Group (2020) Unveiling the 2020 Zeno Strength of Purpose Study, www.zenogroup.com/insights/2020-zeno-strength-purpose (archived at https://perma.cc/8N9K-VN8F)

14 Survey results from Cone (2020) The B2B purpose paradox: How purpose powers business-to-business growth, www.carolconeonpurpose.com/b2b-purpose-paradox (archived at https://perma.cc/CC5T-YYVZ)

15 Quotes from Reason (2005) Rethinking the social responsibility of business, https://reason.com/2005/10/01/rethinking-the-social-responsi-2/ (archived at https://perma.cc/6RAG-VNVE)

16 For more on Apple's purpose audit, see BCG (2018) For corporate purpose to matter, you've got to measure it, www.bcg.com/publications/2018/corporate-purpose-to-matter-measure-it (archived at https://perma.cc/JMJ7-6QU7)

17 Saul, J (2010) *Social Innovation, Inc.: 5 strategies for driving business growth through social change*, John Wiley & Sons.

18 For more on corporate branding, see Hatch, MJ and Schultz, M (2008) *Taking Brand Initiative: How companies can align strategy, culture, and identity through corporate branding*, John Wiley & Sons.

19 For more on employees' response to purpose, see McKinsey (2020) Purpose, not platitudes: A personal challenge for top executives, *McKinsey Quarterly*, www.mckinsey.com/business-functions/organization/our-insights/purpose-not-platitudes-a-personal-challenge-for-top-executives (archived at https://perma.cc/U539-48QF)

20 Mirvis, PH (2008) Can you buy CSR? *California Management Review*, **51** (1), pp. 109–16.

21 Quote from Durocher, K (2019) Gentrification, Whole Foods, and food deserts, *Futurex Network*, https://futurex.network/blog/gentrification-whole-foods-and-food-deserts (archived at https://perma.cc/422H-E6NV)

22 For more, see LTSE (2020) For a new generation of companies, https://ltse.com/about/ (archived at https://perma.cc/7HFJ-K3NS)

23 Klein, P (2012) Defining the social purpose of business, *Forbes*, www.forbes.com/sites/csr/2012/05/14/defining-the-social-purpose-of-business/?sh=114704cd1cac (archived at https://perma.cc/EA3K-QEJW)

Chapter 6

1 For more see Askinosie, S and Askinosie, L (2017) *Meaningful Work: A quest to do great business, find your calling, and feed your soul*, Tarcher Perigee.

2 Pay gap statistics from Mishel, L and Wolfe, J (2019) CEO compensation has grown 940% since 1978, *Economic Policy Institute*, www.epi.org/publication/ceo-compensation-2018/ (archived at https://perma.cc/DSG2-6RJW); Ng, K (2021) Top CEO pay is now 120 times that of average UK worker, says think tank, *Independent*, www.independent.co.uk/topic/high-pay-centre (archived at https://perma.cc/4J4V-UDU3); Jones, J (2021) 5 facts about the state of the gender pay gap, US Department of Labor Blog, https://blog.dol.gov/2021/03/19/5-facts-about-the-state-of-the-gender-pay-gap (archived at https://perma.cc/3KA6-LVDY)

3 For more on how business drives prosperity, see McKinsey Global Institute (2021) A new look at how corporations impact the economy and households, www.mckinsey.com/business-functions/strategy-and-corporate-finance/our-insights/a-new-look-at-how-corporations-impact-the-economy-and-households (archived at https://perma.cc/2TGX-CLNQ)

4 Edelman (2020) Trust Barometer.

5 Marglin, SA and Schor, JB (Eds.) (1991) *The Golden Age of Capitalism: Reinterpreting the postwar experience*, Oxford University Press.

6 Piketty, T (2014) *Capital in the Twenty-First Century*, The Belknap Press of Harvard University Press; Saez, E and Zucman, G (2016) Wealth inequality in the United States since 1913: Evidence from capitalized income tax data, *The Quarterly Journal of Economics*, **131** (2), pp. 519–78.

7 Partington, R (2019) Inequality: Is it rising, and can we reverse it? *The Guardian*, www.theguardian.com/news/2019/sep/09/inequality-is-it-rising-and-can-we-reverse-it (archived at https://perma.cc/52A5-SMJ4)

8 Board of Governors of the Federal Reserve System (2019) *Report on the Economic Well-Being of U.S. households in 2018*, www.federalreserve.gov/publications/files/2018-report-economic-well-being-us-households-201905.pdf (archived at https://perma.cc/DFT6-FJZE)

9 Quote from UNGC–Accenture (2019) The decade to deliver: A call to business action, www.accenture.com/lu-en/insights/strategy/ungcceostudy (archived at https://perma.cc/A9TB-59JQ)

10 As You Sow (2019) The 100 most overpaid CEOs 2019, www.asyousow.org/report/the-100-most-overpaid-ceos-2019 (archived at https://perma.cc/W69G-8GGV)

11 Siddique, H (2019) Britain's ethnic pay gap: Workers of Bangladeshi heritage paid least, *The Guardian*, www.theguardian.com/inequality/2019/jul/09/ethnic-pay-gap-bangladeshi-workers-earn-fifth-less-white-britons (archived at https://perma.cc/Y3FZ-GJE4)

12 Oxfam International (2021) Not in this together, https://policy-practice.oxfam.org/resources/not-in-this-together-how-supermarkets-became-pandemic-winners-while-women-worke-621194/ (archived at https://perma.cc/CZH9-RAFD)

13 Economics of Mutuality (2020) Bruno Roche interview: Cheung Kong Graduate School of Business, https://eom.org/content-hub-blog/bruno-roche-interview-cheung-kong-graduate-school-of-business (archived at https://perma.cc/3Z3M-243T)

14 Mayer, C and Roche, B (Eds.) (2021) *Putting Purpose Into Practice: The economics of mutuality*, Oxford University Press.

15 Felber, C (2019) *Change Everything: Creating an economy for the common good*, Zed Books Ltd.

16 National Center for Employee Ownership (2018) Research on employee ownership, corporate performance, and employee compensation, www.nceo.org/articles/research-employee-ownership-corporate-performance (archived at https://perma.cc/5LEB-B32Z)

17 Freeman, RE and Elms, H (2018) The social responsibility of business is to create value for stakeholders, *MIT Sloan Management Review*, https://sloanreview.mit.edu/article/the-social-responsibility-of-business-is-to-create-value-for-stakeholders/ (archived at https://perma.cc/4586-HBG9)

18 Globescan (2020) GlobeScan Radar: The latest trends that will shape 2020 and beyond, https://globescan.com/radar-latest-trends-that-will-shape-2020-beyond/ (archived at https://perma.cc/6RB6-GFY7)

19 Ton, Z (2014) *The Good Jobs Strategy: How the smartest companies invest in employees to lower costs and boost profits*, Houghton Mifflin Harcourt.

20 See more on gig workers and the economy from Broda, K (2021) Gig economy— the economic backbone of the future? *Brodmin*, https://brodmin.com/case-studies/gig-economy-case-study/ (archived at https://perma.cc/R3LL-HU5S)

21 For more on business engagement with education and good works, see Benioff, M and Adler, C (2006) *The Business of Changing the World: Twenty great leaders on strategic corporate philanthropy*, McGraw Hill Professional.

22 Markovits, D (2019) *The Meritocracy Trap*, Penguin UK.

23 Frank, RH (2016) *Success and Luck: Good fortune and the myth of meritocracy*, Princeton University Press.

24 Institute on Taxation and Tax Policy (2019) Corporate tax avoidance in the first year of the Trump tax law, https://itep.org/corporate-tax-avoidance-in-the-first-year-of-the-trump-tax-law/ (archived at https://perma.cc/CL86-H6AX)

25 Foa, RS and Mounk, Y (2017) The signs of deconsolidation, *Journal of Democracy*, **28** (1), pp. 5–15.

26 Quote and more from Hopp, W (2016) How corporate America can curb income inequality and make more money too, *The Conversation*, https://theconversation.com/how-corporate-america-can-curb-income-inequality-and-make-more-money-too-62339 (archived at https://perma.cc/8FK3-GLLR)

Chapter 7

1 Quote from Crowley, M (2013) How SAS became the world's best place to work, *Fast Company*, www.fastcompany.com/3004953/how-sas-became-worlds-best-place-work (archived at https://perma.cc/3KV5-J3FR)

2 Kane, P (2021) The great resignation is here, and it's real, *Inc.*, www.inc.com/phillip-kane/the-great-resignation-is-here-its-real.html (archived at https://perma.cc/W6TG-T42B)

3 Interest in working for a company with a social conscious is somewhat lower in the UK (51 percent), Germany (60 percent), and Western Europe generally, where government has traditionally assumed a larger role in addressing social ills, but higher in India, China, and parts of Southeast Asia and Latin America (80 percent and more). PwC (2017) *Workforce of the future: The views of 10,000 workers*, www.pwc.com/gx/en/services/people-organisation/workforce-of-the-future/workforce-of-future-appendix.pdf (archived at https://perma.cc/XL5M-A2DD)

4   Martin, RL (2020) *When More is Not Better: Overcoming America's obsession with economic efficiency*, Harvard Business Press.

5   Overwork statistics at Deloitte (2018) Workplace burnout survey, www2. deloitte.com/us/en/pages/about-deloitte/articles/burnout-survey.html (archived at https://perma.cc/JE7W-G94V); Global findings at AIA (2021) The healthiest workplace 2019 across Australia, Hong Kong, Malaysia, Sri Lanka and Thailand, *AIA Vitality*, www.aia.com/en/healthy-living/the-healthiest-workplace.html (archived at https://perma.cc/F3TC-XXAJ)

6   Pfeffer, J (2018) *Dying For a Paycheck: Why the American way of business is injurious to people and companies*, HarperCollins Publishers; On compassion, see Lilius, JM, Worline, MC, Maitlis, S, Kanov, J, Dutton, JE and Frost, P (2008) The contours and consequences of compassion at work, *Journal of Organizational Behavior: The International Journal of Industrial, Occupational and Organizational Psychology and Behavior*, **29** (2), pp. 193–218.

7   Twaronite, K (2019) Five findings on the importance of belonging, *EY*, www. ey.com/en_us/diversity-inclusiveness/ey-belonging-barometer-workplace-study (archived at https://perma.cc/3U7F-WWAQ)

8   McKinsey (2020) Understanding organizational barriers to a more inclusive workplace, www.mckinsey.com/business-functions/organization/our-insights/understanding-organizational-barriers-to-a-more-inclusive-workplace (archived at https://perma.cc/2JRS-5AD6)

9   Blount, S and Leinwand, P (2019) Why are we here? If you want employees who are more engaged and productive, give them a purpose—one concretely tied to your customers and your strategy, *Harvard Business Review* (November–December), pp. 1–9.

10 Survey results from Andrus, D (2021) One-third of employees feel underutilized at work, *Benefits Pro*, www.benefitspro.com/2021/03/08/one-third-of-employees-feel-underutilized-at-work/ (archived at https://perma.cc/B3CW-UKVQ); Bolden-Barrett, V (2020) Workers say they're underutilized and uninformed, *HR Dive*, www.hrdive.com/news/workers-say-theyre-underutilized-and-uninformed/572607/ (archived at https://perma.cc/4PW9-ZCRC)

11 Maslow, AH (1968) *Toward a Psychology of Being*, D. Van Nostrand Company.

12 Hall, DT and Mirvis, PH (2013) Redefining work, work identity, and career success, in DL Blustein (Ed) *The Oxford Handbook of the Psychology of Working*, Oxford University Press.

13 Kegan, R (1982) *The Evolving Self*, Harvard University Press.

14 Tajfel, HE (1978) *Differentiation Between Social Groups: Studies in the social psychology of intergroup relations*, Academic Press.

15 Baker, M (2020) 3 actions to more effectively advance underrepresented talent, *Gartner*, www.gartner.com/smarterwithgartner/3-actions-to-more-effectively-advance-underrepresented-talent/ (archived at https://perma.cc/6MFT-MCCQ); Twaronite, K (2019) Importance of belonging, *EY*.

16 From Fridman, A (2016) Don't call us employees! How corporate culture impacts your internal team and the retaining of employees, *Inc.*, www.inc.com/adam-fridman/dont-call-us-employees--how-corporate-culture-impacts-your-internal-team-and-t.html (archived at https://perma.cc/4B2J-2F5P)

17 LaBier, D (2011) Why it's hard to find your "life purpose" in today's world, *Psychology Today*, www.psychologytoday.com/us/blog/the-new-resilience/201105/why-its-hard-find-your-life-purpose-in-todays-world (archived at https://perma.cc/TPJ5-GB6C)

18 Csikszentmihalyi, M (1993) *The Evolving Self: A psychology for the third millennium*, Harper/Collins.

19 Hunt, V, Prince, S, Dixon-Fyle, S, and Yee, L (2018) Delivering through diversity, McKinsey, www.mckinsey.com/business-functions/organization/our-insights/delivering-through-diversity (archived at https://perma.cc/PU3M-DN4S); Lorenzo, R and Reeves, M (2018) How and where diversity drives financial performance, *Harvard Business Review*, 30, pp. 1–5.

20 Quote from Jackson, AE (2017) The other CEO: Tony Prophet, Salesforce's Chief Equality Officer, *Glassdoor*, www.glassdoor.com/blog/tony-prophet-salesforce/ (archived at https://perma.cc/ZTM2-MZCA)

21 Statistics from Catalyst (2021) Women CEOs at the S&P 500, www.catalyst.org/research/women-ceos-of-the-sp-500/ (archived at https://perma.cc/MN7G-EE66); SpencerStuart (2021) 2021 S&P 500 board diversity snapshot, www.spencerstuart.com/research-and-insight/2021-sp-500-board-diversity-snapshot (archived at https://perma.cc/WXZ6-7M3Y); EWOB (2020) *European Women on Boards Gender Diversity Index 2020*, https://europeanwomenonboards.eu/wp-content/uploads/2021/01/EWoB-Gender-Diversity-Index-2020.pdf (archived at https://perma.cc/93LM-G9LL)

22 Grant, AM (2013) *Give and Take: A revolutionary approach to success*, Penguin.

23 Roberts, LM, Dutton, JE, Spreitzer, GM, Heaphy, ED, and Quinn, RE (2005) Composing the reflected best-self-portrait: Building pathways for becoming extraordinary in work organizations, *Academy of Management Review*, 30 (4), pp. 712–36.

24 Mirvis, P, MacArthur, A, Walsh, M, and Gapeka, T (2020) Global pro bono service: Implications for employees, companies and the communities served, in *Employee Engagement in Corporate Social Responsibility*, Sage.

25 Pinchot, G (1985) *Intrapreneuring: Why you don't have to leave the corporation to become an entrepreneur*, Harper & Row.

26   Grayson, D, McLaren, M and Spitzeck, H (2017) *Social Intrapreneurism and All That Jazz: How business innovators are helping to build a more sustainable world*, Routledge.

27   Courtney, E (2021) Remote work statistics: Navigating the new normal, *Flexjobs*, www.flexjobs.com/blog/post/remote-work-statistics/ (archived at https://perma.cc/6ALP-NVVK)

28   Davenport, TH and Kirby, J (2015) Beyond automation, *Harvard Business Review*, **93** (6), pp. 58–65.

29   Edelman (2021) 2021 Trust Barometer special report: The belief-driven employee, www.edelman.com/trust/2021-trust-barometer/belief-driven-employee (archived at https://perma.cc/HAH3-QJA3)

Chapter 8

1   FAO/WFP/IFAD/UNICEF/WHO (2021) 2021 state of food security and nutrition in the world, United Nations World Food Programme, www.wfp.org/publications/2021-state-food-security-and-nutrition-world-report-and-inbrief (archived at https://perma.cc/5P4L-BR6P)

2   Survey results from Accenture (2018) From me to we: The rise of the purpose-led brand, www.accenture.com/us-en/insights/strategy/brand-purpose (archived at https://perma.cc/G8AZ-XHH9); Haller, K, Lee, J, and Cheung, J (2020) Meet the 2020 consumers driving change, IBM Institute for Business Value, www.ibm.com/thought-leadership/institute-business-value/report/consumer-2020# (archived at https://perma.cc/3NQQ-TKYV)

3   Kotler, P (2015) *Confronting Capitalism: Real solutions for a troubled economic system*, Amacom.

4   Havas Group (2021) Havas' Meaningful Brands report 2021 finds we are entering the age of cynicism, www.havasgroup.com/havas-content/uploads/2021/05/press_release_mb21-final.pdf (archived at https://perma.cc/2SXZ-ESEZ)

5   Tully, SM and Winer, RS (2014) The role of the beneficiary in willingness to pay for socially responsible products: A meta-analysis, *Journal of Retailing*, **90** (2), pp. 255–74.

6   Globescan (2019) High cost and lack of support are key barriers to more healthy and sustainable living, https://globescan.com/healthy-sustainable-living-report-2019/ (archived at https://perma.cc/FG94-DAV3)

7   Rivoli, P (2014) *The Travels of a T-shirt in the Global Economy: An economist examines the markets, power, and politics of world trade. New preface and epilogue with updates on economic issues and main characters*, John Wiley & Sons.

8   Quote from Balch, O (2013) Natura commits to sourcing sustainably from Amazon, *The Guardian,* www.theguardian.com/sustainable-business/natura-sourcing-sustainably-from-amazon (archived at https://perma.cc/G3FK-F3YP)

9   Survey results from Cone (2013) 2013 Cone Communications/Echo global CSR study, www.conecomm.com/news-blog/2013-global-csr-study-release (archived at https://perma.cc/Z2EE-V4EY)

10   Definition from Product Stewardship Institute (2021) What is product stewardship? www.productstewardship.us/page/Definitions (archived at https://perma.cc/MHD3-T58E)

11   See Vitsoe (2021) The power of good design: Dieter Rams's ideology, engrained within Vitsoe, www.vitsoe.com/gb/about/good-design (archived at https://perma.cc/7T8K-NSGY)

12   Heller, C (2018) *The Intergalactic Design Guide: Harnessing the creative potential of social design*, Island Press.

13   For more on social innovation co-creation, see Mirvis, P and Googins, B (2018) Corporate social innovation: Top-down, bottom-up, inside-out and outside-in, in *Business Strategies for Sustainability*, Routledge, pp. 179–96.

14   For background on fair trade, see Bowes, J (Ed.) (2011) *The Fair Trade Revolution*, Pluto Press.

15   For more see, Hatch, MJ and Schultz, M (2010) Toward a theory of brand co-creation with implications for brand governance, *Journal of Brand Management*, **17** (8), pp. 590–604.

16   Graf, N (2019) About four-in-ten U.S. adults say forms should offer more than two gender options, Pew Research Center, www.pewresearch.org/fact-tank/2019/12/18/gender-options-on-forms-or-online-profiles/ (archived at https://perma.cc/6L7N-ZTXM)

17   Fehér, A, Gazdecki, M, Véha, M, Szakály, M, and Szakály, Z (2020) A comprehensive review of the benefits of and the barriers to the switch to a plant-based diet, *Sustainability*, **12** (10), pp. 1–18.

18   Survey from Hubbub (2017) Bright Friday, www.hubbub.org.uk/brightfriday (archived at https://perma.cc/2MQ3-7DQD)

19   Reptrak (2021) 2021 Global RepTrak® 100, Reputation Institute, www.reputationinstitute.com/global-reptrak-100 (archived at https://perma.cc/27EJ-6UES)

20   Quote from interview by Howarth, D (2015) "I want to bring the surprise back to IKEA," says head of design, *dezeen*, www.dezeen.com/2015/02/06/ikea-design-manager-marcus-engman-interview-furniture/ (archived at https://perma.cc/5LFM-CJXV)

21   Statistics from Retail Report Card (2021) How retailers rank on toxic chemicals, https://retailerreportcard.com/grades/ (archived at https://perma.cc/JKC6-D6KZ)

22 See Nielsen (2018) *Sustainable Shoppers Buy the Change They Wish to See in the World*, www.nielsen.com/wp-content/uploads/sites/3/2019/04/global-sustainable-shoppers-report-2018.pdf (archived at https://perma.cc/M8CV-MH4C); Edelman (2019) Edelman Trust Barometer special report: In brands we trust? www.edelman.com/research/trust-barometer-special-report-in-brands-we-trust (archived at https://perma.cc/9V4F-5YXL)

23 Prahalad, CK and Hart, SL (2002) The fortune at the bottom of the pyramid, *Strategy + Business*, **26**, pp. 2–14; London, T (2020) *The Base of the Pyramid Promise*, Stanford University Press.

24 Quote from SC Johnson (2014) The choices we make: SC Johnson 2014 Public Sustainability Report, https://pimsmultimedia.com/sc_johnson_pdf/pics/FINAL_2c_SCJohnson_PR2014.pdf (archived at https://perma.cc/4QZ9-TWY2)

25 Chouinard, Y (2016) *Let My People Go Surfing: The education of a reluctant businessman—including 10 more years of business unusual*, Penguin.

26 Cone (2017) 2017 Cone Communications CSR study, www.conecomm.com/research-blog/2017-csr-study (archived at https://perma.cc/KY6G-2MTA)

27 Madison, N and Klang, M (2020) The case for digital activism: Refuting the fallacies of slacktivism, *Journal of Digital Social Research*, **2** (2), pp. 28–47.

28 Edelman (2020) Trust Barometer special report: Brand trust in 2020, www.edelman.com/research/brand-trust-2020 (archived at https://perma.cc/X6QC-ZFSX)

Chapter 9

1 Kolbert, E (2014) *The Sixth Extinction: An unnatural history*, A&C Black; quote from Kolbert, E (2015) *Field Notes From a Catastrophe: Man, nature, and climate change*, Bloomsbury Publishing.

2 Quote from NPR (2019) Transcript: Greta Thunberg's speech at the U.N. Climate Action Summit, www.npr.org/2019/09/23/763452863/transcript-greta-thunbergs-speech-at-the-u-n-climate-action-summit (archived at https://perma.cc/T8ZA-9FAL)

3 Lovins, AB, Lovins, LH, and Hawken, P (1999) *Natural Capitalism: Creating the next industrial revolution*, Little Brown & Co.

4 Hoffman, AJ (2018) The next phase of business sustainability, *Stanford Social Innovation Review*, **16** (2), pp. 34–39.

5 Steffen, W, Richardson, K, Rockström, J, Cornell, SE, Fetzer, I, Bennett, EM, Biggs, R, Carpenter, SR, De Vries, W, De Wit, CA and Folke, C (2015) Planetary boundaries: Guiding human development on a changing planet, *Science*, **347** (6223). For updates, see Stockholm Resilience Center, The nine planitary boundaries, www.stockholmresilience.org/research/planetary-boundaries/the-nine-planetary-boundaries.html (archived at https://perma.cc/3LGJ-QSDH)

6   Hawken, P (Ed.) (2017) *Drawdown: The most comprehensive plan ever proposed to reverse global warming*, Penguin.

7   Statistics from FTSE Russell (2021) Putting numbers to the global green economy, www.ftserussell.com/blogs/putting-numbers-global-green-economy (archived at https://perma.cc/24YE-HPA9)

8   Pauli, G (2017) The blue economy 3.0: The marriage of science, innovation and entrepreneurship creates a new business model that transforms society, Xlibris Corporation.

9   Survey results from Emmert, A (2021) The rise of the eco-friendly consumer, *Strategy + Business*, www.strategy-business.com/article/The-rise-of-the-eco-friendly-consumer (archived at https://perma.cc/D3MJ-Q8EA)

10   Survey results from World Wildlife Fund (2021) The eco-wakening, https://explore.panda.org/eco-wakening#full-report (archived at https://perma.cc/KUC6-RUT8); Globescan (2021) Breakthrough: Seven unlocks to scaling healthy and sustainable living, https://globescan.com/breakthrough-seven-unlocks-scaling-healthy-sustainable-living/ (archived at https://perma.cc/2TJ6-Z9ZY)

11   History of green brands at Myer, R (2010) The future: The continued growth of green, *Fast Company*, www.fastcompany.com/section/50-years-of-green (archived at https://perma.cc/C5RU-7EUX); Survey results from PwC (2021) The global consumer: Changed for good, www.pwc.com/gx/en/industries/consumer-markets/consumer-insights-survey.html (archived at https://perma.cc/QNX2-WZPY)

12   Raworth, K (2017) *Doughnut Economics: Seven ways to think like a 21st-century economist*, Chelsea Green Publishing.

13   Doughnut Economics Action Lab, https://doughnuteconomics.org/ (archived at https://perma.cc/577X-XSR2)

14   Hollender, J (2015) Net positive: The future of sustainable business, *Stanford Social Innovation Review*, https://ssir.org/articles/entry/net_positive_the_future_of_sustainable_business (archived at https://perma.cc/NC4V-R6E8)

15   Ehrenfeld, JR and Hoffman, AJ (2013) *Flourishing: A frank conversation about sustainability*, Stanford University Press.

16   IPCC (2018) Global warming of 1.5°C: Summary for policymakers, www.ipcc.ch/sr15/ (archived at https://perma.cc/RH9X-WJZK)

17   For more, see Hawken, P (2021) *Regeneration: Ending the climate crisis in one generation*, Penguin.

18   Leiserowitz, AA, Smith, N, and Marlon, JR (2010) Americans' knowledge of climate change, Yale Project on Climate Change Communication.

19   Davies, J (2014) Sustainability and employee engagement, NEEF, GreenBiz, and PwC, www.neefusa.org/resource/sustainability-employee-engagement-state-art (archived at https://perma.cc/HL9K-ZZ4C)

20 McKinsey (2020) Valuing nature conservation, www.mckinsey.com/business-functions/sustainability/our-insights/valuing-nature-conservation (archived at https://perma.cc/Z7FT-3QMR)

21 Jay, J and Gerard, M (2015) Accelerating the theory and practice of sustainability-oriented innovation, MIT Sloan Research Paper No. 5148–15.

22 Jacobson, R and Lucas, M (2018) A review of global and U.S. total available markets for carbon tech, *Carbon 180*, https://static1.squarespace.com/static/5b9362d89d5 abb8c51d474f8/t/5bfc808803ce649d6a0310bd/1543274633164/MS_Exec_Summary. pdf (archived at https://perma.cc/943A-XLXJ)

23 Siegal, RP (2019) Exploring the business case for carbon removal, *GreenBiz*, www.greenbiz.com/article/exploring-business-case-carbon-removal (archived at https://perma.cc/RE7D-3GQF)

24 Stories drawn from Cleantech Group (2021) Global cleantech 100, www.cleantech.com/the-global-cleantech-100/ (archived at https://perma.cc/7GHA-EB5U); Wunderman Thompson (2018) The new sustainability: Regeneration, https://intelligence.wundermanthompson.com/trend-reports/the-new-sustainability-regeneration/ (archived at https://perma.cc/C39T-MQDK)

25 Globescan (2021) The 2021 GlobeScan/SustainAbility leaders survey, https://globescan.com/2021-sustainability-leaders-report/ (archived at https://perma.cc/82AU-DHMK)

26 Corbley, A (2020) Scientists find half the world's fish stocks are recovered—or increasing—in oceans that used to be overfished, *Good News Network*, www.goodnewsnetwork.org/half-the-worlds-oceanic-fish-stock-are-improving/ (archived at https://perma.cc/XY47-TMS6)

27 Carlson, KM, Heilmayr, R, Gibbs, HK, Noojipady, P, Burns, DN, Morton, DC, and Kremen, C (2018) Effect of oil palm sustainability certification on deforestation and fire in Indonesia, Proceedings of the National Academy of Sciences, **115** (1), pp. 121–26.

28 Research and Degrowth (2021) Definition, https://degrowth.org/definition-2/ (archived at https://perma.cc/BB9L-P8UD)

29 Jackson, T (2016) *Prosperity Without Growth: Foundations for the economy of tomorrow*, Taylor & Francis.

30 Kolbert, E (2021) *Under a White Sky: The nature of the future*, Crown.

31 Gates, B (2015) The next outbreak? We're not ready, TED Talk, www.ted.com/talks/bill_gates_the_next_outbreak_we_re_not_ready/transcript?language=en (archived at https://perma.cc/V2XY-JFTP); Gates, B (2021) *How to Avoid a Climate Disaster: The solutions we have and the breakthroughs we need*, Knopf.

32 Quote from ERB (2019) What does society look like in the future of the Anthropocene? A Q&A with Andy Hoffman, ERB University of Michigan, https://erb.umich.edu/2019/04/16/what-does-society-look-like-in-the-future-of-the-anthropocene-a-qa-with-andy-hoffman/ (archived at https://perma.cc/9BCL-GFUY)

Chapter 10

1 Quote from United Nations Global Compact (2020) SDG action manager, www.unglobalcompact.org/take-action/sdg-action-manager (archived at https://perma.cc/47ED-XMQV)

2 Schumpeter, JA (1942) *Capitalism, Socialism, and Democracy,* Harper and Brothers, 3rd Edition 1950.

3 Feldmann, D and Alberg-Seberich, M (2020) *The Corporate Social Mind: How companies lead social change from the inside out,* Greenleaf Book Group.

4 See Tsao, FC and Laszlo, C (2019) *Quantum Leadership: New consciousness in business,* Stanford University Press; Hutchins, G and Storm, L (2019) *Regenerative Leadership: The DNA of life-affirming 21st century organizations,* Wordzworth Publishing.

5 Nelson, J (2017) Partnerships for sustainable development, *Harvard Kennedy School Corporate Responsibility Initiative Report (Commissioned by the Business and Sustainable Development Commission).*

6 Mirvis, PH and Worley, CG (2014) Organizing for sustainability: Why networks and partnerships? In *Building Networks and Partnerships,* Emerald Group Publishing Limited.

7 Stephan, U, Patterson, M, and Kelly, C (2013) Business-driven social change: A systematic review of the evidence, Network for Business Sustainability, www.nbs.net/articles/systematic-review-business-driven-social-change (archived at https://perma.cc/X52J-2ULN)

8 See video by Uren, S (2019) Catalyzing transformational change, www.youtube.com/watch?v=dIQ0NSpr2l4 (archived at https://perma.cc/HT93-87VY)

9 Darwin, CR (1859) *On the Origin of Species (Vol. XI, pp. 1909–14),* The Harvard Classics, PF Collier & Son; quote from Bartleby.com (2001) www.bartleby.com/11/ (archived at https://perma.cc/5NK5-UXXR)

10 Senge, PM, Smith, B, Kruschwitz, N, Laur, J and Schley, S (2008) *The Necessary Revolution: How individuals and organizations are working together to create a sustainable world,* Currency.

11 Waddell, S (2005) *Societal Learning and Change: How governments, business and civil society are creating solutions to complex multi-stakeholder problems,* Sheffield: Greenleaf Publishing; Mirvis, P, Herrera, MEB, Googins, B and Albareda, L (2016) Corporate social innovation: How firms learn to innovate for the greater good, *Journal of Business Research,* **69** (11), pp. 5014–21; Clarke, A and Crane, A (2018) Cross-sector partnerships for systemic change: Systematized literature review and agenda for further research, *Journal of Business Ethics,* **150** (2), pp. 303–13.

12 Austin, JE, Leonard, HB, Reficco, E and Wei-Skillern, J (2006) Social entrepreneurship: It's for corporations too. In A. Nicholls (Ed.) *Social*

Entrepreneurship: New models of sustainable social change, pp. 169–80. For guidance on working with NGO partners, see Grayson, D, Coulter, C, and Lee, M (2018) *All In: The future of business leadership*, Routledge.

13   See Korngold, A (2014) *A Better World, Inc.: How companies profit by solving global problems... Where governments cannot*, Palgrave Macmillan.

14   For more on sustainable fashion coalitions, see Fashion Revolution (2021) Key organisations, www.fashionrevolution.org/key-organisations/ (archived at https://perma.cc/YV8H-GMK8)

15   For more on recycling, see Collin, RW (2015) *Trash Talk: An encyclopedia of garbage and recycling around the world*, ABC-CLIO.

16   Waddell, S (2001) Societal learning: Creating big-systems change, *Systems Thinker*, **12** (10), https://thesystemsthinker.com/societal-learning-creating-big-systems-change/ (archived at https://perma.cc/MPH9-SWQ5)

17   See Eggers, WD and Macmillan, P (2013) *The Solution Revolution: How business, government, and social enterprises are teaming up to solve society's toughest problems*, Harvard Business Press; Mulgan, G and Leadbeater, C (2013) *Systems Innovation*, Nesta; Levey, K (2017) Collaborating for solvable problems: What's next? PYXERA Global, www.pyxeraglobal.org/collaborating-solvable-problems-whats-next/#fb0=1 (archived at https://perma.cc/FLM9-L4JG)

18   There are many more such pressure groups—see Foodtank (2020) 36 organizations helping solve the climate crisis, https://foodtank.com/news/2020/10/36-organizations-helping-solve-the-climate-crisis/ (archived at https://perma.cc/9UJ8-CZ8Y)

19   See Net Zero Climate (2021) Global net zero progress, https://netzeroclimate.org/innovation-for-net-zero/progress-tracking/ (archived at https://perma.cc/2M9A-H4BS); IPCC (2021) AR6 climate change 2021: The physical science basis, The Intergovernmental Panel on Climate Change, www.ipcc.ch/report/ar6/wg1/ (archived at https://perma.cc/VF9Z-EL78)

20   For more on Branson's efforts, see Confino, J (2013) Richard Branson and Jochen Zeitz launch the B Team challenge, *The Guardian*, www.theguardian.com/sustainable-business/blog/richard-branson-jochen-zeitz-b-team (archived at https://perma.cc/754A-P28E)

21   Segal, E (2021) 8 ways CEOs can be corporate activists, *Forbes*, www.forbes.com/sites/edwardsegal/2021/04/05/8-ways-ceos-can-be-corporate-activists/?sh=7ac4d5617ce2 (archived at https://perma.cc/E9RG-BWFJ)

22   Reid, L (2020) Meet the woman who is changing the world one bubble at a time — and preparing for the UK transition, *Wales Online*, www.walesonline.co.uk/special-features/woman-bubble-business-uk-transition-19298144 (archived at https://perma.cc/5267-RK3S)

23 Study and quotes from USC Annenberg (2021) 2021 global communication report: Politics, polarization and purpose, https://annenberg.usc.edu/research/center-public-relations/global-communication-report (archived at https://perma.cc/SB7W-H3XB)

24 Chatterji, A and Toffel, MW (2017) Assessing the impact of CEO activism, Harvard Business School Technology & Operations Mgt. Unit Working Paper; also Toffel, MW (2018), The new CEO activists, *Harvard Business Review*, https://hbr.org/2018/01/the-new-ceo-activists (archived at https://perma.cc/9ELQ-ALJB)

25 Ramaswamy, V (2021) *Woke, Inc.*, Center Street.

26 Antilla, S (2016) Jamie Dimon's makeover: From whiner to would-be statesman, *The Street*, www.thestreet.com/opinion/jamie-dimon-s-makeover-from-whiner-to-would-be-statesman-13478955 (archived at https://perma.cc/5SEJ-E2KH)

27 Dimon, J (2021) Dear fellow shareholders, www.jpmorganchase.com/content/dam/jpmc/jpmorgan-chase-and-co/investor-relations/documents/ceo-letter-to-shareholders-2020.pdf (archived at https://perma.cc/YX65-GLDM)

28 For more examples, see Cooperrider, D and Selian, A (2021) *The Business of Building a Better World: The leadership revolution that is changing everything*, Berrett-Koehler.

29 Quote from Rowley, MJ (2019) How tech is bringing Israelis and Palestinians together, *BBC News*, www.bbc.com/news/business-48053200 (archived at https://perma.cc/GW4A-KBZM)

30 Grayson, D (2012) Essay: The CEO as statesman, *Reuters Events*, www.reutersevents.com/sustainability/business-strategy/essay-ceo-statesman (archived at https://perma.cc/87VG-83PH)

31 McKinsey (2009) The CEO as diplomat: An interview with Richard Haass. www.mckinsey.com/industries/public-and-social-sector/our-insights/the-ceo-as-diplomat-an-interview-with-richard-haass (archived at https://perma.cc/34FR-8A66)

32 Gauthier, A (2008) Developing generative change leaders across sectors: An exploration of integral approaches, *Integral Leadership Review*, pp. 2008–06.

33 Saner, R, Yiu, L, and Søndergaard, M (2000) Business diplomacy management: A core competency for global companies, *Academy of Management Perspectives*, **14** (1), pp. 80–92.

INDEX

CPSIA information can be obtained
at www.ICGtesting.com
Printed in the USA
JSHW012240120522
25871JS00007B/140